ERSITY

This ... m... be returned ...
recalled ... a...
late...

DISPUTED PLEASURES

Recent Titles in
Contributions to the Study of World History

Tsar Paul and the Question of Madness: An Essay in History and Psychology
Hugh Ragsdale

The Orphan Stone: The Minnesinger Dream of Reich
Richard J. Berleth

American Constitutionalism Abroad: Selected Essays in Comparative
Constitutional History
George Athan Billias, editor

Appeasement in Europe: A Reassessment of U.S. Policies
David F. Schmitz and Richard D. Challener, editors

Ritual and Record: Sports Records and Quantification in Pre-Modern Societies
John Marshall Carter and Arnd Krüger, editors

Diverse Paths to Modernity in Southeastern Europe: Essays in
National Development
Gerasimos Augustinos, editor

The Chinese Revolution in Historical Perspective
John E. Schrecker

Cities and Caliphs: On the Genesis of Arab Muslim Urbanism
Nezar AlSayyad

The French Revolution in Culture and Society
David G. Troyansky, Alfred Cismaru, and Norwood Andrews, Jr., editors

Russia and Italy Against Hitler: The Bolshevik-Fascist Rapprochement
of the 1930s
J. Calvitt Clarke III

Germany and the Union of South Africa in the Nazi Period
Robert Citino

"A Policy Calculated to Benefit China": The United States and the
China Arms Embargo, 1919-1929
Stephen Valone

The Politics of Anti-Japanese Sentiment in Korea: Japanese-South Korean
Relations Under American Occupation, 1945-1952
Sung-hwa Cheong

DISPUTED PLEASURES

Sport and Society in Preindustrial England

THOMAS S. HENRICKS

Contributions to the Study of World History,
Number 28

GREENWOOD PRESS
New York • Westport, Connecticut • London

Library of Congress Cataloging-in-Publication Data

Henricks, Thomas S.
   Disputed pleasures : sport and society in preindustrial England /
Thomas S. Henricks.
    p. cm.—(Contributions to the study of world history, ISSN
0885-9159 ; no. 28)
   Includes bibliographical references (p.) and index.
   ISBN 0-313-27453-3 (alk. paper)
   1. Sports—Social aspects—England—History. I. Title.
  II. Series.
  GV706.5.H46 1991
  306.4'83'0942—dc20   90-22619

British Library Cataloguing in Publication Data is available.

Copyright © 1991 by Thomas S. Henricks

All rights reserved. No portion of this book may be
reproduced, by any process or technique, without the
express written consent of the publisher.

Library of Congress Catalog Card Number: 90-22619
ISBN: 0-313-27453-3
ISSN: 0885-9159 189I8212

First published in 1991

Greenwood Press, 88 Post Road West, Westport, CT 06881
An imprint of Greenwood Publishing Group, Inc.

Printed in the United States of America

∞™

The paper used in this book complies with the
Permanent Paper Standard issued by the National
Information Standards Organization (Z39.48-1984).

10 9 8 7 6 5 4 3 2 1

CONTENTS

ACKNOWLEDGMENTS

Although the making of a book seems to an author to be a relatively solitary enterprise, there are typically a number of people who shape the finished product. I wish to thank some of them here.

My principal intellectual debt is to Donald N. Levine at the University of Chicago, who has long believed in this project and in my ability to bring it to a successful conclusion. However, I also wish to thank Professors Bruce Waller and John M. Carter for their encouragements and suggestions.

The National Endowment for the Humanities sponsored a summer of research at the British Museum and University of London libraries. I wish to thank them and the British librarians who assisted me during my stay. I have also been helped by staff at the Duke University and University of North Carolina libraries as well as by my colleagues at the Elon College library. Of these, Teresa LePors, who administers the interlibrary loan system there, deserves special mention.

Linda Martindale at Elon College prepared the final version of the manuscript. I am grateful for her professionalism and cooperative spirit. I would also like to thank our department secretary, Brenda Cooper, who typed earlier versions of chapters with unfailing competence and good grace.

Elon College has provided me with research funds and periods of release time from my typical responsibilities to pursue this project. A professor at a small college cannot flourish without such support.

I wish to thank Cynthia Harris and Sally M. Scott at Greenwood Press for their interest and assistance.

Assistance of a deeper nature has been provided by my mother, Sylvia Henricks. In addition to nurturing many of my intellectual skills, she has persistently encouraged my writing.

Finally, my ultimate gratitude goes as always to my wife, Judy Henricks, for her judgment and support during this long endeavor and to my children, Lizzie and David, for keeping activities such as this in perspective.

DISPUTED PLEASURES

1

INTRODUCTION

To those otherwise employed, the work of the scholar appears all too often to be an exercise in disaffiliation—a flight from the urges and anxieties of modern life. The academic writer is all too willing to replace the concrete with the abstract, the passionate with the dispassionate, the here-and-now with accounts of past and future, the whole with the part, and even the important with the trivial—or so it seems. Indeed, the title of the current work makes it a perfect candidate for such suspicions.

For such reasons, I feel compelled to state at the outset that no flight into the ethereal or trivial is here intended. What follows is a book about the passions of a people who, though separated from us by the boundaries of time and by the social and cultural contexts of their lives, seem modern enough in their urges and anxieties. Preindustrial people *were* different—in their tools and technologies, in their possibilities for organizing themselves, and in many of their beliefs and customs. However, these are merely differences in the resources available to them for comprehending and controlling the world; stripping aside such paraphernalia, we recognize ourselves. This is particularly the case in sporting activities, which are commonly less convoluted than other human endeavors are. Furthermore, although the leisure habits of preindustrial people may seem insignificant enough when viewed in isolation, they were connected to the wider society in ways that were, I shall argue, quite important. Fundamentally, then, this is a book not only about English sport but about English society as well.

The selection of England as the setting for a book about sport and society is, of course, no accident. England played a key role in the evolution of modern sport, a fact that has been recognized widely by students of sport. For example, in the judgment of the great Dutch historian Johan Huizinga, nineteenth-century England can be seen as the "cradle and focus of modern sporting life."[1] Herbert Shoffler and later Richard Mandell both dubbed England "the land of sport" in their historical accounts.[2] J. A. Mangan has claimed that the nineteenth-century British people "taught the modern world to play."[3] Norbert Elias and Eric

Dunning have taken a similar tack by describing what they term the "sportiz-ation" of pastimes, an English approach to leisure that was exported world-wide.[4] In a recent book, Eric Midwinter joins the chorus in noting that "modern sport . . . originated in Victorian Britain."[5] In short, England provides more than a sociologically interesting case study: It is a historically crucial setting for the development of Western sport.

ENGLISH SPORT AND THE HISTORIANS

Because of the path-breaking changes in English sport during the nineteenth century and because of England's role as a great imperialist power, historians have tended to focus on sport in the industrial context.[6] In that setting, readers have been informed of the rise of a modern cult of athleticism, with its school-sponsored sports, hierarchy of athletic associations, large spectator events, and professional-amateur distinctions. This increased "seriousness" (to use Huizinga's term) was expressed ultimately in more or less permanent playing grounds, standardized rules and adjudicating agencies, playing schedules, record keeping, and training procedures. The "rationalization" process that sociologist Max Weber saw as overwhelming every area of Western culture was now claiming the realm of leisure as well.[7]

These changes in sport traditionally have been attributed to the urban-industrial development of the period. In this context various historians have described the migration of a predominantly rural populace to the cities where they found themselves deprived (sometimes forcibly) of their old diversions.[8] As public spaces for play declined, people were forced into more circumscribed environments and even indoors. Commercialized entertainments and spectator sports (aided by such inventions as the railroad, the inexpensive printing of advertisements and newspapers, and improvements in sporting equipment) found a wide audience. By the final quarter of the nineteenth century, a shortening of the work week and an increase in real wages accelerated this process.[9]

If the industrial order created new opportunities for sport (as it closed old ones), so the factory mentality came to prevail in other ways. As Wray Vamplew has explained, the need for synchronized labor meant that the aspirations and habits of working people had to be changed.[10] The agricultural pattern of work alternating with festive release had to be supplanted by a more continuous stream of effort. This regularity (and intensification) of output would allow the lower classes to survive and the higher classes to accumulate. Furthermore, working people should be exposed to new models of corporate duty and efficiency. In this light, team sports, sponsored by civic groups, businesses, and schools, became vehicles for this resocialization process.

This new "games ethic" fit well with the bureaucratic and largely middle-class worldview that was ascendant during the nineteenth century. More specifically, it conformed to liberal, or laissez faire, philosophies about economic activity.[11] By these terms, society could be seen as a great artifice sustained by the self-interested energies of its constituents. The marketplace was the grandest of competitions in which the "best" advanced and the losers took their places below. As the cream was thought to rise to the surface, so society in general was said to be improved. To the extent that the competition was "fair," the victors could comfort themselves with self-congratulation; the vanquished had only themselves to blame. "Modern" sport then emerged as a spectacle comprehended largely in these terms. Collective and individual assertion was praised. Issues of character or will were kept in focus at the expense of more purely social advantages. The quality of self-indulgence found in agricultural sports was replaced by more ascetic virtues. Principles of fair play were extolled in an elaborate amateur code. And somehow the whole process was touted as an agency of social betterment.

As Mangan and others have described, this view of sport was trotted about the globe.[12] In what is perhaps the profoundest form of imperialism, British sport caught the imagination of significant portions of these colonial populations. To capture the public ceremonies of people is to take over their visions of the good life. Once this is done, changes in personal habits, character, and self-regard proceed more evenly. Sport was an evangelism all its own and a symbol of ascendancy that outlasted its originators.

This transformation of leisure into athleticism (a change that touched different sports and social classes in different ways) represents an interesting chapter in the history of sport. It is only one portion of a much longer and much more complicated story, however. For that reason, it is somewhat surprising that the sporting life of the centuries preceding the industrial era should have received so relatively little attention from scholars. Some of this is perhaps attributable to the inclinations of those working in the field—who may wish to reassess British sport in what is arguably its golden age or to find in sport a figuration of the class relations that have been so central to modern historical scholarship. More of this reticence is probably due to the fragmentary nature of early materials on sport. The historian of medieval or early modern sport is hindered by the fact that the writers and account keepers of this age were only under the rarest of circumstances concerned with describing or interpreting sport. Writing was used largely to keep track of the possessions (both goods and people) of the powerful and to make permanent their administrative and judicial decisions. Sporting accounts appear largely by inference, as occasions for civil disturbance, theft, debt, and so on.[13] Writing was also used to produce fawning (or, alternately, villifying) accounts of the powerful. Here, again, sport was used to illuminate biography or philosophy; it was rarely the focus of discussion. Gradually, literature assumed a more independent status. However, even here, sport appeared primarily as metaphor or allegory—for example, as a vehicle to reveal heroic character or its opposite. Like decorations at the margins of a manuscript, sport has been used to illuminate matters thought to be more pressing.[14]

All this is not to say that no important contributions have been made to this part of English sporting history. Any list of such efforts might well begin with the work of the antiquarian Joseph Strutt. His book, *The Sports and Pastimes of the People of England*, first published in 1801 and subsequently edited and expanded by J. C. Cox, remains a valuable compilation of references to early sports.[15] Throughout the nineteenth century, there were efforts to pool these references into "stories" of individual sports. Occasionally, these appeared in book form or in antiquarian journals; more commonly, they were produced for the literary magazines of the time.

By the end of the century, some worthy accounts had appeared. One notable event in this process was the establishment in 1882 of the Badminton Library of Sports and Pastimes.[16] This series of volumes on individual sports was composed of works written by educated sportsmen, rather than by professional historians. While rather uneven in quality, the books uniformly convey the aficionado's romance with the language and lore of his sport. Not surprisingly, the sports given best treatment in these early books were those that had military and economic relevance (and, therefore, made their way into the record on those terms). In this vein, we find the works of C. J. Longman and H. Walrond on archery and Egerton Castle on fencing.[17] Just after World War I, two fine works on the military tournament—by Francis Cripps-Day and R. Coltman Clephan—were published as well.[18]

The histories of ball play have accumulated more slowly. Folklorists such as Andrew Lang and Robert MacGregor gave some attention to this in articles during the last quarter of the nineteenth century and Julian Marshall produced his great work on tennis in 1878.[19] Generally, however, one must wait until the 1930s for substantial treatments of this topic.[20]

In every instance the works cited are basically descriptions of early sports. They are not—and are not intended to be—analyses of sports or explanations of the relationship between sport and society. This same pattern occurs with the general treatments of early sports. The books that followed Strutt—from those by Henry Alken and J. Aspin in the early 1800s to the works of Christina Hole and Norman Wymer in the 1940s—are essentially colorful, if thought-provoking, summaries.[21]

Within the last two decades, however, the historical ambience has changed dramatically. Sport history has become not merely a recounting of people and events, but also an opportunity to ascertain the values and preoccupations (and, increasingly, the social tensions) of the wider society. A landmark in this shift is Dennis Brailsford's book on sport in Tudor/Stuart times.[22] In his hands sport reappears at the intersection of religion and politics. Another celebrated account is Robert Malcolmson's portrait of the recreations of ordinary folk at the close of the preindustrial period.[23] Here, the tensions between the property-owning classes and poorer people appear even more conspicuously. Indeed, the transition between the pre-industrial and industrial period (from the late eighteenth to mid-nineteenth century) has been described in a number of substantial accounts of recreation and leisure; in these the specifically social context of sport becomes clear.[24]

The studies of individual sports (or categories of sports) have followed a similar pattern. Sport history has become social history. Books on hunting by Michael Brander and Charles Trench and more recently, Edward P. Thompson and P. B. Munsche have increasingly become treatises on class relations.[25] In a similar spirit, valuable social and economic accounts of boxing, cricket, horse racing, and football have now been produced.[26]

If class relations have preoccupied many writers, the older, more "cultural" approach has also found renewed vigor. Such medieval scholars as C. H. Hoskins, G. G. Coulton, and H. S. Bennett include sport among their panoramic visions of society.[27] Sport was a significant form of human expression and, thus, a vehicle for the understanding of mental life. This approach, which sometimes relied on literary sources, has been continued by such writers as Francis P. Magoun and Marcelle Thiebaux.[28] Two current scholars who seem especially noteworthy in this regard are Joachim Rühl and Heiner Gillmeister.[29] They use literary as well as other sources to consider such problems as the origins and patterns of diffusion of early sport.

The current work attempts to stand, somewhat precariously, astride this widening chasm between the older and newer types of studies. On the one hand, it is offered as a kind of summary of sport during the preindustrial era. Although others have focused on play or recreation over long periods in England[30] and still others have offered even more general treatments of English sport,[31] no other work to my knowledge has attempted to chart the changes in sport during the centuries preceding the so-called modern era. For the general reader, then, or for one acquiring a fresh interest in sports studies, the following may serve as an introduction to this subject. Furthermore, the work is intended to be a conduit to the writings of the historians and others whose works are cited throughout.

On the other hand, the book is motivated by a more limited set of theoretical concerns. In particular, I shall try to trace the relationship between sport and shifting social and cultural patterns. In so doing, my ambitions are largely sociological in nature; I wish to comprehend some of the various ways in which sports have been developed and to assess the significance of these patterns. Following the encouragement of the sociologist Pierre Bourdieu, a great range of sporting activities will be considered.[32] By this approach, it is hoped that a sense of the different (and historically shifting) contexts of sport should be gained.

DEFINITIONS AND THEIR IMPLICATIONS

In academic work the act of definition is commonly a fateful choice. By this process, selected phenomena are brought into focus, others are seen dimly about the edges of the image, and still others are lost forever. The decision about definitions has been especially significant in the case of sport.[33]

As the reader will have noted from the title, this book is not about the historical transformation of "play," the subject of Huizinga's great work, *Homo Ludens*.[34] Huizinga sought out play in a wide range of human institutions and endeavors (for example, law, war, poetry, and politics). Play, then, was not an institution itself, but rather a quality of experience characterized by, among other elements, freedom, seclusion, and make-believe. As such, Huizinga saw play as the seedbed of creativity and a dynamo of progress. The thesis of *Homo Ludens*—that the forces of modernism (including formality, gigantism, and bureaucratization) have diminished our possibilities for playfulness—is a profound, if largely misunderstood, challenge for modern scholarship.[35] The current book, about the changing contexts of sport, clearly pursues a different path. By considering the extent to which early sport was playful, however, the following may shed some light on the broader problem that Huizinga addressed.

In a similar fashion, the book is not specifically about changes in leisure, recreation, or amusement. Just as sport is not a subset of play, so it may or may not illustrate the various categories above. For example, sport commonly presents itself as a variety of leisure; often, however, it is much more than this. Furthermore, the term *leisure* is a particularly problematic one for a study of preindustrial society.[36] It carries with it, among other things, a compartmentalized view of existence (particularly the separation of work from other spheres) that is especially pertinent to the working classes of industrial society but less relevant to other classes and times. The terms recreation and amusement are equally unsuited for this study. In addition to being somewhat too broad, they draw attention to the psychological rather than the social aspects of the activity in question—either wholesome and refreshing (in the case of recreation) or trivial and evanescent (in the case of amusements).

Instead, this study restricts itself to sport, a term that has few equivalents outside the English language. In practical terms, this means a focus on vigorous, usually outdoor activities featuring adults in interpersonal or intergroup competition. Descriptions of children's games, card or table games, dancing, indoor activities such as billiards, courtship games, and so forth will not for the most part be provided here. As noted above, restricting one's focus in this way means that a range of significant questions such as, How did changes in sport compare to changes in other adult amusements?) can no longer be answered. A narrower focus, however, does permit a more detailed analysis of the ways in which social forces operated on the activity in question. In general, then, I have tried to strike a balance between the particular (changes in a single sport such as cricket or a somewhat broader category like hunting sports) and the general (the broader transformation in recreation).

To define sport somewhat more precisely, I should say that this category of activity refers to a set of institutionalized games in which the outcome is determined primarily by gross physical skills. To say that an activity is "institutionalized" is to say that it is built into and maintained by other enduring patterns in society. To say that it is a "game" is to describe it as a contest following more or less agreed on rules. The existence of these rules transforms sport from a purely psychological or social experience into a cultural form—a pattern or model that channels the energy of people.

The decision to define sport as a set of cultural forms is quite intentional. By so doing, attention can be placed on the ways in these forms have been organized or given expression *socially.* Again, I will emphasize that I do not consider the term sport to be identical to its big-time bureaucratic manifestations in Western society. The development of sport by schools (a contribution largely of the nineteenth century) or as a profession (a variety that is even now ascending) or as an instrumentality of the nation-state (as best exhibited in the Eastern European countries) is a mere manifestation of the sporting impulse; such examples do not exhaust it.[37]

SPORTING EVENTS AS IDENTITY CEREMONIES

The following chapters may be interpreted as a fundamentally symbolic analysis of early sports. By saying this, I do not wish to disregard completely the material or practical consequences of sport. Sport has been used as training for war; as a health regimen; as a provider of food and clothing; and as an employment for thousands of government officials, grounds-keepers, animal breeders, equipment manufacturers, writers and publishers, gamblers, and servants. These matters will be given some attention. My primary interest, however, is the connection of sport to conceptions of public order—that is, to the understanding of society as a whole and, more particularly, to the placement of various categories of people within that order.

One way of accomplishing this objective is to conceive of sports as identity ceremonies—as occasions where individuals and groups present themselves before others. As Huizinga and later Gregory Stone emphasized, games very easily lend themselves to *display.*[38] Not only do we compete against others, but also we perform before them—and sometimes before a collection of spectators as well. In other words, we make a public accounting of ourselves. Sometimes we are lost in play and are hardly conscious of being watched; at other times our behavior is crafted with all the care of a dramatic performance.

This dramatic quality is assisted by the eventfulness of games—by their customary separation from routine existence. Huizinga, it may be recalled, detailed the kinds of separation that might occur.[39] The first is the failure of the game to issue any material product; games are "inconsequential." For that reason, much can be made of their symbolic (rather than practical) meanings. Another kind of separation is the curious nature of the playing rules of games. To surrender to these rules is to enter an order of things quite unlike the world left behind. A third type of separation is achieved by the special use of space and time. In their more developed forms games employ playing surfaces that are distinctive of almost any other human endeavor. Similarly, they follow their own internal logic or "clocks" that are pointedly disconnected from outside time. Yet another separation is achieved by clothing and other material contrivances.

Costumes and playing equipment are often outlandish. By putting on a silly costume and prancing about, the player signifies commitment to the play sphere.

For all these reasons games are "dramatic" in ways that routine existence typically is not.[40] Games package experience in limited, predictable, and safe forms. Action has stipulated beginnings and ends; success and failure are etched in the clearest terms; opportunities for gallantry abound. Furthermore, because sports tend to rely on the conversation of physical gestures, rather than language, they are eminently watchable, even at great distances. Most are simple enough in outline to be understood by a child yet admit at other levels to endless perturbation and calculation. Indeed, their meaning for spectators can be different from—and even greater than—their meaning for the players themselves.

To speak of sports as identity ceremonies then is to focus on such events as structured, public opportunities for personal and collective expression. In the social sciences, "identity" refers to the more or less complete, enduring pictures or conceptions of persons (and groups) in society.[41] Entailed in these definitions are physical characteristics, cultural traits (values and beliefs), social standing (positions within society), qualities of personality and character, and biographical details. My argument is that sports have provided one substantial forum for the display of such traits. In other words, sports have been vehicles of identity construction and management. By contending with others on the field of play, we participate in a public evaluation of our own qualities and character.

Simply because sport constitutes this opportunity for personal and social expression, access to sport has been restricted historically. Indeed, a most fundamental question for sports studies is, Who gets to play what with whom before whom (and in what ways)? In the social sciences, studies of social stratification have tended to focus on the differential access people have to certain "key" resources—for example, wealth and property (the key themes of a "class" analysis), political power, prestige, knowledge, and so forth. Singly or in combination, these may be used to facilitate control of other valued resources, such as health care, housing, and justice before the law. Different societies emphasize different resources and possess quite different systems for their distribution. Likewise, they justify the resulting patterns of inequality in different ways. The current book will examine sport as such a valued resource. Patterns of access to sport will be given primary emphasis; I shall also be concerned, however, with the ideas that have justified sports participation and with the more general connection of sport to the other resources mentioned above.[42]

The significance of this matter can be seen by a quick look at two categories of potential sports participants. The first—women—hardly appears in this book. This is partly because the male-female distinction is not the one at issue here; more practically, it is because women historically have been kept off the fields of play to such a large degree. We find them here and there in illustrated manuscripts tossing a ball, but, for the most part, women were pressed into more sedentary, domestic amusements or toward dances and games with communal, rather than individual, implications. When they were involved in public sports, women were more often supporters or spectators to competition and violence, rather than participants. A strong queen such as the first Elizabeth (who hunted and hawked) could stretch the definitions pertaining to sex; even she, however, yielded ultimately to proprieties about the more aggressive forms of participation, such as tennis, jousting, and wrestling.

The second example—the sporting life of working people—is central to this book; yet, we learn more of it by inference than by description. As indicated previously, poor people enter the historical record largely as elements within (and often disruptions to) the administrative schemes of those who controlled writing. For example, we learn about the origins of football because the government suddenly decided to ban it or because some poor soul lost his temper in a game and killed someone. History tends to be written from the top of society downward. We know a good bit about the lives of the powerful and successively less as we descend the social scale. This book tends to focus upon the wealthier and more politically prominent groups in England because that is where the information (and, thus, the interpretations of earlier historians) has been concentrated. This bias (which is being corrected to some degree by the most recent generation of historians) is a substantial and unfortunate one. However, this methodological problem is itself an indicator of the wider issue at hand: the ability of different groups to define themselves (through sport and otherwise) in an enduring, public way.

To facilitate the historical descriptions, each of the substantive chapters will be organized in a similar way. A brief introduction to the social life of the times will be followed by presentations of patterns within individual sports. This will be followed again by a summary of dominant themes in sport during the era. In this process few assumptions about the knowledge of the reader will be made. Historians may find some fairly elemental and shopworn themes on display; sociologists will be subjected to the explication of some standard concepts; other students of sport may find needless descriptions (for them) of archaic pastimes. Such is the dilemma of one who tries to serve a variety of audiences at once.

The analysis will begin with the early Middle Ages (roughly 1066–1272). This represents the period when England was arguably a feudal society. The following chapter treats the decay of feudalism during the later Middle Ages. The transformation of the military elite and the rise of new status groups are themes expressed in sporting life. These developments accelerate with the centralized administration and "middle-class" appeal of the Tudors (1485–1603). By the time of the Stuarts (1603–1714), a certain elitist nostalgia and French influence are at work, themes counterpointed by the Puritan Revolution. Sport becomes a showcase for the contrasting worldviews. Finally, Georgian England (1714–1830), with its celebration of private property and its curious mixture of snobbery and social mingling, brings us to the dawn of the modern age. Any attempt to divide a longer period into shorter ones is problematic. In general, I have chosen what is, for the most part, a dynastic division of the preindustrial era because it is fairly traditional one, because royal families commonly impart a certain style to national life, and because the transitional points are sometimes marked by broader political and social shifts. In the concluding chapter, then, I will attempt to draw these themes together into a set of more general sociological reflections.

NOTES

1. Johan Huizinga, *Homo Ludens: A Study of the Play Element in Civilization* (Boston: Beacon, 1955), 18.

2. Herbert Shoffler, *England: Das Landes des Sports* (Leipzig: 1935) and Richard Mandell, *Sport: A Cultural History* (New York: Columbia University Press, 1984), chapter 7, "England: Land of Sport."

3. J. A. Mangan, Introduction to *Pleasure, Profit, Proselytism: British Culture and Sport at Home and Abroad: 1700–1914,* ed. J. A. Mangan (London: Frank Cass, 1988), 1.

4. Norbert Elias and Eric Dunning, *The Quest for Excitement: Sport and Leisure in the Civilizing Process* (New York: Basil Blackwell, 1986), 22.

5. Eric Midwinter, *Fair Game: Myth and Reality in Sport* (London: George Allen & Unwin, 1986), 2.

6. See William J. Baker, "The State of British Sport History," *Journal of Sport History* 10, no. 1 (Spring 1983): 54–55.

7. For a quite explicit attempt to apply Weber's ideas about rationalization to the development of modern sport, see Allen Guttmann, *From Ritual to Record: The Nature of Modern Sports* (New York: Columbia University Press, 1978).

8. See, for example, J. H. Plumb, *The Commercialization of Leisure in Eighteenth Century England* (Reading, England: University of Reading Press, 1973). See also John Rickard Betts, "The Technological Revolution and the Rise of Sport: 1850–1900," *Mississippi Valley Historical Review* 40 (September 1953): 231–56, for a discussion of sport and industrialization in America.

9. See Richard Holt, *Sport and the British: A Modern History* (Oxford: Clarendon Press, 1989), 5–7.

10. Wray Vamplew, "Sport and Industrialization: An Economic Interpretation of the Changes in Popular Sport in Nineteenth-Century England," in *Pleasure, Profit, Proselytism: British Culture and Sport at Home and Abroad: 1700–1914,* ed. J. A. Mangan (London: Frank Cass, 1988), 7–21.

11. See Randall Collins and Michael Makowsky, *The Discovery of Society*, 4th edition (New York: Random House, 1985), chapter 5, "Do-Gooders, Evolutionists, and Racists."

12. See, for example, J. A. Mangan, ed., *Pleasure, Profit, Proselytism: British Culture and Sport at Home and Abroad: 1700–1914* (London: Frank Cass, 1988). See also J. A. Mangan, *The Games Ethic and Imperialism: Aspects of the Diffusion of an Ideal* (Harmondsworth, England: Viking, 1986).

13. See John Marshall Carter, *Sports and Pastimes of the Middle Ages* (Columbus, Ga: Brentwood University, 1984), for an interesting account of medieval sources and their uses.

14. See Heiner Gillmeister, "Medieval Sport: Modern Methods of Research-- Recent Results and Perspectives," *International Journal of the History of Sport*, 5, no. 1

(May 1988): 53–68, for a discussion of medieval pictorial resources for the study of sport.

15. Joseph Strutt, *The Sports and Pastimes of the People of England* (London: Metusen, 1801, reprint, ed. J. C. Cox, 1901).

16. A. Briggs, "The View From Badminton," in *Essays in the History of Publishing in Celebration of the 250th Anniversary of the House of Longman, 1724–1974*, ed. A. Briggs (London: Longman, 1974), 187–218.

17. C. J. Longman and H. Walrond, *Archery* (New York: Frederick Unger, 1894); Egerton Castle, *Schools and Masters of Fence from the Middle Ages to the End of the Eighteenth Century* (London: Arms & Armour, 1885, reprint, 1969).

18. Francis Cripps-Day, *The History of the Tournament in England and France* (London: Bernard Quaritch, 1918); R. Coltman Clephan, *The Tournament: Its Periods and Phases* (London: Methuen, 1919).

19. For example, Andrew Lang, "Cricket," *English Illustrated Magazine* (August 1889): 747–57; Robert MacGregor, "The Game of Bowls," *Belgravia* 36 (September 1878): 352–59. Julian Marshall, *The Annals of Tennis* (London: Horace Cox, 1878).

20. See especially Francis P. Magoun, "Football in Medieval English Literature," *American Historical Review* 35 (1929–30): 33–45 and Francis P. Magoun, "Shrove Tuesday Football," *Harvard Studies and Notes in Philology and Literature* 12 (1931): 9–46.

21. J. Aspin, *Ancient Customs, Sports and Pastimes of the English* (London: Harris, 1832); Henry Alken, *The National Sports of Great Britain* (London: T. McClean, 1821); Christina Hole, *English Sports and Pastimes* (Freeport, N.Y.: Books for Libraries, 1949); Norman Wymer, *Sport in England* (London: George Harrap, 1949).

22. Dennis Brailsford, *Sport and Society: Elizabeth to Anne* (London: Routledge and Kegan Paul, 1969).

23. Robert Malcolmson, *Popular Recreation in English Society: 1700–1850* (Cambridge: Cambridge University Press, 1973).

24. See, for example, James Walvin, *Leisure and Society, 1830–1950* (London: Longmans, 1978); Hugh Cunningham, *Leisure in the Industrial Revolution 1780–1880* (New York: St. Martin's, 1980); and Peter Bailey, *Leisure and Class in Victorian England: Rational Recreation and the Contest for Control* (London: Routledge and Kegan Paul, 1978).

25. Michael Brander, *The Hunting Instinct* (London: Oliver & Boyd, 1964); Charles C. Trench, *The Poacher and the Squire: A History of Game Preservation in England* (London: Longmans, Green, 1967); Edward P. Thompson, *Whigs and Hunters: The Origins of the Black Act* (New York: Pantheon, 1976); P. B. Munsche, *Gentlemen and Poachers: The English Game Laws 1671–1831* (Cambridge: Cambridge University Press, 1981).

26. John Ford, *Prize Fighting in the Age of Regency Boximania* (Newton Abbot, England: David & Charles, 1971); John Ford, *Cricket: A Social History 1700–1835* (Newton Abbot, England: David & Charles, 1972); Wray Vamplew, *The Turf: A Social and Economic History of Horse Racing* (London: Allen Lane, 1976); James Walvin, *The People's Game: A Social History of British Football* (Bristol, England: Allen Lane, 1975).

27. See, for example, C. H. Hoskins, "The Latin Literature of Sport," in *Studies in Mediaeval Culture* (New York: Frederick Ungar, 1958), 105–23; H. S. Bennett, *Life on the English Manor 1150–1400* (London: A. Sutton, 1989); G. G. Coulton, *Medieval Panorama* (Cambridge: Cambridge University Press, 1939).

28. See, for example, Magoun, "Football in Medieval English Literature"; Marcelle Thiebaux, *The Stag of Love: The Chase in Medieval Literature* (Ithaca, N.Y.: Cornell University Press, 1969).

29. Representative works include Joachim Rühl, "Methodological, Technical, and Organizational Aspects of Research in Medieval Sport," in *Practising Sport History,* ed. Roland Renson, Manfred Lämmer, and James Riordan (Academia Verlag Richarz: Sankt Augustin, 1987), 41-48; and Heiner Gillmeister, "The Gift of a Tennis Ball in the Secunda Pastorum: A Sport Historian's View," *Arete: The Journal of Sport Literature* 4 (1986): 105-119.

30. John Armitage, *Man at Play: Nine Centuries of Pleasure-Making* (New York: Frederick Warne, 1977); Teresa McLean, *The English at Play in the Middle Ages* (Windsor Forest, England: Kensal, 1984).

31. H. A. Harris, *Sport in Britain: Its Origins and Development* (London: Stanley Paul, 1975).

32. Pierre Bourdieu, "Program for a Sociology of Sport," *Sociology of Sport Journal* 5 (1988): 153-161.

33. One of the more astute sociological considerations of this is John Loy, "The Nature of Sport: A Definitional Effort," *Quest* 10 (May 1968): 1-15.

34. An enthusiastic interpreter of Huizinga is Theodore Roszak, "Forbidden Games," in *Sport in the Socio-Cultural Process*, ed. M. Marie Hart (Dubuque, Iowa: W. C. Brown, 1972), 91-104.

35. See T. S. Henricks, "Huizinga's Legacy for Sports Studies," *Sociology of Sport Journal* 5, no.1 (March 1988): 37-49.

36. See Kendall Blanchard and Alyce Taylor Cheska, *The Anthropology of Sport: An Introduction* (Boston, Massachusetts: Bergin and Garvey, 1985), 38.

37. An interesting treatment of the development of sport in the English public school system is J. A. Mangan, *Athleticism in the Victorian and Edwardian Public School* (Cambridge: Cambridge University Press, 1981). The use of sport is well described in Martin Barry Vinokur, *More Than a Game: Sports and Politics* (Westport, Conn.: Greenwood, 1988).

38. Huizinga, *Homo Ludens*, 13; Gregory Stone, "American Sports: Play and Display," *Chicago Review* 9 (1955): 83-100.

39. Huizinga, *Homo Ludens,* chapter 1, "Nature and Significance of Play as a Cultural Phenomenon."

40. See Huizinga, *Homo Ludens*, chapter 1, "Nature and Significance of Play as a Cultural Phenomenon." See also Mary Gluckman and Max Gluckman, "On Drama, Games, and Athletic Contests," in *Secular Ritual*, ed. Sally Moore and Barbara Myerhoff (Amsterdam: Van Goroum, 1977), 227-43.

41. See, for example, G. J. McCall and J. L. Simmons, *Identities and Interactions* (New York: Free Press, 1978); and Morris Rosenberg, *Concerning the Self* (New York: Basic, 1979).

42. For a sophisticated appraisal of different approaches to this matter, see John Hargreaves, "Sport, Culture, and Ideology," in *Sport, Culture, and Ideology*, ed. Jennifer Hargreaves (London: Routledge and Kegan Paul, 1982), 30-61.

2

SPORT IN FEUDAL ENGLAND

ENGLISH SOCIETY: 1066–1272

When Edward the Confessor died childless in 1066, he relinquished a kingdom that was prosperous, even wealthy, by the standards of the times. Anglo-Saxon England was an economically stable country of perhaps 1.5 million people. Urbanization was beginning, and trade with the Baltic and North Sea ports was well established. There had been a tradition of strong kingship, and such institutions as the territorial militia, land tax, county sheriffs, and minting of money were in place. London had a population of 30,000 and other large towns like Lincoln, York, and Oxford were growing. Wool was becoming a valuable export. Clearly, this was a prize worth taking.

The most fundamental accomplishment of the Norman invasion of that year was a reconnection of England to the patterns, policies, and ruling families of continental Europe. At the most obvious level, this meant a replacement of the native thegns (lords) and freeholders with the adventurers who had enlisted in Duke William of Normandy's cause. One-quarter of the country was kept by the new king as his own. The rest was distributed to 1,400 lay and ecclesiastical tenants-in-chief. The division, of course, was not equal; ten of his more trusted affiliates received another quarter of the land. In short, England was now possessed by a foreign-speaking aristocracy.

From a sociological viewpoint, a more substantial change was the introduction of feudalism on English soil.[1] As a form of political administration, feudalism drew its inspiration from the Germanic custom of binding warriors to a leader through oaths of loyalty and pledges of service. On the Continent (and especially in France) it became common for the leader to provide a benefice of conquered land in exchange for such support. Fundamentally, this was a conditional arrangement that could be revoked by the lord should the vassal fail in his obligations.[2] Just as the lord divided his territory in this way, so the vassal parceled out his holdings among his own supporters. In short, feudalism appears as a glittering pyramid of obligations, in which landholders owe loyalty to those immediately above them and, thus, quite indirectly, to the king.

Despite the elegance and scope of feudalism as a model, the feudal polity was characterized by strong centrifugal forces. Much of this weakness was attributable to the limited economic resources of the king. Like other lords, he had the power of patronage over his vassals (that is, the right to demand service, money, and property on specific occasions) and the spoils of war. However, the prosecution of war became increasingly expensive, and a losing effort could be financially disastrous. Without a regular system of taxation, there could be no police force, no standing army, and only the rudiments of a civil service. Instead, centralized administration depended on the cooperation of the local lords. Just as they were expected to build castles, raise and equip armies, and lead these armies in battle against the enemies of the king, so they were asked to participate in the king's administrative units, the shires. As the armed force of the state, knights were charged increasingly with the duties of keeping order, apprehending criminals, and supporting the assizes (the periodic sessions of superior courts). They could be called to the king's court to offer their advice, settle civil and criminal suits, and provide financial support for some dubious venture.

Of the various obligations owed a superior for rights to the soil, knight service is distinctive of feudalism.[3] In contrast, the abbeys and monasteries held their vast lands primarily on the condition of providing spiritual benefits for the soul of the donor. Notably, this was the great era of church and cathedral building in England. The Normans and their Angevin successors raised their own cathedrals and appointed bishops to sanctify their power. However, this activity was also an expression of the growing power of Christianity. In Europe, the papacy was ascendant; four Crusades (from 1096 to 1271) were mounted, and England was drawn in. In an age of faith, kingship needed the legitimacy provided by the church. Furthermore, the social order was stabilized by such Christian ideals as vassalage (service) and by a focus on the other-worldly rewards that came from the spiritually, rather than the materially, successful life. Moreover, the church provided life stations for younger sons and others who could find no place in the secular order.

However, the church was not simply a conservative force. Its scheme of values countered and softened secular beliefs. Its denial of sacraments to the egregious sinner was considered terrible punishment. It was, after the king, the principal landholder of the country. It controlled, for the most part, formal education and literacy. Those in holy orders were exempt from criminal prosecution. Most profoundly, the church controlled the intellectual resources for comprehending an unpredictable world.

A third source of power, as yet in the shadows, was the developing towns. By 1300 there were perhaps five million people in England; fewer than 10 percent lived in towns.[4] Some towns grew up as trading ports; others arose about the great cathedrals; most were market centers for the locality. In general, town life was both an expression of and a response to the feudal order. Towns typically were established by some local lord who wished to derive income (in the form of fees, taxes, and rents) from their presence. Gradually, this lord, requiring special household or military expenses, signed away portions of his authority by charter. By the close of the period then, more than 100 English towns had become exempted from manorial payments.[5] Ultimately, they gained the right to tax, hold courts, and otherwise manage their affairs. Town corporations or guilds were the effective administrative units; within these, the category of merchants rose to power and workers in other crafts either dropped out or formed their own guilds. At their height, perhaps 25 percent of craftsmen and merchants belonged to the guilds; many towns were too small to sponsor them, and many crafts never organized in this fashion.[6]

The vast majority of the population worked outside the city in agricultural occupations. While landed estates controlled by powerful lords were common in Anglo-Saxon times, the Normans extended and gave legal footing to this pattern. Their creation, the manorial economy, represents a meeting of established farming practices and feudal inclinations. In this system, land is distributed to resident villagers working strips in huge open fields; portions of this are reserved for the lord, and this, too, is worked by the villagers at designated times. According to the Domesday Survey of 1086 (undertaken by the Normans to assess the extent of their new country), nearly 80 percent of the population could be reckoned in the category of "unfree" peasants.[7] These families were legally attached to the land and were bought and sold with it. They owed the lord not only their labor, but also a host of other services or "incidents." Their produce was ground at the mill of the lord, and their lesser disputes were settled at his court; they worshipped at the parish church that he established and endowed. While a small percentage of freeholders continued to exist after the conquest, this lord-serf distinction became the fundamental division of the Middle Ages.

It is commonly observed that feudal society was divided into those who fought, those who prayed, and those who worked for their living. As might be expected, reality was more complicated. Knight service was sometimes a condition of religious tenure, and bishops were commonly secular lords as well. Working people were expected to support the mounted warriors as infantry. Some knights never received land and instead slept in the hall of their lord. Various categories of freeholders in both town and country broke their chains of obligation to a superior. Hereditary rights overwhelmed the original, conditional nature of land tenure. Religious organizations were accorded special status as were the corporations of towns.

In short, the great pyramid was never complete. It was broken at various points by pockets of relative independence and by different principles of association. From this vantage point, then, the stratification system of this period may be visualized as a set of interlocking triangles representing church, town, and the nobility-dominated rural world. Just as these three estates jockeyed for power, so within each order there were significant vertical tensions.

The Middle Ages was a profoundly hierarchical age, and the domination of lord over vassal, lord over serf, master over apprentice, abbot over monk, and husband over wife was personal as well as positional. Nevertheless, society featured important horizontal dimensions. Farmers were members of a village community that long preceded the Normans; monks and nuns were bound as brothers and sisters; knights were encouraged to enter orders of chivalry; guilds were essentially communal orders regulating both working and non-working life. Significantly, then, people took on the values and obligations of the corporations to which they belonged. They shared in the rights and prestige won by the wider group. In the terminology of the sociologist, such memberships were "diffuse"; that is, they were not merely occupations, but also statuses detailing a great range of human expression.

These differences were manifested in various ways. The fighting man was distinguished from the monk or tradesman by such equipage as weapons and dress.[8]   Naming, including the possession of a surname or title, became a designation of rank.   Language, including French for the conquerors and Latin for the clerics, divided these groups, while connecting them to similar categories on the continent.   The mystery of writing separated status groups further. Punishment before the law was differentiated. As a Norman lawyer explained it: "There is a distinction of persons in condition, in sex, according to profession and order, and according to the law which should be observed, which things must be observed by the judge in all matters."[9] It is within this pattern of privilege and prohibition—of status groups gaining special liberties for themselves and guarding them against others—that we must examine sporting life. Like the other matters mentioned above, sport became a chief mechanism for maintaining social distance—that is, for keeping the conceptions of the different life stations clear and distinct.

HUNTING RIGHTS

One of the interesting issues posed by feudal social structure was the assignment of hunting rights. In a society based largely on agriculture, land was the primary source of both wealth and prestige. As landowners (beginning with the king) granted acreage to their social inferiors, the question became, Which of the several layers of tenants should have rights to the wild beasts residing on those lands? Hunting privileges, thus, became an important way to illustrate the superiority of station. Indeed, the history of hunting has been anchored about the twin concepts of exclusion (by means of forest, chase, park, and warren) and poaching.[10]

To understand the significance of hunting in the medieval imagination, it is first important to understand the economic base of the activity. Because of the difficulty in providing winter feed for livestock, animals not kept for breeding typically were slaughtered in the fall. This meant relatively long periods during which there was no fresh meat. Wild game was more than a dietary supplement; it was the centerpiece of a meal. That this dish should have been extracted from nature's bounty (or, more specifically, from the provinces of a lord or neighbor) only added to its appeal.

Before the Norman Conquest, freeholders generally were permitted to hunt on their own grounds. However, the Conqueror was intent on dramatizing his new status. Therefore, he annexed vast areas of relatively unpopulated woods and wasteland as the king's forest—that is, as ground on which only he or his officials could take game. Charles Young has estimated that the new areas of royal prerogative ultimately reached one-fourth of all England. This extension was resented not only on principle, but also because it sometimes involved the removal of villages.[11] The best known of the seventy or so new preserves was New Forest in Hampshire, created in 1079. Here William added some 20,000 acres to 75,000 acres of wasteland already there, an act that involved the destruction of thirty-two villages. The creation of such a forest worked a hardship on those remaining in or living near that land as well. Not only was hunting prohibited, but other uses of the land, such as assart (making new clearings for crops), waste (removing wood for lumber and fuel), and purpresture (raising fences to keep animals away from neighboring cropland), were forbidden as well.

Why should the Norman kings have reserved such vast domains in this way, particularly when some of this land could have been turned to agricultural use? The modern eye looks to the economic advantages of the new arrangement, and, to be sure, the kings were quite aware of these. Privileges to use the forest for various purposes could be sold, and fines could be exacted from captured trespassers. As a final recourse, the king might relax all claims to the land in exchange for money or political support, a policy that led to the diminution of the forest during the thirteenth and fourteenth centuries.

The task of managing such vast and generally uncharted regions was enormous. In response, the administration of the forests became increasingly elaborate.[12] Heading the management was a lord warden, who was often a person of high birth; beneath him was a hierarchy of verderers, foresters, rangers, woodwards, agisters, regarders, bow bearers, and underkeepers. Some were responsible for the condition of the game; others the trees, hedges, and fences. Regarders were to keep track of the local populace, specifically those who possessed bows and arrows and large dogs. Agisters supervised the herding of cattle within these territories. Verderers were local landowners who lent their authority to criminal arrests and prosecutions.

To enforce the royal prerogative, a system of forest courts was established.[13] By this process, forest law became separated from common law. After 1225 three separate courts were arranged under the administration of the justices in eyre. The Woodmote and the Court of Attachment (or forty-day court) were preliminary courts that recommended cases to the Swainmote. Here, a jury of appointed freeholders oversaw a trial before the forest officials. The most serious crimes might be passed up to yet another level, the eyre of the forest. As always, the king was sensitive to the revenue that could be produced by such procedures, and the more successful administrators were those such as the de Neville family in the twelfth and thirteenth centuries who oversaw these finances carefully.

Although several years might pass between the visits of the justices in eyre, the forest courts were resented and feared by the local populace. On the one hand, they were the culmination of a more active policing of society, including regular patrolling or searching for violators; on the other, they represented a departure from the customs of the common law, an occasion in which seemingly arbitrary rule was visited on a locality. If financial interests provided one basis for the forest administration, at least as important a reason for such jealously guarded preserves was the royal love of hunting. By all accounts the Saxon and Danish rulers were enthusiasts for the chase; with the Normans, hunting seems to have become a passion. Well known is the depiction of William I from the Anglo-Saxon Chronicle:

> He made great protection for the game
> and imposed laws for the same.
> That he who slew hart or hind
> should be made blind.
> He preserved the harts and boars
> and loved the stags as much
> as if he were their father.
> Moreover, for the hares did he
> decree that they should go free.[14]

William II (reigned 1087–1100) was equally a lover of the chase; he was killed during a hunting party. His successor, Henry I (r. 11001135), was perhaps more passionate about the revenues to be made from the forest system, but was known to be an enthusiast for boar hunting as well.[15] Less is known of the "habits of Stephen" (r. 1135–1154) in this regard, but Henry II (r. 1154–1189) was most decidedly a hunter. As Walter Map remembers the first Plantagenet king, he was "a great connoisseur of hounds and hawks and most greedy for the vain sport."[16] Of his sons, Richard (r. 1189–1199 was only in England for a few months of a ten-year reign, but John (r. 1199–1216) made up for it by assembling a large hunting establishment.[17] Finally, Henry III (r. 1216–1272) was not by inclination a great sportsman; however, he, too, spent many days at his hunting lodges at Clarendon and Geddington.[18] In an age of martial prowess, hunting was one standard by which the vigor of the king was proclaimed; as such, it was as much expectation as pleasure.

The early kings defended their domain to a degree remarkable by modern standards. Richard, for example, added castration to the list of punishments for forest offenses. When mere threat was not sufficient to prevent trespassing, measures were taken to restrict the possession of hunting implements. One example of this is the "lawing" of dogs during the reign of Henry II.[19] By statute all mastiffs—and later all larger dogs—living near the king's forests (and thereby constituting a hazard to royal game) were to have three toes on each forepaw amputated by hammer and chisel. Similarly, by an act of Henry III in 1225, wearing green in the forest (presumably as camouflage) became an offense.[20] Even clerics, who were immune from the common law, were subject to the wrath of the forest administration.

The royal forests reached their largest dimensions and most systematic administration during the reign of Henry II and then slowly diminished throughout the period. Three documents indicating the decline in monarchical prerogative are the so-called Forest Laws of Canute during the reign of Henry I, the Assize of Woodstock (1184), and the Forest Charter (1217). The first is believed to be a Norman forgery, designed to give their own severe policies some legal precedent.[21] In these "laws," penalties were differentiated between freeman and villein, with the latter receiving such punishments as the loss of a hand, the immersion of his arm in boiling water, and ultimately death itself. The second document, the Assize of Woodstock, is important in part for its preamble, which explained that this was not an arbitrary act of the ruler, but a joint act of king and council.[22] It codified forest policy and checked some of the worst abuses of the forest officials. Finally, the Forest Charter ended the worst punishments, replacing these with fines or, for an offender unable to pay, imprisonment for a year and a day.[23] Furthermore, the process of afforestation was reversed, and magnates (including bishops) were granted rights to take a limited number of beasts of the forest when traveling through the king's preserves. As a political document it is corollary to the new balance struck by the Magna Carta of 1215.

Even though the kings were jealous of their hunting territories (a jealousy that extended to areas they might never visit), one need not feel sorry for the knightly class. For the most part, knights had their hunting rights. Such rights could be acquired in two ways. First were the "rights by soil." Freeholders (and this included yeoman farmers) could take game on their own land provided it was outside the king's forest. Second, there were "rights by privilege." That is, one could apply to the monarch for permission to use his lands. These rights were granted not only to lords, but also to leaders of the clergy and to important citizens of towns. As John Marshall Carter has indicated, there was a growing ecclesiastical acceptance of sport between 1150 and 1200.[24] Some of this he attributes directly to the influence of Bishop Odo (William I's half-brother and the man who commissioned the Bayeux Tapestry). However, many other "secular" clergy-including Thomas Beckett—continued their leisure habits after their appointments. As a contemporary in the twelfth century put it: "Does the knight swear, then so does the bishop, and with far stranger oaths. Does the knight follow the chase; the bishop must go a-hunting. Does the one boast of his hounds; they are the other's only joy."[25]

Thus, access to land was a basic means of discrimination. Beyond this, rights were demarcated by the kind of animals that could be taken.[26] A first category was the beasts of "venery" or "hunting." These included the red deer (both hart and hind), the boar, and sometimes the wolf and hare. They were so termed not only because they provided excellent hunting, but also because they were typically roused and sought in woodland. A second category was the beasts of the "chase," including fallow deer (both buck and doe), marten, and roe deer.[27] These were more often pursued in open country. For legal purposes, both groups might be considered "beasts of the forest." When a person with the right of forest or chase was allowed to enclose an area for his own use, the result was termed a park. Finally (and least prestigious), there was the right of "warren." This permitted the taking of smaller game such as rabbits, pheasants, and partridge, which were more often captured in open wasteland. Warren seems to have been the privilege most commonly granted.[28] Typically, such privileges were not granted categorically, but were the result of individual compacts between king and vassal.

For the most part, then, the powerful of both the sacred and the secular estates had their hunting. Hunting was not merely a pastime; it was a central part of the life style of a rurally situated nobility. As Leon Gautier explains, the life of the feudal elite was governed by three passions—war, hunting, and the tournament—and the last two were preparation for the first.[29] This military emphasis was especially pronounced in the *à force* hunting of the stag (a hart of at least five years), which the Normans popularized. An unsympathetic account of this is provided by John of Salisbury, writing about 1159:

> In our time, hunting and hawking are esteemed the most honourable employments and most excellent virtues by our nobility and they think it the height of worldly felicity to spend the whole of their time in these diversions, accordingly they prepare for them with more solicitude, expense, and parade than they do for war, and pursue the wild beasts with greater fury than they do the enemies of our country.[30]

The earliest hunting manual to comment on this type of hunting is *La Chace dou Cerf,* written anonymously around 1250 in Norman French. From it, the following picture emerges. Early in the morning, the forester with his lymer (or scenting hound) located the stag to be pursued. After marking the way to the spot, he returned to the assembled hunting party. These mounted riders would be led in the actual chase by a huntsman. In heavily forested or boggy country the going would be very slow indeed, and the party would depend on the deep-voiced chime of the hounds. When the beast was finally brought to bay, it was the prerogative of the host or whomever he appointed to dismount, close quickly, and kill it with his sword.[31] This sort of hunting was an opportunity to exhibit not only riding skills, but also courage, and the triumphant return was attended by a parade and feasting.

This relationship between performance in the chase and noble character has been emphasized by Marcelle Thiebaux.[32] As she has demonstrated, the chase by this time had become a metaphor for noble aspiration in medieval legend and literature (for example, Tristan, Roland, and Beowulf). Similarly, the stag and boar had become symbols of noble accomplishment.[33] This relationship becomes even clearer in the period that follows.

The pursuit of the boar offered similar opportunities. While deer hunting was customarily done in the summer, boar hunting was essentially winter sport.

Here, the chase was less critical than the kill. Again, the appointee was expected to ride in and dispatch a dangerous beast with a special spear. In contrast, the hunting of the hare focused on the chase. Hare hunting was permitted throughout the year, and its twisting and turning runs were considered excellent training for both greyhounds and running hounds.

Beasts further down the hierarchy were accosted in less vigorous and ceremonious ways, all of which involved the omnipresent hound. Fallow and roe deer were driven within range of the crossbow, which, because of its mechanically produced power and accuracy, was preferred over the longbow. Smaller game, however, were driven into nets called "hays" and clubbed; some of the burrowing animals were smoked out and beaten or killed by ferrets. Women and children trapped birds and small mammals as well.

What game was left for the poorest segments of rural society? Although they possessed no universal rights as a group, they might well be granted rights to take partridge or rabbits in their own fields or on common land. Second, animals considered vermin (such as foxes, badgers, and wildcats) were usually considered fair prey, although these were difficult to kill and had limited utility once caught. Third, large areas of wasteland were not supervised in any meaningful way. Finally, there was the dangerous, but attractive, alternative of poaching on the grounds of others—an activity that became a central element in the later Robin Hood mythology.[34] How much the sporting and economic motives mixed in poaching is not known. In a time when much of the population relied on salted meat (and many others had none at all), fresh game was a great temptation. It was facilitated by the rudimentary state of criminal detection and by local conspiracies of silence.

Barbara Hanawalt has gone further to argue that hunting (and, most particularly, poaching) was closely related to male identity.[35] Basing her conclusions on thirteenth-century forest eyre cases, as well as literary sources, she describes poaching as a "game" between foresters and poachers. For the poacher, it combined the thrills of being in the woods, of outwitting one's prey and—as significantly—owners of the preserve, and of being bound into a conspiracy with fellow violators. In short, poaching was both a pleasure and a way of solidifying connections with fellow poachers. Venison was commonly the center of a holiday meal, and the source of the food was the subject of much merriment. Indeed, stories of prominent guests invited to partake (unknowingly) of their own game were treasured. Hanawalt also contends that hunting featured a variety of male symbols (horns, knives, sticks and the like) and that ack-nowledged gestures of defiance (placing the head of the prey on a stake facing the castle or, alternatively, the setting sun—to indicate daytime transgression) were common. Certainly, hunting was an accepted form of masculine assertion, and the killing of the first deer by a young male was a ritualized occasion.

In summary, hunting rights illustrate the tensions of the feudal polity. The great (beginning with the king) extended their pleasures at the expense of the small. Smaller men garnered what special privileges they could, poached from their superiors, and defended their rights against others. As expressed in the

Forest Laws, this pyramid of privilege reinforced the idea of individual rights at the expense of common rights.

HAWKING

In contrast to the relative immobility of the rural peasants, life for the wealthiest members of the kingdom was spent on the move. A lord who owned manors in different parts of the country was forced (due to problems in transporting and storing foodstuffs) to travel with his retinue from one to another during the year. These caravans, which are a characteristic feature of the Middle Ages, carried as well the furniture and decorations to be used at each stop. Relieving the drudgery of travel was sport. Hunting was an enjoyable way of garnering fresh meat for the ensemble, both along the way and at each destination, where it was the major male amusement. Also important was hawking, that long-neglected pastime which Annie Abram considers the distinctive sport of the Middle Ages.[36] Early portraiture suggests that the possession of a hawk may have been a mark of nobility before the Norman invasion. To be sure, hawking was of special importance to the Anglo-Saxon and Celtic nobility. In Wales, which was well known for its peregrine falcons, the falconer ranked fifth in a noble household, behind the head of the household, priest, steward, and judge, and before the huntsman. In the Bayeux Tapestry (which celebrates the history of the invasion), Harold Godwinson is depicted with a hawk on his fist as he embarks from Normandy as is Count Guy, a vassal of William's.[37] Likewise, English illuminators may have distinguished the portrait of King Stephen in this manner to indicate his noble, rather than royal, birth. Medieval calendars sometimes represented the month of May by picturing a wealthy youth riding out to hawk, and the antiquarian Joseph Strutt argues that "no act could be reckoned more dishonourable to a man of rank than to give up his hawk."[38]

By the Forest Charter of 1217 the privilege of owning a hawk was extended formally to every free man. Even then, however, the sheer economics of owning a hawk put the matter beyond the means of most. The birds themselves, when imported from Scandinavia, the Mediterranean, or Iceland, were expensive and required long periods of training and special diets. King John, for example, had a pet falcon named Gibbun that he fed a special diet of goats, hares, and chicken. While William Fitzstephen notes that "many of the citizens [of London] delight in taking their sport with birds of the air, merlons, falcons, and the like," few commoners could afford such an expensive hobby.[39] As Frederick II, emperor of Germany and Sicily, summarized it in his classic work on the subject, *De Arte cum Avibus* (1247): "Since many nobles and but few of the lower rank learn and carefully pursue this art, one may properly conclude that it is intrinsically an aristocratic sport."[40]

There also seems to have been a ranking of the different kinds of birds.[41] According to Frederick, the most prestigious of the true falcons (those long-winged birds of prey who hit their target by a long dive or stoop) were the gyrfalcons. Ranking second was the saker from Eastern Europe. Of this, Daude de Pradas in the early thirteenth century remarked: "No bird can fly under it . . . it is suitable only for a lord."[42] Completing Frederick's list of "noble" birds were the peregrine (a native of the British Isles) and the lanner. Smaller and less powerful falcons included the merlon, the hobby, and the kesterel. Of the true hawks (those that seize their prey through swift horizontal maneuvers), probably the most prestigious was the goshawk. These, too, were valuable, as there is a record that Henry III purchased two of them at a price higher than what he paid for two gyrfalcons.[43]

The value of the birds was indicated in other ways as well. Hawks figured historically in peace agreements and Saxon wills. In the Domesday Book, hawks and their eyries (nesting spots) are considered among the more valuable pieces of property. The exchange of falcons was a form of correspondence between royal courts in the Northern Atlantic, and the birds were sometimes accepted in lieu of money payments. As the twelfth-century writer of the *Dialogus de Scaccario* explains:

> Sometimes royal birds are promised to the King for various reasons; that is, hawks or falcons. But if the person promising specifies a "hawk of this year" or "mewed" [i.e., trained,] or names the place of origin, "I will give an Irish, Spanish, or Norway hawk," he must make his promise good. But if neither the giver nor the receiver of the promise has settled the point, the giver may please himself whether he is to pay a mewed hawk or not. But if it is passed by the King's ostringers [keepers of goshawks] as perfect and sound, it will be accepted, wherever hatched. Again, if the debtor being summoned, brings an acceptable hawk to the Exchequer, and there is nobody there to receive it, even though the Summons be put off for a year or two, he need only pay which he prefers. . . .[44]

As in hunting, there was also a hierarchy of prey.[45] The larger prey, such as herons and cranes, presented more spectacular sport and required the larger and more powerful falcons. Hawking at rabbits or other small prey along the ground constituted more modest sport.

The care and training of the birds suggest something about the devotion of their owners. Falcons were exotic and high-strung, and their supervision was a painstaking process. If not acquired fully trained, very young birds were preferred for it was difficult to accustom the older ones to human contact.

The falcons were kept at the mews, a timber and wattle structure with perches inside and places for frequent bathing. Nearby were the dovecot and cranehouse, where practice prey was kept. The whole establishment might be surrounded by hedges and guarded by mastiffs. The care and feeding of the hawks was expensive enough that they were sometimes farmed out to subordinates, particularly during the moulting season. Such practice is indicated by a letter of instructions written by John in 1216 to one of his sheriffs:

We send you by William de Merc and Richard de Erleham three girefalcons and Gibbun the Girefalcon than which we do not possess a better, and one falcon gentle, commanding you to receive them and place them in the mews and provide for their food plump goats and sometimes good hen and once every week let them have the flesh of hares; and procure good mastiffs to guard the mews.   And the cost which you incur in keeping these falcons . . . shall be accounted to you at the Exchequer.[46]

For the training itself, the eyelids were sewn shut and the talons blunted.[47] Leather thongs (jesses) were attached to their feet, as were bells. Held on the gloved hand, the bird would be walked for hours in a darkened room. Gradually, the room would be made lighter and the eyes would be half opened. Always the trainer would reassure the bird and reward it for its docility with scraps of meat.

In training the bird to strike on command, long tethers (creances) were used. So controlled, the now unhooded bird would be taught to attack a feathered target or lure. After a suitable period, free flights would be made, with the falcon returning to its lure; hawks normally would be trained to return to the fist.

Falcons were trained to attack hares first and then small birds. Ultimately, they were taught to kill live cranes, though these at first not only had their claws blunted and their beak tied, but also had fresh meat tied to their back. Finally, the falcon was allowed to kill the crane and in reward was fed its heart. Such were the passions of a martial age.

Equal care was given to deportment. The hoods that the falcons wore were elaborately embroidered. Their bells were sometimes made of silver and tuned differently for a more pleasing effect. They were always carried on the left "fist" by proud owners of both sexes. This connection between aristocratic behavior and hawking was close enough that Gerald of Wales could turn it to allegorical purposes. His comments capture the spirit of the activity and, at the same time, insinuate something about the unsuccessful attempts of Henry II (in 1157 and 1165) to extend his dominion in Wales:

King Henry the Second of England (or his son Richard: I name both, but shun to distinguish clearly since my tale is to his dishonour) in the early days of the reign cast off his best falcon at a heron for the sake of that cruel pastime. The heron circled higher and higher; but the falcon being swifter, had already well-nigh overtaken him, when the king felt certain of victory and cried aloud, "By God's Eyes or His Gorge . . . , that bird shall not now escape, even though God himself had sworn it.". . . At these words the heron turned forth-with to bay; and by a most miraculous change from victim to tormenter, stuck his beak into the falcon's head, dashed out his brains, and (himself whole and unhurt) cast the dying bird to earth at the king's very feet.[48]

THE TOURNAMENT

Perhaps as old as war itself are military games. The Romans had their *ludus Troiae* and the early European tribes, such as the Celts and the Teutons, sponsored similar exercises.[49] In these, the role of the mounted warrior assumed increasing importance; and by the eleventh century in France, the feudal tournament had begun.

As Doris Stenton notes, this *conflictus gallicus* or *bataille francais* was always something of an exotic plant in England.[50] Its center remained on the Continent, and, for the most part, during this period English knights found it necessary to pursue the pastime there. William the Conqueror, his son William Rufus, and Henry I all prohibited these gatherings. While tournaments surfaced during the generally weak kingship of Stephen, they were again opposed by Henry II. Henry's sons, however, were all tourneyors during their youth. With Richard in particular these events found a friend, and they became more prevalent in England after that time.

The rise of the tournament is intimately connected to the institution of knighthood and cannot be understood apart from it.[51] Although the term *knight* derives from the Anglo-Saxon cnicht, the parallel terms of *chevalier* and *ritter,* used on the Continent, better capture the notion of the mounted warrior. If kings had been able to equip their own armies, the glorification of the knight would not have occurred. Instead, the considerable expense of horses, arms, armor, and attendants, as well as the time needed for developing and maintaining the requisite skills, was afforded by the fief system. By such terms, knights had an essentially private economic base from which to support their military activities. Furthermore, those who held castles had virtual political in-dependence as well. How then to draw a geographically isolated and socially diverse collection of military leaders into a relatively cooperative and loyal band of supporters? Knighthood (and the broader ethic of chivalry associated with it) was this device.

It may be remembered that knighthood was not an ascribed status, but rather one conferred in solemn ceremony by another knight, commonly one to whom some allegiance was owed. For his part the knight undertook various vows of service. These included feudal chivalry (vows of loyalty to a superior) as well as obligations to other knights (for example, an agreement not to attack an unarmed foe) and pledges to the church and its missions. Furthermore, during the latter part of the twelfth century, chivalry focused on the respect—and even adoration—of noblewomen, especially those whose marital or social status made them unattainable. Finally, knighthood entailed significant economic implications; one was expected to maintain the status now acquired. In brief, chivalry was a normative order, civilizing a warrior caste and integrating it across the boundaries of regional and political allegiance.

This civilizing process was implemented by the educational system. Youth of the military estate were placed at an early age in the households of relatives or powerful lords. In this colder, less familiar setting they were taught the essentials of horsemanship and military bearing. This apprenticeship continued until military necessity, economic circumstance, or the favoritism of a patron enabled their appointment. Until then they lingered hopefully—assisting knights and trying to distinguish themselves in private skirmishes.

Technically considered, the skills of the knight were difficult to master and maintain. In addition to maneuvering a large horse under difficult conditions, the use of lance and sword required considerable strength and practice. As noted previously, armored cavalry had become elevated over infantry in the military scheme. At the Battle of Hastings, the defenders dismounted and fought on foot. The Normans, on the other hand, used their cavalry as a sort of shock troop, breaking apart the line of defenders. The use of cavalry in this fashion was made possible by earlier changes in the saddle and stirrup. The rider could now absorb the tremendous shock of the lance thrust without becoming unhorsed; similarly, he could fight in close quarters without being pulled off easily. In summary, horse and man had been bound together as an integrated fighting machine.

The obligations of the knights to their respective lords varied, as might be expected of any system featuring essentially private agreements between individuals. A common pattern was the provision of forty days of military service a year; if the lord was attacked, something more might be expected. In addition, knights (or their subalterns) might be expected to provide guard duty at castles, military escorts, and shows of force at ceremonial occasions. In battle each lord was expected to bring his own supporters into the field and they fought under his banner.

It has been argued that the rise of the tournament around 1100 corresponded to the relative decline of private warfare and the growing authority of feudal princes.[52] If somewhat more circumscribed than the real thing, tournaments were not mere mimicry. As the events sharpened military skill and fostered martial enthusiasm between wars, so they fulfilled some of the functions of real war. The military relevance of the events was always recognized. As Roger of Hoveden comments in the twelfth century, "A youth must have seen his blood flow and felt his teeth crack under the blow of his adversary and have been thrown to the ground twenty times. Thus, will he be able to face real war with the hope of victory."[53] As such, the activity was always dangerous. Among the records of important persons killed is that of Geoffrey de Mandeville in 1216. As Ralf of Ceggeshall recalls it, he died "of a wound received while in the French manner, riding horses very quickly they mutually attacked each other with horses and spears."[54] Sometimes the death of a leader precipitated a riot. Matthew Paris records the accidental death of the Earl of Pembroke at Hertford in 1241.[55] At that point the meeting degenerated into a full-scale battle where an important member of his retinue and many other knights were killed. On the Continent, the largest number of deaths seems to have occurred at a tournament at Nuys near Cologne in 1240. There sixty knights died, though many of them suffocated in the dust and heat.[56]

These early events, then, were quasi-battles featuring the barons and their retinues.[57] Two sides (sometimes numbering as many as 200 knights apiece) were drawn; and the battle was fought in the typical fashion of the day. All the knights took part at once, and the fighting (which was termed the melee) might spread over an area of several square miles. Each lord took his normal war retinue, including foot soldiers. Indeed, to the casual observer it would have been difficult to tell the difference between this and real warfare. However, agreements were made about the duration of the fighting and the types of weapons to be used—that is, sharp (*à outrance)* or dulled (*à plaisance).* Furthermore, boundaries were established, as were safety zones (*recets).* Sides were sometimes composed by region (as in north vs. south) or by political affiliation (as in host country vs. foreigners). However, there are no records of judges in the early accounts, and regulation, once fighting had begun, was difficult in any case.

Such occasions represented true training for war. The secret of mounted warfare was organization. Cavalry learned to charge together and to reform quickly. Once the ranks were broken, valuable lessons in skirmishing (or more individual fighting) were learned. Broadswords now replaced lances.

However, the tournament would have been far less popular had it been only a military exercise. Instead, it featured important sociopolitical and economic incentives. At the highest social level it was a place for barons to display their military strength. Allegiances were formed, plots hatched, and able knights recruited. Further down the scale, tournaments held out hopes of social mobility for landless knights. Success on the battlefield might attract the attention of a powerful lord or result in the more tangible benefits of booty and ransoming. Horses, armor, and even the person of fallen knights were claimed by the squires of the victors. Ransoms were determined by the presiding lords, and after arrangements for payment had been made, a knight might return to the fray. Thus, the twelfth-century tourney was a magnet for younger sons of the knightly class, professional warriors with no fief, and those who had been dispossessed. There seem to have been few requirements regarding admission to the sides; thus, an energetic knight-errant might attend one every fortnight on the Continent.[58] In summary, the tournament trail was in part a way of circulating and displaying young warriors to the powerful. It also kept a restless and potentially troublesome group occupied, and provided a framework or filter for their mobility.

The best descriptions of the tourney at this time are found in the biography of William the Marshal, an originally landless knight, who through his skill in tourneying and his talent for social contacts, rose to prominence and eventually became guardian to the young Henry III.[59] Born in 1147 as the fourth son of a minor baron, William was sent at thirteen to Normandy as a squire. At twenty, he fought (unsuccessfully) in a battle to defend Eleanor of Aquitaine, queen to Henry II of England. She arranged for William's release and two years later he became tutor of chivalric exercises for their son Prince Henry. A few years later, the Marshal was included in the entourage of the prince as they made the rounds of European tourneys; the biography includes descriptions of twelve of these events.

From these accounts it appears that the meetings might last several days, with the first given over to exercises for squires (*behourds*). Ladies and other spectators do not seem to play prominent roles; rather, the knights got together afterward to discuss the day's events and to find out about captured friends and relatives. Furthermore, the economic incentives are clear. In 1177 the Marshal began a two-year partnership with Roger of Gaugi. In one ten-month span during that period they ransomed 103 captives.[60] Notably, the desire for individually acquired booty or ransoms could sometimes cause the defeat of the entire group because coordination was required. At any rate, team victory was proclaimed by the side holding the field at the end of the day or by the side holding the most booty.[61]

Qualities of sportsmanship seem dubious. Philip of Flanders, for example, is accused of dashing in with his men after everyone had tired; yet Prince Henry and William were quick to copy the maneuver. Still, prizes were given to those who showed the most prowess, and the Marshal was as interested in glory as he was in money. As Sydney Painter puts it, chivalry had become something of a fad by the end of the twelfth century, and decorous behavior, along with softer manners and even courtly love (inspired by Eleanor's court at Aquitaine), was just beginning to emerge.[62] As part of this process, epic poetry was shifting away from the *chansons de geste*—the accounts of war and violence—and toward romantic or troubador forms. In these new creations, the knight (Perceval, Tristan, Lancelot, and others) was also a zealous, if duty-bound lover. A new vision of castle life as a prosperous and peaceful world was being put forth. This ethic would make its way across Europe in the following century.

Another important influence on the growth of chivalry was the church with its Crusades to the Holy Land. Beginning in 1095 and occurring intermittently throughout the twelfth and thirteenth centuries, the Crusades transformed the rough military man into the Christian knight. Many landless knights entered such orders as the Templars and Hospitallers (organizations that had religious as well as military implications, and the general ethic of piety, sobriety, and honesty influenced the secular orders of knighthood as well. The tournament, then, was a place where these virtues could be proved. However, the church's attitude toward the tourney was always ambivalent.[63] By 1130 papal opposition was strong enough that the Council of Claremont threatened to excommunicate participants, to confiscate their lands and goods, and to treat those killed in tourneys as suicides. Tournaments were seen as leading not only to needless deaths but also to performance of the seven deadly sins; likewise, it was felt that knights could better use their energies crusading. The church also needed trained warriors for its excursions against the Muslims, however, and it was on that basis that John XXII lifted the prohibition in 1316.

In England, papal opposition resulted in new regulations for tournaments under Richard I.[64] It was in response to such an order by Celestin III that Richard sent a letter to the archbishop of Canterbury in 1194 setting forth a scheme for organizing the events. Henceforth, all English tournaments were to be held at five royally approved sites south of the Trent River (the north being less predictable in its loyalty). Three of Richard's most trusted earls were to oversee the events—in particular, to see that they did not devolve into real war. Those breaking this vow of peace might lose horses or armor or even risk imprisonment. Those not getting the required license (such as Robert Mortimer in 1195) also lost their land to the king and were forced to regain it through fines. As with most royal plans, there was money to be made from the arrangement. For the privilege of participating, an earl was to pay twenty marks, a baron ten, a knight with land four, and a landless knight two. Noel Denholm-Young has calculated that the typical tournament of perhaps thirty a side produced in this way about 200 marks.[65] No foreign knights were allowed, although English knights might travel to other countries not hostile to the Plantagenet dynasty.

In general, the tournament posed dangers as well as opportunities for the king. Any large gathering of men at arms represented a danger to the crown, as in 1215 when tourneys became a prelude to the barons' rebellion. Likewise, they led to disorderly conduct and to feuding among rival lords. The genius of Richard's scheme was to place this almost irresistible impulse of the barons under the auspices of the crown. Church (represented by two clerics) and crown (represented by two knights of the Justiciar) thus recorded the participation of legal entrants.

As indicated above, all members of the knightly class (including landless knights and squires) were allowed to participate during this period. Nonmilitary persons (however rich) were not. While the presiding lords initially served as social gatekeepers, increasingly this function was taken over by heralds. During the Crusades the practice of wearing coat armor became popular; by the mid-thirteenth century, heraldry (the study and recording of such insignia) was fairly well established. It became the task of the herald to know the coats of arms of the participants and to extract the proper fees. Like the formalization process, this movement toward social exclusivity would accelerate in the period that follows.

COMBAT SPORTS FOR OTHER GROUPS

Dominant social classes tend to inspire imitation from those below. Feudal society, at least in its secular version, was controlled by a caste who claimed a monopoly on the highest levels of prowess and daring. Similarly, the ethical implications of knighthood—i.e., the vows, quests, and ascetic ordeals—captured the popular imagination. The trappings of knighthood were spectacular as well, and when a prominent baron and his retinue made their way through an area, great throngs gathered to see the costumes, equipment, and menageries of animals.

For such reasons, the various activities of knights, including the tournament itself, spawned mimic forms. For example, tilting at a fixed object was part of knightly training. Such a target or "quintain" had originally been a post or mark attacked by foot soldiers wielding axe, sword, or spear. By the feudal period the target might be dressed as a Turk or Saracen and was constructed so that a sword or bag of sand would swing about and hit the contestant who missed the center of the target. There seems to have been at least two variants of this.[66] In one, the target was attached to a cross piece that would swing about horizontally. In the other, the target would swing vertically and was suspended between two posts through which the contestants rode. Thus, precision with the lance was developed. For the nonknightly class, however, the activity had no military relevance. Still, tilting matches of this sort were set up in towns.

Under such terms, the event lost its knightly solemnity. Indeed, quite the opposite, a sort of comic perversity prevailed. Such a picture is provided by Fitzstephen, writing about 1180, of a "water quintain" by London youth.

> At the Easter festival they play a kind of naval warfare. A shield is firmly bound to a tree in mid-stream, and a small boat, swiftly impelled by many an oar and the current of the river, carries on the stern a youth armed with a lance with which to strike the shield. If he breaks the lance by striking the shield, and yet keeps his footing, he has achieved his aim and gratified his wish, but if he strikes the shield firmly and the lance remains unbroken, he is thrown overboard into the flowing river, and the boat, impelled by its own motion, rushes past him. . . . On the bridge and the terraces fronting the river stand the spectators, ready to laugh their fill.[67]

At another point, he notes a sort of jousting on ice skates, "two of them run against each other in this way from a great distance, and lifting their poles, each tilts against the other."[68] Juliet Barker has collected other examples of this, including jousting upon barrels, on wooden horses pulled by footmen, and from a swing against a man sitting on a stool.[69]

The wealthier citizens and courtiers might also engage in free-for-all jousts from horseback. As Fitzstephen continues:

> Every Sunday in Lent after dinner a fresh swarm of young men goes forth into the fields on war- horses, steeds foremost in the contest, each of which is skilled and schooled to run in circles. From the gates there sallies forth a host of laymen, sons of citizens, equipped with lances and shields, the younger ones with spears forked at the top, but with the steel point removed. They make a pretense at war, carrying out field exercises and indulge in mimic combats. Thither too come many courtiers, when the king is in town, and from the households of bishops, earls and barons come youths and adolescents, not yet girt with the belt of knighthood, for the pleasure of engaging in combat with one another. Each is inflamed with the hope of victory.[70]

Again, the emphasis is on the high spirits of the contestants, for as he continues, "it is not fitting that a city should be merely useful and serious-minded, unless it be also pleasant and cheerful."

Seventy years later, Matthew Paris records that these two groups (citizens and courtiers) were competing in a similar fashion (*quod quintena vulgaritur dicitur*).[71] The Londoners had been challenged by members of the king's household who teased them and called them names. However, the citizens won and then put the courtiers to rout with their broken lances.

As might be expected, there were special tensions between town dwellers and the feudal class. Great lords normally built their castles on the edges of towns (as in London) where they could participate in the defense of a town or, alternatively, defend themselves against it. The citizens' victory in this particular informal skirmish was significant enough to be noted by the chronicler. It was also, in ways he could not have foreseen, a harbinger of deeper social transformations to come.

Another activity of London youth noted by Fitzstephen is archery. At least since Saxon times the bow had been an instrument of hunting (used by all classes) and a weapon (by the lower ranks).[72] Harold had used archers both in his defense against the Danes and later at Hastings. Likewise, the Normans used archers to support their cavalry charges, and they continued to use them in their campaigns against the Welsh and Scots. Indeed, the popularization of the longbow in England is usually attributed to the Welsh, who showed its advantages in defending a fortified or hillside position. Unlike the crossbow (which could be wound mechanically and then shot with relative ease), however, the longbow required great strength and considerable practice. For such reasons, it was not a central weapon in the military scheme.

Perhaps the best indication of the status of archery is the Assize of Arms of Henry II in 1181.[73] By that proclamation Henry ordered all men with property worth more than sixteen marks to take the field with lances, hauberks of mail, and helms; those with between ten and sixteen marks were to have hauberks, lances, gambesons, and steel caps. Finally, the poorer sort were to appear unarmored and with swords, knives, or any sort of smaller arms. Remarkably, there is no specific mention of bows and arrows.

Seventy years later, in another assize, a major change is recorded. Now all citizens with between forty and 100 shillings in land (and burgesses with between nine and twenty marks) are commanded to possess a bow with arrows. Archery practice becomes mandated. Still, until the end of the period, a crossbowman was paid more for a day's work (four pence to two pence) than a longbowman.[74]

OTHER PASTIMES OF COMMON FOLK

It is the nature of history to memorialize the exceptional. The great moments of the great are captured and embellished for public recollection. The ordinary activities of the ordinary escape notice—a dark backdrop to the age. Such is the problem of accounting for ordinary people's play.

As Carter has argued, then, the history of medieval sport must be extracted largely from the public records—the various accounts of deaths, expenditures, public proclamations, court actions, directives to royal officials, and the like.[75] From these we know that people played a great variety of games, that they gambled and fought and sometimes died in their enthusiasm. We know much less about the frequency of their play, about its rules or consequences, or even about the names they ascribed to it.

One significant exception to this general lack of description is the accounts of Fitzstephen. In describing the activities of Londoners about 1180, he notes:

> On feast days throughout summer the young men indulge in the sports of archery, running, jumping, wrestling, slinging the stone, hurling the javelin beyond a mark and fighting with sword and buckler. Cutherea leads the dance of maidens, and until the moon rises, the earth is shaken with flying feet.[76]

While there is some debate over the meaning of "slinging the stone" (*in iactu lapidum*), it seems most likely that this refers to the game of bowls. This pastime is illustrated in a psalter from this time and is known to have been an occasion for gambling.

The wrestling matches are described more fully by Roger of Wendover. On St. James's Day in 1222, the inhabitants of London defeated men from the surrounding districts. Disturbed by the defeat, the seneschal of the abbot of Westminister

> fixed on the following plan of revenge, he offered a prize of a ram on St. Peter's Day and sent word throughout the district for all to come and wrestle at Westminister, and whoever should prove himself the best wrestler should receive the ram for a prize. He, in the meantime, collected a number of strong and skillful wrestlers, that he might thus gain the victory; but the citizens, being desirous of gaining another victory, came to the sport in great strength. The contest having been commenced by both parties, they continued to throw each other for some time. The Seneschal, however, with his suburban companions and fellow provincials, who sought revenge rather than sport, without any reason flew to arms, and severely beat the citizens, who had come unarmed, causing bloodshed among them.[77]

The awarding of a ram or a cock seems to have been typical during the Middle Ages, as these were symbols of virility. The wrestlers themselves usually fought naked except for a loincloth and sometimes a scarf. While there were regional variations in style, the emphasis seems to be on upper body strength used in pulling a man down. Londoners were particular enthusiasts for the sport, and Clerkenwell was a favorite spot for matches on St. Bartholomew's Day.

Less formal than wrestling was sword and buckler play. The weapons here were a short sword and a small round shield (sometimes spiked) permitted to the non-knightly class. The swords were sometimes dulled or even made of wood. Such fights were sometimes the outcome of meetings between gangs of youths who roamed London streets; and it was on this basis that they were prohibited in 1281.

Another sport motivated by gambling was animal fighting. As Fitzstephen explains, "In winter on almost every feast day before dinner either foaming boars, armed with lightning tusks, fight for their lives 'to save their bacon,' or stout bulls with butting horns or huge bears do battle with the hounds let loose on them."[78] Of similar nature was cockfighting: ". . . every year on the day called Carnival . . . scholars from the different schools bring fighting cocks to their masters, and the whole morning is set apart to watch their cocks do battle in the schools, for the boys are given a holiday that day."[79] Competitors were matched by pulling names out of a hat, and through a process of elimination, the cocks killed one another until only one remained. Furthermore, the victory of the owner removed him from certain Lenten obligations at the school, so it was hotly contested.

Likewise, Fitzstephen directs his readers to ball games—though the specific games played are unclear:

> After dinner on the day of Carnival all the young men of the town go out into the fields in the suburbs to play ball. The scholars of the schools have their own ball, and almost all the followers of each have theirs also. The seniors and fathers and the wealthy magnates of the city come on horseback to watch the contests of the younger generation.[80]

Finally, although in another discussion, Fitzstephen notes the popularity of horse racing:

> Just outside the city gates there is a field which is as smooth in fact as in name [Smithfield]. Here every Friday unless it is a major festival, there is a wonderful show of fine horses for sale. All the earls, barons, and knights who happen to be in the city and many of the citizens come either to look on or to buy . . . . When a race is to be run by these horses and by such of the draft horses as are also good runners, the common beasts are led away with a great shouting and hullabaloo. The riders are boys . . . all trained in managing horses. They have special bits for the unbroken animals; the great point is not to let a competitor get in their way. . . . The riders, urged on by love of praise and hope of victory, use spur and whip, and shout at the beasts.[81]

As indicated, these races were "sale" races—occasions to demonstrate the value of horses for market. In a world on horseback, horse breeding was important business. For their part, the kings of the period imported stock from Europe and Arabia and maintained their own royal studs for a variety of breeds. In addition to these sale races, there were major races at Whitsuntide and Easter. Indeed,

Richard I put up a purse of £40 for one of these. Clearly endurance was as important as speed; for the races were set at three miles and more.

In general, Fitzstephen's descriptions are remarkable because they indicate the various settings for Medieval sports. Each activity seems to have had its own time and place. Certain sports occurred on "Sundays in Lent," "at the Easter Festival," on "feast days through Summer," and so on. Likewise, the events were clearly sanctioned by the groups in authority. The schoolmasters permitted their charges to bring their cocks to school on Carnival Day, the wealthy came out to supervise the ball games, and great crowds gathered to watch the naval jousts. Finally, these descriptions reflect some of the divisions of medieval life—the girls danced while the boys played more competitive games, representatives from the various guilds and schools each had "their own ball," the locals challenged the lads of surrounding areas to tests of strength and skill.

All this points to the significance of the holiday in the life of the ordinary person. While summer evenings and Sunday afternoons provided time for informal play, holidays and market days were special days giving vent to more elaborate productions. The great religious holidays included Christmas, Twelfth Day (Epiphany), Shrove Tuesday (the carnival referred to by Fitzstephen), Easter, May Day, and the Feast of St. John the Baptist (Midsummer). Added to this were Whitsuntide (Pentecost), Halloween, All Saints Day, and the days for the patron saints of the various parishes, guilds, orders, and other groups. Each was marked by communal celebrations. Mummery, mystery plays, morris dancing, gambling, animal baiting, cockfighting, ale drinking, and sexual adventure were all elements in this stepping out of routine.

Institutionalized escapism was most developed during the carnival season (originally January 6 to Shrove Tuesday). In France there was a well-established custom among clergy known as the Feast of Fools. Traditionally, on January 6 the monks and clerks would be elevated from their lowly ranks; one might even be elected "bishop" and receive services from those normally his superior. And there would be much feasting and foolery. In England in 1236 Bishop Grosseteste tried to prohibit the custom as "it was replete with vanity and foul voluptuosity."[82]

To some extent, all holidays partook of this foolery. Through comic excess, the fool ridiculed the society of which he was a part. He mocked not only himself (as player of the role), but also the superior whose role he performed so ludicrously. Thus, Fitzstephen's account of the comic jousts comments as well on the excesses of the knightly class. However, the holiday—even when it permitted moments of status reversal—generally had a conservative, rather than revolutionary, effect. Social dissent was safely managed; the ascriptive and hierarchical aspects of feudal life were buffered by calculated moments in which the reverse prevailed. In this sense sport—even foolish sport—offered occasions for individual license in a world dominated by corporate duty.

CONCLUSIONS

For the most part, feudalism constitutes a system of personal, rather than categorical, domination.[83] In other words, people were tied to each other within a context of special arrangements and local customs. Individuals and groups lived by the bargains they were able to strike with superiors. Correspondingly, individualism (as a broader ethic regarding the rights and responsibilities of people in general) or even class consciousness (as a sentiment transcending local affiliations) was not yet well developed. To use the terminology of the sociologist, relationships were commonly "particularistic"—that is, dependent on the special situation or characteristics of the people involved.[84]

This is the theme that seems to dominate sporting life at this time. Hunting is perhaps the key example. That activity expressed the special privileges groups and individuals struck with superiors, be they kings or lords of lesser degree. The listing of more or less prestigious kinds of prey was a way of refining the system. While falconry was guaranteed to all freemen by the Forest Charter of 1217 (which may only have formalized existing practices), it also was dependent on special circumstances, such as the time and skill for training, possession of nesting spots, and other economic support for the birds themselves. The final sport in the noble triumvirate was the tournament. In this, status as a military vassal does seem to have been a categorical restriction. However, here again there was a certain looseness. Any knight who could manage the costs of horse, armor, and squires, as well as the expenses of traveling on the Continent, could participate. In each of these activities, stricter, *categorical* exclusion became more prevalent in the period that follows.

For the upper classes, recreation was not clearly separated from the business of life. Hunting was pleasure, but it also produced food. Before the age of the gun, hawking was a principal means of fowling. Furthermore, the tournament was perhaps more a political event than sport. In this latter setting one gave credence to his value as a warrior or even as a leader of men in battle. In a military caste where security of station depended upon the loyalty of inferiors and the wariness of equals, this was a significant consideration.

Although play was still embedded in economic and political circumstance, ritualized expressions were developing. Certainly, by the latter part of this period, one did not kill a stag or cast a hawk or mount a charge haphazardly. The chivalric orders and the Medieval romances of the era were unifying the ideal of the knight. While he was still a fairly rough character, prowess was becoming more than mere ferocity.

If the elite tradition of games as ritualized expressions of group solidarity and manners was just beginning, the folk tradition was already well developed. As Eric Dunning and Kenneth Sheard have explained, folk games tend to be informal, unspecialized, emotionally spontaneous, and sometimes violent.[85] They also feature a blurring of the spectator and player roles and a general submersion of the individual within the group. To use the terminology of the first chapter, they are fundamentally playful ceremonies, rather than ritualistic ones.

Much of what we know about the play of common folk during this period seems to fit this pattern. Especially on Sundays and holidays, life spilled out onto village commons and city fields. As Teresa McLean has emphasized, interior accommodations for the majority were cramped and uncomfortable.[86] A sunny day was an exhilarating gift. People were made strong by the habits of their work, and their play in these public settings was often rowdy. Gambling was sometimes a part of it, as were occasional fights and even killings. Indeed, this is how much of it finds its way into the historical record.

However, even at this point, there were occasions, for example, the wrestling matches and horse races mentioned, where the participation of ordinary people was sponsored by wealthy or powerful interests. In such settings, there were opportunities for personal recognition—the ram for the best wrestler, the love of praise that motivated the able jockey, and so forth.

If some of this sounds fairly modern, it should be remembered that the preindustrial era was different in more ways than just the kinds of sports that were favored. There were major differences in the extent and enforcement of discrimination in sports; different values were embodied; sports were less formally organized and connected to the other social institutions in somewhat different ways. Such matters will become clearer as the record becomes more fully developed.

NOTES

1. The classic work on feudalism is Marc Bloch, *Feudal Society,* 2 vols. (Chicago: University of Chicago Press, 1974). See also Carl Stephenson, *Medieval Feudalism* (Ithaca, N.Y.: Cornell University Press, 1942) and F. L. Ganshoff, *Feudalism* (New York: Harper & Row, 1964).

2. M. L. Bush, *The English Aristocracy: A Comparative Synthesis* (Manchester, England: Manchester University Press, 1984), chapter 7, "Formation."

3. Some of the more curious and complicated aspects of feudal tenure are discussed in Austin Lane Poole, *Obligations of Society in the XII and the XIII Centuries* (Oxford: Clarendon, 1946).

4. Brian Murphy, *A History of the British Economy: 1086-1970,* (London: Longmans, 1973), 16.

5. George Holmes, *The Later Middle Ages* (London: Nelson, 1962), 38.

6. J. F. C. Harrison, *The English Common People: A Social History from the Norman Conquest to the Present* (Totowa, N.J.: Barnes & Noble, 1984), 64.

7. Maurice Ashley, *The People of England: A Short Social and Economic History* (Baton Rouge: Louisiana State University Press, 1982), 40–41.

8. Pictures of English costume are found in Marjorie Quennell and C. H. B. Quennell, *A History of Everyday Things in* England, vol. 1 (1066-1499) (London: B. T. Batsford, 1930).

9. Quoted in Poole, *Obligations of Society,* 2.

10. See Charles C. Trench, *The Poacher and the Squire: A History of Game Preservation in England* (London: Longmans, Green, 1967), chapter 1, "The Second Oldest Profession."

11. Charles Young, *The Royal Forests of Medieval England* (Philadelphia: University of Pennsylvania Press, 1979), 5.

12. The best descriptions of these are found in Young, *The Royal Forests*.

13. See Young, *The Royal Forests,* 74-113. See also Barbara Hanawalt, "Men's Games, King's Deer: Poaching in Medieval England," *Journal of Medieval and Renaissance Studies* 18, no. 2 (Fall 1988): 178-79.

14. Dorothy Whitelock, ed., *The Anglo-Saxon Chronicle* (New Brunswick, N.J.: Rutgers University Press, 1961), 165.

15. Patrick Chalmers, *The History of Hunting* (London: Seeley, Service, 1936), 97.

16. Walter Map, *De Nugis Cuiralium,* 261, discussed in Young, *The Royal Forests,* 59.

17. Roger Longrigg, *The History of Foxhunting* (London: Macmillan, 1975), chapter 2.

18. Margaret Wade Labarge, *A Baronial Household of the Thirteenth Century* (New York: Barnes & Noble, 1965), 166.

19. Teresa McLean, *The English at Play in the Middle Ages* (Windsor Forest, England: Kensal Press, 1983), 37-38.

20. Longrigg, *The History of Foxhunting,* 24.

21. Trench, *The Poacher and the Squire,* 22.

22. The articles of the Assize are summarized in Young, *The Royal Forests,* 28-29

23. The Forest Laws are reproduced in John Manwood, *A Treatise and Discourse on the Laws of the Forest,* 4th ed. (London: n.p., 1717), 402-406.

24. John Marshall Carter, "Muscular Christianity and Its Makers: Sporting Monks and Churchmen in Anglo-Norman Society, 1000-1300," *British Journal of Sports History* 1, no. 2 (Sept 1984): 109-124.

25. Quoted in Michael Brander, *The Hunting Instinct* (London: Oliver & Boyd, 1964), 20.

26. William Twiti, *The Art of Hunting,* ed. Bror Danielsson (Uppsala, Sweden: Almquist & Wikell, 1977).   See also Chalmers, *The History of Hunting,* Chapter 5, "Norman Influence."

27. The roe was sometimes demoted to the status of warren because it disrupted the feeding of the more prestigious kinds of deer.

28. See Doris M. Stenton, *English Society in the Early Middle Ages* (London: Penguin, 1965), 105.

29. Leon Gautier, *Chivalry* (London: Phoenix House, 1959), 9-31.

30. John of Salisbury, *Policraticus,* quoted in Joseph Strutt, *The Sports and Pastimes of the People of England,* (London: Metusen, 1801; reprint, edited by J. C. Cox, 1901), 4.

31. This type of hunting receives a colorful description in the fourteenth century poem *Sir Gawain and the Green Knight,* trans. James Rosenberg (New York: Holt, Rinehart, & Winston, 1967), 39-67.

32. Marcelle Thiebaux, *The Stag of Love: The Chase in Medieval Literature* (Ithaca, N.Y.: Cornell University Press, 1969), chapter 1.

33. Marcelle Thiebaux, "The Mouth of the Boar as a Symbol in Medieval Literature," *Romance Philology* 22 (February 1969): 281-99.

34. See Maurice Keen, *The Outlaws of Medieval England* (London: Routledge and Kegan Paul, 1961).

35. Hanawalt, "Men's Games, King's Deer."

36. Annie Abram, *English Life and Manners in the Middle Ages* (London: George Routledge, 1913), 230.

37. See John Marshal Carter, "Sport in the Bayeux Tapestry," *Canadian Journal of the History of Sport and Physical Education* 2 (May 1980): 36–60.

38. Strutt, *The Sports and Pastimes of the People of England,* 21.

39. William Fitzstephen, "Description of the City of London (1170–1183)," in *English Historical Documents: 1042–1189,* ed. David Douglas (London: Eyre & Spottiswoode, 1968), 961.

40. Frederick II, *The Art of Falconry Being the De Arte Venandi Cum Avibus of Frederick II,* trans. and ed. Casey Wood and Marjorie Fyfe (Stanford, Calif.: Stanford University Press, 1943), 5.

41. See the discussion of this in Robin Oggins, "The English Kings and Their Hawks: Falconry in Medieval England to the Time of Edward I" (Ph.D. Diss., University of Chicago, 1967), 36–111.

42. Quoted ibid., 48.

43. Labarge, *A Baronial Household of the Thirteenth Century,* 171.

44. Charles Johnson, ed., *Dialogus de Scaccario: The Course of the Exchequer (1176–1179)* (London: Nelson, 1950), 122.

45. McLean, *The English at Play in the Middle* Ages, 53.

46. Quoted in Brander, *The Hunting Instinct,* 34.

47. See Oggins, "The English Kings and Their Hawks," chapter 3, "The Training of Medieval Hawks."

48. Giraldus Cambrensis, *Gemma Ecclesiastica,* D.i.c. 54 (R. S. Vol. II), 161.

49. See R. Ewart Oakeshott, *A Knight and His Horse,* (London: Lutterworth, 1962), chapter 4, "The Tournament."

50. Stenton, *English Society in the Early Middle Ages,* 83.

51. Works stressing this connection include Richard Barber, *The Reign of Chivalry* (New York: St. Martin's, 1980); Raymond Rudorff, *Knights and the Age of Chivalry* (New York: Viking, 1974); and Maurice Keen, *Chivalry* (New Haven, Conn.: Yale University Press, 1984).

52. Stephen Jeffreys, *Tourney and Joust* (London: Wayland, 1973), 14.

53. Quoted in Oakeshott, *A Knight and His Horse,* 203.

54. Quoted in Stenton, *English Society in the Early Middle Ages,* 83.

55. Matthew Paris, *Chronica Majora.* See Noel Denholm-Young, "The Tournament in the Thirteenth Century" in *Studies in Medieval History Presented to Frederick Maurice Powicke,* ed. R. Q. Hunt (Oxford: Clarendon Press,), 253.

56. Francis Cripps-Day, *The History of the Tournament in England and France* (London: Bernard Quaritch, 1918), 47.

57. For discussions of the early tournament, see Juliet Barker, *The Tournament in England: 1100–1400* (Wolfeboro, New Hampshire: Boydell Press, 1986). Also, see Barber, *The Knight and Chivalry* (London: Butler & Tanner, 1970).

58. See Denholm-Young, "The Tournament in the Thirteenth Century."

59. Jean d'Erlee, *L'Histoire de Guillaume le Marechal, Comte de Striguil et de Pembroke, Regent d'Angleterre de 1216 a 1219,* 3 vols. (Paris: Paul Meyer, 1901). The English version is Sidney Painter, *William Marshal: Knight-Errant, Baron and Regent of England* (Baltimore: Johns Hopkins, 1953). See also Georges Duby, *William Marshal: The Flower of Chivalry* (New York: Pantheon, 1985).

60. Painter, *William Marshal,* 41.

61. Barker, *The Tournament in England,* 143.

62. Painter, *William Marshal,* 57.

63. The clerical prohibitions have been collected by Cripps-Day, *The History of the Tournament,* 39–40.

64. Roger of Hoveden, *Annals,* discussed in R. Coltman Clephan, *The Tournament: Its Periods and Phases* (London: Methuen, 1919), 247.

65. Denholm-Young, "The Tournament in the Thirteenth Century," 243.

66. Frederick Hackwood, *Old English Sports* (London: T. Fisher Unwin, 1907), 96–101.

67. Fitzstephen, "Description of the City of London," 960-961.

68. Ibid, 960.

69. Barker, *The Tournament in England,* 151.

70. Fitzstephen, "Description of the City of London," p. 960.

71. Matthew Paris, *Chronica Majora ,* 5: 367, discussed in A. L. Poole, "Recreations" in *Medieval England,* ed. A. L. Poole (Oxford: Clarendon, 1958), II: 619.

72. See Robert Hardy, *Longbow: A Social and Military History* (Cambridge, England: Patrick Steves, 1976), chapter 1.

73. C. W. Oman, "Military Archery and the Art of War," in *Companion to English History: The Middle Ages,* ed. Frances Barnard (Oxford: Clarendon Press, 1902), 53–89.

74. Charles C. Trench, *The History of Marksmanship* (London: Longman, 1972), 61.

75. John Marshall Carter, "Sports and Recreations in XIIIth Century England: The Evidence of the Eyre and Coroners' Rolls," *Journal of Sport History* 15, no. 2 (Summer 1988): 167–173.

76. Fitzstephen, "Description of the City of London," 961.

77. Roger of Wendover, *Annals,* volume 2, recorded in R. B. Morgan, ed., *Readings in English History* (Cambridge: Cambridge University Press, 1923), 103–104.

78. Fitzstephen, "Description of the City of London," 360.

79. Ibid., 961.

80. Ibid., 960.

81. Quoted in Edith Rickert, comp., *Chaucer's World,* ed. Carl Olson and Martin Crow (New York: Columbia University Press, 1948), 228–29.

82. Quoted in Poole, "Recreations," 609.

83. Marc Bloch, *Land and Work in Medieval* Europe (New York: Harper Torchbooks, 1969), 33.

84. Talcott Parsons, *The Social System* (New York: Free Press, 1951).

85. Eric Dunning and Kenneth Sheard, *Barbarians, Gentlemen, and Players: A Sociological Study of the Development of Rugby Football* (New York: New York University Press, 1979), 33–34.

86. McLean, *The English at Play in the Middle Ages,* chapter 1, "Out of Doors."

3

SPORT IN THE LATER MIDDLE AGES

ENGLISH SOCIETY: 1272-1485

During the later Middle Ages, the economic and political foundations of English society shifted, and with these movements came changes in social relationships as well.[1] Villeinage was dying, as was "strenuous" or military knighthood. The lord of the manor was becoming increasingly a landlord; and kings were depending on a Parliament that included wealthy burgesses and gentry. England was acquiring its own distinctive system of law, its own architecture and universities, and a flourishing export trade. The kings lost most of their continental possessions, and English itself became the language of both courtly and common life. Such changes served to differentiate England from other countries and correspondingly produced a new pride in national membership.

Patterns of social stratification changed as well. At the top there was an extension and consolidation of the power of the major landholders. In particular, this meant the development of a peerage. In 1300 there was only one hereditary title, the earl—and only thirteen holders of that. In 1337 dukes were added; then marquisates (1385), baronies by patent (1387), and viscounts (1440). By 1420 there were forty peers; by 1450 there were sixty.[2] By the end of the period, a small and graded class of 50 to 60 had emerged as the central social and political actors in the kingdom.[3]

This dominance was expressed in various ways. While the feudal era featured relatively few legal distinctions for highest nobility, the later Middle Ages saw the evolution of special rights for peers.[4] These included freedom from arrest for many crimes, freedom from imprisonment for debt, a jury by peers, freedom from certain taxes and from various administrative duties such as serving in a posse, and enhanced protection from searches of property. Such differences were further articulated in sumptuary legislation, laws specifying the clothing and possessions appropriate to the different ranks. For example, the *Black Book of Edward IV* (r. 1461-1483) suggests the proper household expenditures attending social rank. A duke was to have 4,000 pounds and 240 attendants, a marquis 3,000 pounds and 200 attendants, and so on.

Another indication of dominance is the institutionalization of this group as a body of advisors to the king. The later Middle Ages is characterized by incessant warfare, including attempts to subdue the Welsh and Scots and later the Hundred Years War (1337–1453) with France. For such business, kings needed military support and cooperation in levying special taxes. The first Parliaments were essentially congregations of the landed elite, and during the fourteenth century, a true House of Lords developed. As the military fortunes of the king fell, the power of this body rose.

Fewer, though defined, privileges were available for somewhat more modest property owners. In particular, lesser knights and squires were called to become justices of the peace in the king's administrative system. Along with substantial burgesses, knights were called to Parliament to advise the king—a process that led to a House of Commons during this time. In one landmark instance Edward I in 1295 summoned two knights from each shire and two burgesses from each borough to his "model" Parliament, and he is credited generally with being the first king to make extensive use of larger councils. Between 1258 and 1311 the Commons attended only ten of seventy parliaments; from 1311 to 1327 they attended all but two. After 1327 they were always in attendance.[5]

An important change affecting this group was the decline of chivalry. As Annie Abram has explained, chivalry (as a voluntary ethic of military commitment) became separated from landownership during this time.[6] While the great landowners continued to take vows of knighthood, fewer middling property holders were doing so. In 1324 there were 1,200 knights in England; by 1490 there were only 375.[7] This was due in part to the increasing expense of military paraphernalia. However, a more important cause was the changing nature of warfare. Because of the protracted warfare of the period, the traditional feudal levy (under which knights served forty days a year) was not adequate. An alternative became the professional soldier—paid at a certain rate a day. Magnates were still charged with bringing their own armies into the field, but their connection to these men was less likely to be land tenure and more likely to be household obligation or money. McFarlane has referred to these changes of the fourteenth and fifteenth centuries as "bastard feudalism."[8] In essence, the status of the military man, when detached from other social and economic criteria, sank. His status was further eroded by an increasing reliance on archery and scientific strategy in war. By the end of the period, such elements—and gunpowder—had more or less displaced the knight.

By 1400, then, a civilian rather than a military ethic had come to prevail for the small rural freeholder; and the word "gentleman" enters the English language about this time.[9] The term reflected the growing legitimacy of careers in law, civil service, church, and education as well as war; and it tended to combine all of these within a broader class ethic that included polite manners, respect for noble women, religious piety, physical vigor, and a smattering (or at least tolerance) of education. The concept was, furthermore, an adaptation to primogeniture as a system of inheritance. When only eldest sons inherit, there is a great deal of downward mobility. These families were now accumulating within a landed class of knightly origins—a fact that accounts for the granting of coats of arms (traditionally armigerous symbols) to mere gentry.

Crucial changes were occurring at the bottom of the social scale as well. During this time, villeinage more or less disappeared. Feudal tenants owing work to their lords were replaced by renters and even freeholders. This change was greatly accelerated by the great plague of 1348–49, by which a population of about 4 million was reduced by one-half to one-third.[10] The sudden absence of laborers produced not only unworked fields, but also new opportunities for the peasant. The villein might enlarge his own holdings or flee to another estate and become a free laborer, extracting what wages he could. If successful, he might purchase acreage and become a small freeholder (yeoman), or he might rent land and sell his produce in a nearby town. In all of these instances the lord-serf relationship was replaced by a more purely economic arrangement. The Black Death affected the status of artisans as well. Workers at every level could demand higher wages or seek new employment.

Predictably, landowners and employers were disturbed by these changes. The Statute of Laborers of 1351—which attempted to force wages back to preplague levels—was one response. Another response of the landowner was to re-evaluate his holdings. The manor became less a place to travel to and more a way to raise money. Where possible, the desmesne might be consolidated and worked to produce a surplus. Common land might be turned into pasture for sheep, or the landlord might try to exact heavier seigneurial dues from his remaining peasants.

This discrepancy between the wishes of the governing groups and the new economic conditions was given clear expression in the Peasants' Revolt of 1381.[11] Begun as armed resistance to new taxes required for the Hundred Years War, it developed as a much wider critique of the social order. Both religious and secular authorities were accused of abusing their privileges. Lower rents and the abolition of serfdom were key demands of the insurgents. Although London was taken and much property destroyed, the rebellion only lasted a few months, and no more than a few thousand persons were involved. What is significant for our purposes is the display of medieval social tensions. Artisans, lower clerics, and even a few gentry were involved. What they celebrated were themes from *Piers Plowman* (circa 1370) and the Robin Hood legends: the universal right to justice and the dignity of the ordinary person.[12]

In general, the later Middle Ages features a heightened class consciousness. In other words, people came to be perceived more as members of societywide categories and less as participants in local groups. This change is reflected in the sumptuary legislation of 1363 (itself a response to the higher wages of the period). Parliament ordained a dress code that included knights with more than 400 marks in land (a mark being worth one-third of a pound), knights with less than 400 marks, esquires and gentlemen with over 100 pounds a year, merchants (those with less than 1000 pounds were considered equal to landowners with 200 pounds rent), artisans, and eventually laborers with less than 40 shillings.[13] As one can see, money as well as status was now important. Another indication of this change is the outlawing of subinfeudation after 1300.[14]   Landholders of all types were now somewhat freer of their immediate superiors.   Slowly, their sense of obligation was shifting toward the king and his administrative machinery.

Into this context of declining military enthusiasm, the growing importance of money, broader literacy, softer manners, and competitive display fits sporting life. As will be shown, sports reflected the desire both to prop up the old order and to make way for the new.

HUNTING

The study of the chase is now aided immeasurably by the development of a hunting literature.   During these two centuries, several English and French accounts of the activity appeared. In terms of sheer quantity of information, the writings are somewhat disappointing because the later works tend to plagiarize the earlier ones. However, this copying is not without significance. It suggests both the similarity of French and English customs and the extent to which hunting technique must have been codified during this time.

The first work on hunting in French, *La Chace dou Cerf,* has already been mentioned. Written anonymously in 1250 (or a little later), it is a pamphlet of 180 lines discussing certain aspects of *à force* hunting, including the etiquette of the kill. The first work oriented to an English audience is *Le Art de Venerie* by William Twiti (the spelling of the name varies) in 1327.[15] Twiti was huntsman for Edward II, and his work—in Norman French—was quickly translated into English by another huntsman named Gyfford. The work again is short (about 280 lines) and consists of descriptions of the various beasts and their habits, the techniques for hunting each, and directions for flaying them. Of special interest are comments on the horn calls used to mark each stage of the hunt.

A later work (in English) is *The Master of Game* by Edward, the second duke of York, which was written early in the fifteenth century (between 1406 and 1413).[16] Edward, who was killed at Agincourt in 1415, held the position of master of game during the reign of Henry IV; and his book is intended as a set of instructions for the future Henry V. Of thirty-six chapters, only five (along with part of the prologue and a short epilogue) are original. The rest is taken from a 1390 French work by Gaston, comte de Foix and Bearn. Gaston was one of the great sportsmen of his age, and his estate in Southern France was said to have boarded 600 hunting horses and 1,600 hounds.[17] His work is again a description (at greater length) of the various prey and their characteristics, hunting techniques and terminology, hounds, and horn calls. Edward omitted sections on snaring (perhaps not favored in England), added some material on the fox and hare, and wrote about the events of a particular deer drive.

A final hunting manual in English is *The Boke of St. Albans* (1486), apocryphally attributed to Dame Juliana Berners, a prioress at Sopwell

Nunnery.[18]   Also cribbed from earlier sources, the work focuses on hunting terminology and on instructions for hunting, flaying, and dressing various beasts. While the above sources represent primarily technical accounts, more vivid descriptions are provided by the literary works of the period. Among these, *Sir Gawain and the Green Knight* (written during the last quarter of the fourteenth century) recounts the hunting of the stag, boar, and fox, though in a somewhat allegorical way.   Likewise, from Mallory's *Le Morte d'Arthur,* one learns something of hunting customs of the time (circa 1470).

From such works, a fairly uniform picture emerges. The chief beasts of prey were the red and fallow deer, the boar, the roe deer, and the hare. Somewhat surprisingly, the hare is given precedence in the three English manuals, a fact that reflects not only the sporting motive, but the taste for hare in the national diet. Worthy sport, though less prestigious because they were vermin, were the wolf, fox, and badger. Indeed, at three points during this period (1355, 1356, and 1413) all subjects were encouraged by royal proclamation to take these latter three without penalty.[19]

The weapons of the hunt included the longbow, Oriental or short bow, crossbow, javelin (or boar spear), ordinary spear, hunting sword, and hunting knife. Hounds such as the Talbot and Gascon were becoming more specialized, and horses were used increasingly. The hunts themselves were fairly slow and ceremonious, with special responsibilities taken by the generally unmounted hunt servants, who located and unharbored the game and assisted at various points along the way. Such assistance might involve driving the game, erecting hays or nets to channel it, keeping the dogs, positioning relays along a possible route, and so forth. Different horn signals were used to mark unharboring, the uncoupling or unleashing the hounds, bringing the hounds up, setting them off on the correct line of scent, and, of course, the death.

The most complete summary of upper-class hunting customs from the later Middle Ages has been provided by Marcelle Thiebaux.[20]   Focusing on the pursuit of the stag, she has identified ten stages of the hunt, each quite formalized.

The first is the unharboring or starting of the deer from its lair. Before dawn, one or more harborers with their scenting hounds would be sent to locate a likely quarry. Telltale signs would be the shape and pressure of the "slots" (hoofprints), the character of the "fewmets" (droppings, which might, for example, indicate the deer's age and value), and the height and depth of the "frayings" (marks made by the antlers as they rubbed against brush or trees).

After dropping branches along the way to indicate the direction of the prey, the harborer would return to the "gathering," as the assembled hunting party was called. Often this was a breakfast spread upon cloths in the forest. Each harborer would present his evidence regarding a stag, and each description was to be as detailed as possible.

Relays of hounds were then posted at various points along a prospective route and maintained by valets. The hunting party was now ready to depart. With all the major participants mounted, they retraced the path set by the harborer. At the point where the signs of the stag were strongest or where it had last been seen, the running hounds were finally released. Three long notes on the horn were blown, and a series of calls to the hounds was begun.

Sometimes the stag would throw the hounds off the scent by a series of clever ruses—for example, by retracing a part of its path and leaping dramatically in one direction. On such occasions, the huntsman would lead the pack in ever-widening circles hoping to pick up the scent.

Ultimately, the stag would tire, and its signals of exhaustion (short rusing runs, downwind flight, and the narrowing of the toe prints) would be evident to the trackers. Sometimes, in desperation it would race through villages or take to the water. This latter course was especially dangerous for the dogs, many of whom might be pushed under and drowned.

With all its alternatives exhausted, the stag would finally turn at bay. The dogs were allowed to gather until there was no avenue of escape. The huntsman would then attempt to move the deer from the thicket where it stood so that it could be shot with an arrow or hamstrung. As a final stroke, the huntsman or his honored designé was to rush forward and pierce the beast's neck with his sword or knife.

The final stage, dividing the quarry, was the most formalized of all. The stag was laid on its back with its feet in the air. In the case of a deer drive (when many might be killed by arrows), the positioning was also crucial. *The Master of Game* explains: "And all the while that the hunting lasts, the carts should go from place to place to bring the deer to the curée. There the server of the hall should be to arrange the curées and to lay the game in a row, all the heads one way and every deer's feet to the other's back."[21] In each case, the breaking up or disjointing of the animal was critical; as the writer of *La Chace dou Cerf* notes, a mistake here could bring "a blow without pity."[22] First the testicles were removed and fastened to a forked stick to which other morsels would be added before it was borne off on the homeward journey. The deer was slit from throat to tail; and each portion was removed in a specified order. For example, there was a proper sequence for the removal of the forelegs as well as stipulations for handling the entrails. All blood was to be captured by the hide; none should touch the ground.

Finally, various organs (such as the heart and lungs) were cut into pieces and arranged on the hide for the dogs, who had been waiting impatiently throughout the entire event. All assembled for this final act, which was attended by much shouting and hallooing, as well as by the blowing of the "death" on the horn. The division of the carcass also was formalized, but seems to have followed local custom. Sometimes, the right forefoot was reserved for the most eminent member of the party. Each huntsman was granted a certain portion in accordance with his role in the hunt—though Twiti notes that if the master huntsman of the king was present, he should get the neck and head of each beast taken.[23] The remainder was arranged for the triumphal journey homeward. The whole procedure is viewed with a sarcastic eye by Erasmus, writing about 1509: "A yokel can butcher an ox, but it takes a noble to butcher a wild animal.

Regard him, bareheaded, knees bent, holding the appropriate knife and no other—making the ritual gestures and carving, according to the rites, certain limbs in a certain order."[24]

In her account, Thiebaux emphasizes the system of horn calls and shouts that was central to the progress of the hunt. One might also point to the development of hunting terminology. For example, the act of dislodging an animal was specified as "unharboring" a hart, "starting" or "moving" a hare, "rearing" a boar, "raising" a wolf, "bolting" a coney, "rousing" a buck or doe, and so forth.[25] Likewise, it might be noted that a group of hart or hind was a "herd"; that of hare was a "hushe" or "down"; that of boars, a "singular" (though for wild swine, it was a "sounder"); that of foxes, a "skulk"; and of wolves, a "rout." Furthermore, two greyhounds were called a "brace" and three a "leash," but two spaniels or harriers were a "couple." Indeed, a prized beast such as the red deer might have a different name for each year of its life. Such jargon may well have facilitated communication; however, it seems more clearly to be a mechanism for distinguishing knowing insiders from the outsider.

The preceding suggests that aristocratic hunting had become fairly formal by the later Middle Ages. The various hunting manuals both expressed and perpetuated that state of affairs. While the works tend to be dedicated to or oriented toward the young noble, one must wonder about the intended audience of the writing. The works may have been recopied for the rural elite, though this group would have had firsthand instruction in such matters. If so, the books helped unify aristocratic behavior. Or the audience may have been the burgesses and gentry, groups that were anxious to simulate the behavior of their social superiors. At any rate, this begets the broader question of who was hunting at this time.

For the most part, the feudal patterns of prerogative continued. Though the royal forests were shrinking, the kings continued to maintain large hunting establishments. Edward I was described by a contemporary as a "vigorous lover of woods and wild beasts."[26] Edward II's queen Isabella even had her own hounds,[27] and Edward III reputedly took sixty couples of deerhounds and an equal number of harriers with him on one of his campaigns to France.[28]

Furthermore, this seems to have been a golden age for clerical hunting. In Chaucer's *Canterbury Tales,* his monk is first of all a hunting man:

> This monk was therefore a good man to horse;
> Greyhounds he had, as swift as birds, to course.
> Hunting a hare, or riding at a fence
> Was all his fun, he spared no expense[29]

Some real-life clerics spent much of their time in the pursuit as well. In this vein, Joseph Strutt records the activities of a thirteenth-century bishop of Rochester who, in his declining years, devoted all his energy to hunting, at the expense of his other duties.[30] In another thirteenth-century example the prior and canon of Bridlington in Yorkshire wrote a letter of complaint to the pope regarding the habits of one archdeacon who brought his hawks, hounds, and attendants with him and overstayed his welcome.[31]   Another, a bishop of Worcester, left a manuscript in which he pleaded for six couples of deerhounds from another bishop.[32]   Perhaps the best example of the hunting cleric, however, is William Clown, who filled the abbey of St. Mary's during the reign of Edward III. He is described by one of his canons, Henry Knighton:

> In the coursing of hares he was considered the most celebrated and renowned
> Master of Hounds among all the lords of the kingdom. So much was this so
> that the King himself and his son Prince Edward and several of the magnates
> of the kingdom used to have an annual engagement of coursing with him.[33]

Likewise, the citizens of the towns continued to press for hunting rights. Rights to the royal forest or other private land might be purchased, as was the case when a thirteenth-century group of burgesses bought most of a private hunting ground of the earl of Leicester for 1,000 pounds.[34]   Hunting was so popular in London that in 1379 the first "Common Huntsman," John Charney, was appointed to "do all things concerning hunting and fishing."[35]

This popularity of hunting (particularly in the towns) resulted in a new means of discrimination, the property qualification. It resulted from a complaint by the Commons to Richard II in 1389:

> Foreasmuch as divers artificers, laborers, and   servants and grooms keep
> greyhounds, and other dogs, and on holidays, when good Christian people be
> at church hearing Divine service, they go hunting in parks, warrens, and con-
> negries of lords to the very great destruction of same.[36]

In response to this purported problem, a property qualification was introduced to restrict those who could rightly keep hounds, ferrets, nets, or "other engines to take and destroy deer, hares, or coneys, or other gentlemen's game."[37]   The qualification for keeping such instruments was forty shillings a year for a layman and a benefice worth ten pounds for a clergyman. The punishment for infraction was one year's imprisonment.

Again, one must note the political context of this legislation. The 1380s had been a period of political unrest; thus the Commons insinuated that "sometimes under such colour, they [the above-named artificers, laborers, and so on] make their assemblies and conferences and conspiracies to rise and destroy their allegiance."[38]   One demand of the ill-fated Peasants' Revolt of 1381 had been free hunting and fishing rights; now such privileges were even more sharply circumscribed.

This, then, was the beginning in England of game law legislation—laws that applied to all hunting territory, public and private. The attempt to deny the lower ranks the use of sporting implements set in motion a process that would last for over 400 years. The changes in hunting were paralleled, predictably enough, by the continued development of hawking. Indeed, this period represents the apogee for hawking.[39] The land was still largely unenclosed, so practitioners could follow their birds on horseback without interference. The Forest Charter of 1217 had guaranteed the right of owning a hawk to every freeman, a factor encouraging wider participation. And refinements in the practice itself, represented by Frederick II's great work near the end of the previous period, suggest new levels of sophistication.

The chief enthusiasts of the sport were still the rural nobility and gentry. Along with hunting, hawking facilities were part of any substantial sporting establishment, and the vision of the good life was to hunt deer, like Chaucer's Sir Thopas,

> and ryde on hawkynge by the river
> with grey goshawke in hande.[40]

Ladies, as a number of manuscript illustrations reveal, were hawking as well, both in single-sex groups and in company with the men.[41] Indeed, so familiar were hawks that there were perches in the bedchamber for a favorite bird.[42]

The interest did not diminish during the fifteenth century, for, as a contemporary manuscript put it, "Manye gentlemen will do almoste nothing els, or at the leste can do that better than any other thing."[43] A picture is formed, then, of ladies and gentlemen spending many hours in the taming and training of their birds, carrying these around with them while traveling, going out with their friends to hawk, and in general treating the birds as pets. It is confirmed by Sebastian Brandt's *Ship of Fools* (first published about 1485 and soon translated into English) in which the gentry are satirized for bringing their sparrowhawks and falcons to church.[44]

Likewise, the interest of royalty continued. Jean Froissart records that Edward III (who took all those hounds with him to France) also took along thirty falconers mounted on horseback.[45] Members of the sacred estate were discouraged by their superiors from excessive interest, but indications of just this phenomenon occur. For example, a fourteenth-century bishop of Ely excommunicated a number of laymen who stole his falcon during divine service.[46] Likewise, in 1384 the dean of St. Martin Le Grand received a special right from Richard II to "hunt, hawk, fish, and carry the same away at pleasure" from the royal forests.[47]

While the lower status groups were permitted to hawk, there is little evidence of their doing so. In fact, a proclamation by Edward III in 1360 suggests some continuing opposition to the ownership of hawks by poorer citizens.[48] By that notice, anyone finding a hawk of any description was obliged to deliver it to the sheriff of the county, who in turn would announce the finding of such a bird within the principal towns of the district. The owner could reclaim the bird on payment of costs and proof of ownership. If the hawk was not claimed within four months, the ownership of the bird would revert to the finder, if he was a gentleman. However, if the finder was not a gentleman, the sheriff could keep the hawk and merely recompense the finder. On the other hand, if a person finding a hawk tried to conceal this fact, he was subject to payment of the value of the hawk and a two-year prison sentence. If he could not pay the price (as the poor man undoubtedly could not), "he shall the longer be in prison." It was likewise made a felony to steal the eggs of a falcon, even if these were found on one's own land. Punishment in this instance might be a sentence of a year and a day and a fine at the king's pleasure.

This connection between sporting activities and social rank is given a fanciful expression in the aforementioned *Boke of St. Albans.* In that work the author lists the types of birds considered appropriate for the various stations of human life:

> The eagle, the vulture, and the merlon
> for an emperor
> The ger-falcon and the tercel of the
> ger-falcon for a king
> The falcon gentle and the tercel for a
> prince
> The falcon of the rock for a duke
> The falcon peregrine for an earl
> The bastard for a baron
> The sacre and the sacret for a knight
> The lener and the leneret for an esquire
> The marylon for a lord
> The hobby for a young man
> The gos-hawk for a yeoman
> The tercel for a poor man
> The sparrow for a priest
> The musket for a holy water clerk
> The kesterel for a knave or servant.[49]

There is no indication that this elaborate classification was ever followed. The prince, duke, and earl all have peregrines under different names, and the eagle and the vulture are of little use as sporting birds.[50] What the listing does indicate is the continuing interest of the medieval mind in sumptuary rights or behaviors appropriate to station.

In general, then, hawking maintained its status as a major amusement throughout the period. The royal falconers continued to be important persons with grants of land, and hawks were still offered as gifts, though by now money payments were customary. Something of this change is reflected in John Paston's letter to his brother during the fifteenth century: "I axe no more worldly goods of you for all the servyse that I shall do you whyll the world standeth but a gosshawke."[51] This sentimental affection of the English for their hawks is reflected as well by a much earlier story of Edward I recorded by the contemporary Nicholas Trivet.[52] Edward was hawking along a river when he saw a companion on the other side who had neglected to help a falcon that had captured a duck among some willows. The king reproved the man for his neglect, and when the man was still slow in responding, the king berated him further. The fellow then made the mistake of noting that a river lay between the two; whereupon Edward forded the stream with his horse and, sword drawn, took out after the fugitive. When Edward caught up with the man, the latter bared his head to take punishment. However, Edward returned his sword to its sheath, and the two then returned to assist the falcon. Whatever the intended lessons of the writer regarding Edward's character, it seems apparent that hawking was serious business indeed.

THE TOURNAMENT

No sport better illustrates the social transformations of the period than the tournament. As noted above, the character of the landowning class was changing. Fewer were taking the vows of knighthood; money had replaced feudal service. Within this context, then, the tournament developed as a way of both affirming the old virtues of military fealty and establishing a new solidarity among the smaller numbers who participated.

This social (rather than military) rationale effected many changes in the organization of the event. The tourney became socially exclusive and display-oriented. The wider setting now included ladies and courtly festivities. Changes in weapons, armor, and types of fighting took place. Rules became more elaborate. In short, the tournament developed as an increasingly artificial environment for the display of individual honor.

This new formality is indicated by the *Statuta Armorum* of Edward I, which was first issued in 1267 and made statutory in 1292.[53] Edward himself had been involved in violent and even riotous tourneys abroad during the preceding decade; his rules were an attempt to control such disagreements in England. By the terms of these regulations, only knights, squires, and tournament officials were allowed swords—and even the nature of these was specified. Others were not allowed to be armed, even with pointed sticks or clubs. The number of attendants was restricted, and these were to wear their lord's colors. In summary, these rules were to keep onlookers from interfering in the melee, and they were enforced by the threat of seven years' imprisonment.

Richard Barber has noted that the number of participants in the European tourneys continually diminished from the one hundred or so a side that pertained around the beginning of this period.[54] Part of this decline may be attributed to the increasing cost of maintaining the equipage of knighthood, including horses, armor, squires, and other servants. Indeed, Rodney Hilton has argued that by 1250 it was five times as expensive to undertake these requirements as it had been seventy-five years before.[55] Likewise, expensive plate armor was replacing the mail protection of Norman tradition. By the fourteenth century tourneying was a hobby that only the rich could maintain.

The trend toward social exclusiveness was perpetuated by other means as well. Whereas invitations to the earlier tournaments had been more or less

publicly broadcast a week or two before the event, now they were directed to specific grandees and issued months in advance. Furthermore, a set of qualifications based on courtly behavior and pedigree (requiring proof of one's descent from four noble grandfathers) became more important.[56]

Enforcing such restrictions and in general acting as social gatekeepers were the heralds. While shields of arms had been in existence since 1130, heralds as a specific group are first mentioned in 1265.[57] It was their task to know the coats of arms of the participants (a rather complicated symbolism featuring country of origin, families related to, position in family, presence of royal blood, and so forth), to display these symbols, and to proclaim the entrance of the participants and the stages of the event. For this, they received a variety of payments including the cost of armor falling to the ground and retrieved, the helmet of a knight at his first tourney, and charges for nailing the shields to the pavillion.[58] Significantly, capture and ransom had declined; poor knights could no longer make a fortune as William the Marshal had done. Indeed, at the à plaisance events only prizes were awarded.

This trend toward exclusivity was aided by the creation of the Order of the Garter by Edward III in 1349 or 1350. Before the formation of this select group, there had been roughly two categories of knights, knights bachelor (generally poorer knights who fought under another's banner) and knights banneret (more substantial men who might lead 25 to 50 men into the field under their own pennant).[59] The Order of the Garter instead identified twenty-five of the greatest nobles who were to stand with the king, observe the peace, and more generally behave in the manner of Arthur's legendary group. Notably, the order was dedicated to St. George, the patron of men of war, and its formation was soon followed by letters patent proclaiming an annual joust in London. The order was divided into two groups headed by Edward and his son, the Black Prince; these represented England in tourneys abroad. Because of the idea's success, it was copied by the king of France's Order of the Star in 1351 and much later by the Duke of Burgundy's Order of the Golden Fleece in 1429.

Perhaps the most thorough exploration of the socio-political significance of the Order of the Garter has been made by Juliet Vale.[60] In part, the order represented a quite conscious attempt by Edward III to identify his kingship with that of his successful grandfather. Both sought to legitimize their reigns within the fanciful tradition of Arthur and his Round Table. Indeed, Edward I had ceremoniously opened the graves of Arthur and Guinevere in 1278 and moved their remains to a more prominent setting. The order was, furthermore, an attempt to perpetuate the atmosphere created by the great triumph over the French at Crecy in 1346. The blue and gold colors of the garter itself were pointedly the colors of France and thereby symbolized Edward's claim to that throne. The members of the order—arranged along the divisions of two tournament teams—were the heads of England's most prominent families. By this act of unification a commonly rivalrous group could be made to bow to a higher "English" tradition and purpose. Significantly, too, the secular nature of the order (in contrast to the religiously inspired orders of the Crusades) meant that the arbiter of this higher purpose would be the king, and not the church.

The new emphasis on courtliness was reflected as well in the change of setting for the tourney. Whereas the early events were held in open country, now they were more likely to be held in city squares or other special enclosures where accommodations for spectators could be provided. Sometimes the instructions for the field were quite specific:

> The kynge shall fynd the feelde for to fight in, and the listes shal be made and devised by the constable. And it is to be considered, that the listes that shall bee of sixtie peases of length, and fortie paces of brede in goode manner, and the erth be ferme and stabill, and harde, and evyn made, withoute grete stoones, and that the erth be platt, and that the listes be strongly barred rounde aboute, and a gate in the Est, and an oothir in the West, with gode and stronge barriers of sevn fete of heith or more.[61]

In London, favorite sites were Smithfield, a familiar place for fairs, and Cheapside, one of the widest streets in the city.

Furthermore, ladies were now central figures. Not only did they inspire and cheer their favorites; typically they awarded prizes. And at tourneys in 1383 and 1390, they led the competitors into the lists by threads of silver and gold.[62] Such involvement did not escape the criticism of Henry Knighton, writing about 1348:

> In these days a rumor and a great complaint arose among the people that when tournaments were held, in every place a company of ladies appeared, somewhat like performers during the time between combats, in the diverse and marvelous dress of a man, to the number sometimes of about forty, sometimes fifty, ladies from the more handsome and the more beautiful, but not from the better ones, of the entire kingdom; in divided tunics ... even having across their stomachs, below the middle, knives which they vulgarly called daggers placed in pouches from above. Thus they came, on excellent chargers or other horses splendidly adorned, to the place of the tournament. And in such manner they spent and wasted their riches and injured their bodies with abuses and ludicrous wantonness that the common voice of the people exclaimed.[63]

Fortunately (in Knighton's view), God "put their frivolity to rout" with rainstorms. Ladies were also hostesses for the dances and festivities that became increasingly important parts of the event, and a knight who failed in his courtly duties to a lady here might be excluded from the tourney or even beaten by the other knights. By the time of Duke René's *Treatise on the Form and Devising of a Tourney* in the fifteenth century, these festivities might occupy several days before and after the actual fighting.[64]

Along with the emphasis on display and festivity was a softening of the events themselves. Perhaps the most noteworthy example of this change is the introduction of the round table, mentioned by Matthew Paris in 1252.[65] While there is some disagreement over the meaning of this expression, a round table generally is considered to have been an English invention in which "arms of courtesy" (that is, blunted weapons) were used within a circular or oval enclosure.[66] Furthermore, as the name implies, the event was swathed with chivalric fantasies and festivities. The round table seems to have enjoyed special popularity during the reign of Edward I (1272-1307). In 1279 Roger de Mortimer held one for one hundred knights and an equal number of ladies at Kenilworth.[67] Likewise, a tournament at Windsor in 1278 may have been one because the knights were given armor of boiled leather, shields of wood, and swords of whalebone and parchment to use.[68] It was then repatronized by Edward III seventy years later and is closely associated with his Order of the Garter.

Another practice growing in popularity was the *pas d'armes*. In its strictest sense the term referred to a narrow bridge or passage that was defended by a number of contestants (*tenans*) against invited challengers (*venans*). In a somewhat broader context the defenders (*ceux de dedans*) might protect an enclosure or territory from the attackers (*ceux de dehors*) or meet them in some artificial set of challenges. One of the best known of these occurred near Dijon in France in 1443.[69] At that event, which lasted two months and spread into three castles, the host Charny family displayed their coat of arms on a "Tree of Charlemagne." Challenges were registered by touching one of two shields with a lance (to indicate whether the fighting was to be on horse or on foot); and anyone beating the defenders received five hundred gold crowns.

Another was hosted by Edward IV at Smithfield in 1467.[70] For this, the special concessions to display are clear because special lists and galleries were created. A first set of stands had areas for knights, squires, and royal orders of the guard (in descending order of importance). A second was for the mayor and aldermen of London, and the king and the tournament officials occupied a third reviewing area. This was followed in the next year by a more elaborate event celebrating the marriage of Edward's sister Margaret to the duke of Burgundy. For this, a tableau of the twelve labors of Hercules was created, and the whole affair (which lasted ten days) was cast within this mythology.

Another change in the nature of the event was the growing popularity of the joust as opposed to the melee. In contrast to the team event, jousting highlighted individual prowess and provided conspicuous opportunities for winning the favor of the ladies. The joust typically began with three passes of the lance. If, after those encounters, both contestants remained on their horses, they dismounted and continued their fighting on foot. To prevent the collision of the horses, a "tilt" or barrier (first of cloth and later of wood) was added early in the fifteenth century. This barrier was a completely social artifice, a recognition of the sport that the tournament had become.

This transformation of the joust into sport continued with the development of special rules for jousting. One well-known set of regulations was created by John Tiptofte, earl of Warrene and constable of England, in 1466.[71] According to these, unhorsing an opponent was the most prized feat. This was followed by the act of striking "coronal to coronal" (hitting the crownlike lance tip) three times. Lesser awards were allotted for striking the crest of the opponent's helmet three times and for breaking the most spears. Striking an opponent's horse was grounds for disqualification.

In general, then, the tournament became a vehicle for the display of individual skill and aristocratic character. At its heart was the old-fashioned emphasis on military prowess. As a fourteenth-century enthusiast, the chronicler Froissart, exclaims:

> Prowess is so noble a virtue and of so great recommendation that one must never pass over it too briefly, for it is the mother stuff and the light of noble men and as the log cannot spring to life without fire, so the noble man cannot come to perfect honor or to the glory of the world without prowess.[72]

Yet, onto this emphasis were grafted softer, more courtly virtues. Dancing, festivity, and even theatricality were now central. When Edward IV tried to reanimate the chivalric tradition of his namesakes in the 1470s, it was clear that the requisite military skills were falling away.[73] Hence, a book printed by Caxton shortly thereafter could claim:

> Alas, what do ye, but sleep and take ease, and are all disordered from Chivalry? I would demand a question if I should not displease—How many knights be there now in England that have the use and exercise of a knight? That is, to wit, that he knoweth his horse, and his horse him. . . ."[74]

ARCHERY

Much of the decline of the tournament as a military exercise can be traced to the rise of archery as a national weapon. The reasons for this rise were both social and military. On the one hand, England was less entrenched than France and Germany in the traditions of chivalry; thus, it turned more readily to the use of commoner-specialists to assist in the fighting. Certainly, the increasing reliance on archers was a rather unchivalric practice. Instead of a "proper" confrontation between men of similar rank with equal weapons in hand-to-hand combat, the English first softened up their opponents with a rain of arrows from hundreds of yards away. Both the knight and (perhaps worse) his horse might be killed before ever reaching the line of fighting. The use of archery brought about the development of plate armor (for knight and horse) and signaled a movement toward scientific strategy in warfare.

While other European armies tolerated their foot soldier, the English glorified him. Indeed, it is the archer who seems to be the hero of the English victories of the period. Edward I had relied on archers against the Scots, and later they prevailed in the victories at Bannockburn (1314) and Halidon Hill

(1333). At Crecy in 1346 a French force of 35,000 was defeated by an English army one-third that size.[75] Around 8,000 of these were archers who cut down the French knights as they made repeated assaults on the English position. While the French had their own artillery force, a contingent of mercenary crossbowmen, its effectiveness was reduced by rain showers, which slackened their strings. The English, on the other hand, relied on long bows, which had been covered in cases.

Archers were also instrumental in the other two spectacular English victories of the Hundred Years' War. At Poitiers in 1356 the French dismounted, so the fighting was more balanced and protracted. Still, the defense, led by the archers, prevailed. At Agincourt in 1415 the French charge was so deep into the English ranks that the archers were pressed into the melee. In all three battles, archers were used to halt or weaken enemy charges.[76] While archery was less useful as an offensive maneuver, it came to be believed that the defense of England rested in large part on the quality of its archers.

Throughout the period, then, efforts were made to enforce archery practice. The first indication of this is the Assize of 1252 in which Henry III commanded all subjects with between 40 and 100 shillings in land (and burgesses with between 9 and 20 marks) to possess a bow and arrows.[77] This was affirmed and extended by Edward I in the Statute of Winchester (1285).[78] Now all persons with an income of less than 100 pence in land were to possess a bow and arrows and to practice on Sundays and holidays. Those living within the king's forests were to have headless arrows (called "bolts") for the safety of the king's deer.

Such proclamations make the class basis of archery and archery practice quite explicit. Just as upper status groups were encouraged to take up the sword and lance, the lower orders were urged (somewhat more forcibly) to adopt the bow. Notably, the bow with arrows referred to was the longbow, an implement that required much strength and years of training. The knightly class (and even ladies) used the crossbow for hunting. For this purpose (and, of course, for poaching too), it was an extremely accurate weapon. However, the crossbow was relatively slow to rewind and it could not shoot the tremendous distances (300–400 yards) of the longbow.[79] Hence, the latter became the distinctive weapon of the common man. In 1417 all those with less than 200 marks were prevented from owning a crossbow.[80]

The ordinary man began archery practice at age seven, and eventually he was expected to maintain a six- to seven-foot bow with two dozen arrows.[81] "Butts" (turfed earthen mounds with paper targets affixed to them) were established near all villages and towns, and on Sundays and holidays the local men would compete with one another, occasionally for prizes. The distances at which they shot seem incredible by modern standards, and undoubtedly the strength and skill of the English yeoman fed such legends as that of Robin Hood and his followers. Indeed, as Patrick Chalmers notes, just as Lancelot was the idealized knight of the thirteenth and fourteenth centuries, so Robin Hood (who is first mentioned in *Piers Plowman* about 1377) was the idealized yeoman.[82] In this light, Chaucer's yeoman was also an archer:

> This yeoman wore a coat and hood of green,
> And peacock-feathered arrows, bright and keen
> And neatly sheathed, hung at his belt the while—
> For he could dress his gear in yeoman style,
> His arrows never drooped their feathers low—
> And in his hand he bore a mighty bow.[83]

With the onset of the Hundred Years' War came increased efforts to enforce archery practice. In 1337 Edward III strictly forbade all other plays and pastimes on pain of death.[84] In 1365 this same Edward ordered his sheriffs to issue a proclamation forbidding all able-bodied men under pain of imprisonment to "meddle in hurling of stones, loggats, and quoits, handball, football, club ball, cambuc, cock fighting or other games of no value." Instead, they were constrained to practice archery, for thus "by God's help came forth honor to the kingdom."[85] This proclamation was made statutory in 1388 and reissued periodically throughout the period. For example, in 1477 the Commons petitioned Edward IV to the effect that "no person should use any unlawful plays, as dice, quoits, football, and such like plays, but that every person mightly and able should use his bow, because that the defense of this land standeth much by archers."[86]

Such proclamations stemmed from the growing reliance on archery in warfare. At Crecy, about 5,000 of the 9,000 English troops were archers. Seventy years later at Agincourt, the proportion had risen to 5,000 of 6,000.[87] Properly directed, archers could devastate great sections of an opposing army. Plate armor proved to be some protection, but the relatively unprotected horses were brought down or disoriented by the rain of arrows. A heavily armored horse was too immobile for battle. By the time attacking soldiers had made their way through the barrage, they were forced to contend with relatively fresh opponents.

Coupled with the enforcement of practice were efforts to increase the quantities of bowstaves and arrows. In 1371 the bowyers and fletchers of London were given official guild status for the making and selling of these.[88] However, procuring wood for bow staves became a problem, and in 1436 bow staves were imported from Prussia.[89] Still, the supply was inadequate, and in 1472 Edward IV complained "that great scarcity of bowstaves is now in this realm, and that the bowstaves that be in the realm be sold of excessive price, whereby the feat of archery is greatly discontinued and almost lost."[90]

In response, every merchant bringing merchandise into England was to include four bowstaves for every ton of goods. Still, the exorbitant prices of the English bowyers continued, so Richard III in 1483 added that each shipment of wine include a certain quantity of staves as well.

By the end of the period, archery as a military weapon was in decline, and the force that defeated Richard III at Bosworth Field in 1485 included its descendant: guns manned by French mercenaries.[91] Despite all efforts, archery could not be maintained. Just as the knightly class lost its military vigor, so the common man found new, more thoroughly civilian enthusiasms.

THE ORIGIN OF TENNIS

There is no evidence that the military elite of Anglo-Norman times were ball players. While there are some indications of the importance of ball games for women and youth,[92] the men seemed to have preferred the more vigorous pursuits provided by horses, hawks, and hounds. Such activities promoted the martial prowess that had forged their position in society. Ball play did not. Even by Chaucer's time, the "parfait knight" of his prologue is hardly a gamester.

During the fourteenth century, however, this antipathy to ball play began to soften. The change was apparently due to French influence, for *jeu de paume,* an early form of handball, was played in the courtyards of castles and monasteries there. During this time the first walled-in courts appeared and *jeu de courte paume* (the indoor game) became differentiated from *jeu de longue paume* (the outdoor game).[93] The French origin of court tennis in England is attested by the fact that the earliest prosecutions of unlawful tennis in England come from towns near the French coast (for example, Canterbury and later Lydd) and by the terminology of the game (*dedans, grille,* and the like).[94]

The position that court tennis has Northern French or Flemish origins has been most fully developed by Heiner Gillmeister.[95] He has argued that the game was carried to England by Protestant refugees and that the terms of the modern game are Anglicizations of their words. *Love* is thus thought to be a transformation of the Flemish *lof,* meaning to play for honor rather than money. *Tennis* itself derives from the French *tenez* (literally, to hold), a call to announce the readiness to serve. The mysterious counting by fifteens is attributed to a common stake in the game, the French sou, which was worth fifteen deniers.

Gillmeister also argues that the game was initially a team game with several players on a side and that there was no net until the sixteenth century. Even in its early stages, the game was complicated by the architectural encumbrances that make it among the most complicated ball games in the world. By the sixteenth century these had become more or less formalized. A roofed shed, known as the penthouse, ran around three sides of the court; and there were netted recesses in the walls under this roof known as the *dedans, grille,* and galleries. Furthermore, an abutment, called the *tambour,* projected from one of the longer walls. These elements and the penthouse were "in play" and introduced some of the strategy of billiards into the contest. Points were scored when a ball was hit into one of the recesses or when it was netted or hit out of play by the opponent. A point might also be scored when the ball bounced twice on the opponent's side of the court. However, on such occasions the site of the second bounce was recorded at one of several "chase" lines. The opponent then had the opportunity to "play off the chase" during the next rally by hitting the ball on its second bounce closer to the wall than the original point (in effect, to surpass the previous point). As one might guess, the game featured not only hard hitting, but also delicate placement and, perhaps more than anything, acute judgment regarding the positioning of the ball.

The game was adopted in England because it afforded exercise in winter and provided a relished occasion for gambling. By the last quarter of the fourteenth century tennis was established enough that Chaucer could assume a general familiarity with it in his *Troilus and Criseyde* (1379-1383): "But canstow pleyen racket to and fro, Nette in, dokke, now this, now that, Pandare."[96]

While the wealthy pursued the game within the closed quarters of their great houses or at "public" courts in town, the poor did not have these opportunities. Like hunting and military exercises, tennis history is a record of discrimination. To a large extent this was imposed by the nature of the activity. The elite version required special courts and balls, and by the latter part of the fourteenth century, rackets were in use. As Julian Marshall notes, such rackets would have been a luxury beyond the capacities of the poor.[97] Likewise, the complicated system of scoring must have distinguished the elite version from humbler forms.

Nonetheless, tennis became an object of legal discrimination. The first of the pronouncements thought to be aimed at tennis (among other games) was the prohibition in favor of archery practice by Edward III in 1365. This was repeated in 1388 by Richard II, though that edict was directed especially to the lower classes.[98] By 1410 Henry IV slapped a punishment of six days' imprisonment on the offenders.[99]

During the fifteenth century tennis rated more specific attention in these pronouncements. The Proceedings of the Court of the Common Council in London for 1476 records the following:

> My lord the Maire chargeth and comaundeth that manner persone what degree
> of condicion he be haff suffer any temys playing, play at the Cloich [bowls]
> or the Cailes [ninepins] to be used in his hous or his ground.[100]

By 1477 Edward IV proclaimed that no "person should use any unlawful Games as Dice, Coits, Tenis, and such like Games . . . upon Pain to have Imprisonment of three years. . . ."[101] In London the Common Council in 1480 again focused this ordinance more specifically on laborers, servants, and apprentices.[102]

Such prohibitions argue for the increasing popularity of tennis. By the mid-fifteenth century the demand for tennis implements was substantial enough that Edward IV was petitioned to prevent the import of tennis balls. In response, a monopoly was granted to the ironmongers for this purpose. The Register of the Ironmongers' Company during 1454-1533 makes it apparent that they sold balls in large quantities throughout the period.[103] In fact, the size of some of the orders (ten gross, twenty gross, and more) and the repetition of certain names suggests that some of the sales may have been to the proprietors of tennis courts.

Seemingly, the wealthier citizens had their tennis and the poor continued to play where they could. Often their playground was the street or churchyard, as this complaint by the bishop of Exeter Cathedral in 1447 makes plain:

Atte whych times, and in especial, in tyme of dyvyne, ungoodly ruled people, most customably yong people of the said comminalte have exercise unlawful games, as the toppe, penny prykke, and most atte tenys, by the which the walls of saide Cloistre have been defowled and the glas wyndowes all to brost, as it openly sheweth, contraries to all good and goostly godenesse.[104]

Such activity, however, represents merely the beginning of tennis in England. The game was concentrated in the towns, and the knightly class maintained a certain suspicion. Such ambivalence appears in Raphael Holinshed's account of the reaction of Henry V (r. 1413–1422) to a gift of tennis balls:

Whilest in the Lente season the King laye at Kenilworth, there came to him from Charles, Dolphin of Fraunce, the Frenche King's eldest sonne, certayne ambassadours, that brought with them a barrell of Paris Balles, which they presented to hym for a token from their master, which presente was taken in verie ill parte, as sent in scorne, to signifie that it was more mete for the King to passe the tyme with such childish exercise, then to attempt any worthy exploite. Wherefore the Kyng wrote to him that ere long, hee would send to hym some London balles, that should breake and batter downe the roofs of his houses about his eares.[105]

The more general acceptance of the game came only in the following century.

MASS BALL GAMES

The village communities had other traditions of ball play, activities that owed little or nothing to the influence of wealthier groups. Participation in mass sports, such as football (closer to soccer than to its American equivalent), hurling, and their variants became an important part of village and town life during the Middle Ages. It is, however, particularly difficult to assign a period of origin to these games. On the one hand, earlier historians and folklorists have considered such mock battles to be expressions of ancient tribal antagonisms.[106] Indeed, many of the later games on festive occasions acquired a mythical significance. For example, the later Derby game was purportedly a re-creation of a victory over the Romans in the third century, at Chester the first football was supposedly the head of a Dane who had been captured and ritually sacrificed, and the quarrymen of the Isle of Purbeck commemorated the original granting of their rights by kicking a ball over the ground they claimed.[107] On the other hand, there is almost no reference to the game before the fourteenth century and no description of this activity before the end of the fifteenth.

During the reign of Edward II (c. 1314) comes the first unambiguous reference to football:

Proclamation issued for the
Preservation of the Peace

By virtue of this notice Nicholas de Farndon, then Mayor, has by trustworthy men of the several wards caused inquiry to be made concerning malefactors and nightprowlers, and has caused a proclamation . . . to be proclaimed throughout the entire city: Whereas our Lord the King is going towards the parts of Scotland in his war against his enemies and has especially commanded us strictly to keep his peace. . . . And whereas there is a great uproar in the City through certain tumults arising from the striking of great foot- balls in the fields of the public, from which many evils perchance may arise . . . we do command and do forbid, on the King's behalf, upon pain of imprisonment, that such game shall not be practiced henceforth within the City . . . .[108]

This beginning of the football record in England represents the start of a fairly consistent pattern: the successive prohibition of the activity because it was disruptive of ordinary routine and responsibility and because it was dangerous to persons and property.

This is confirmed by the second indication of football.[109] About 1321 two young men collided while playing. One of them, a cleric, was wearing a knife, a fact that resulted in the death of his friend and ultimately a dispensation from Pope John XXII. Royal prohibitions appear in 1331 and 1365.[110] In the latter, football receives special attention as one of the "dishonest and unthrifty or idel games" that distracted men from archery practice. As noted previously, this pronouncement was reissued by Richard II in 1388.

In 1409 Henry IV forbade the custom of levying money for football on the occasion of marriages. This is the first indication of a custom that is more evident in later times—married and unmarried men playing against one another at weddings. Apparently, some officials were winking at the custom, for Henry in the following year placed a fine of twenty shillings on the mayor and bailiffs of towns where misdemeanors occurred. His successor, Henry V, was equally adamant. As he prepared his new offensive in the Hundred Years' War, he issued another proclamation forbidding football in favor of archery.

A response of fining participants was tried by the city of Leicester in 1467:

that no man of the town nor of the cuntray play withinne the fraunchys of this town . . . at no unlawfull gamons that has been defended by the statute and lawe and by the parlement, that is to sey at dyce . . . tenes . . . foteball . . . in pain of imprisonment. And the owner of the hows, gardens or places where the playes has been used as often as it is so founded and used shall paye to chamberlains iiii d. and every player vi d. to the same chamberlains to the use of the commons.[111]

It must not have worked very well, for it was repeated again in 1488, as were the royal prohibitions in 1474, 1477, and 1478.

Like the legal record, literary sources first note the presence of football in the fourteenth century. Piecing these together, Francis P. Magoun has offered the following picture: Football at this early stage was probably more a fight than a game.[112] The object of the game was to move the ball toward some goal or boundary. There were very likely few rules, and regulation, once the contest had begun, would have been difficult in any case. Finally, the "teams" were probably of no specified size.

A game of this type that retained many medieval elements in later times was the Haxey Hood Game from Lincolnshire.[113] In this, the articles of play were not balls, but rather twelve pieces of tightly rolled canvas and a thirteenth roll of leather, which legend asserts was once quit rent for the locality. One team consisted of twelve "boggans" led by a "king" or "lord" and a "fool," who, like the boggans, was dressed in scarlet. This group was opposed by men of the neighboring villages. The game began when the lord tossed one of the canvas hoods into the air; the villagers attempted to seize it and carry it to a boundary before it was touched by a boggan. After all the canvas hoods had been played in this fashion, the thirteenth hood was thrown up. The object in this instance was for the villagers to compete against themselves in bringing the hood into their respective towns.

The game was preceded by a ceremonial procession through the local villages. This procession was headed by the fool, his face smeared with soot and red ochre and his body attired in a comical fashion. At the village church, he would call an assembly and repeat the legends of the game. In this context he claimed that two and one-half bullocks had been killed and that the other half was still roaming the fields. Afterward, the fool was tied to a bough and swung to and fro over a fire of damp straw. E. O. James has interpreted this to indicate a mid-winter festival, in which the hood symbolized the head of a bull sacrificed to fertilize the newly ploughed fields and where the smoking of the fool was a ritual fumigation. In his terms, the whole ceremony was "the last stage of a ritual combat between local groups."[114] One might note that it also displays some of the tensions between peasants and their rulers.

Whether football began as a peasant custom or as a town game, it does seem to have been the province of ordinary people. In this regard an interesting thesis had been put forth by Gillmeister.[115] He argues that the various forms of ball games (including football) were initially adaptations by the lower classes of certain principles inherent in the medieval tournament. As these groups were unable to participate in these martial contests, they developed their own contests under much the same terms. In particular, he cites the *pas d'armes* mentioned previously. This defense of a passage or gateway was transformed by ball-players into the defense of a goal mouth. Some of the same terms are used to describe activities in both tournaments and ball games, and both feature an evolution toward more or less equal sides. Although ball play itself seems to have preceded these developments in the tournament, it is also likely that a spectacular event like the tourney cast its shadow over other, less formally organized types of activities.

Perhaps the clearest sociological account of the significance of football has been provided by Norbert Elias and Eric Dunning:

> Semi-institutionalized fights between local groups arranged on certain days of the year, particularly Saints' Days and Holy Days, were a normal part of the traditional pattern of life in medieval societies. Playing with a football was one way of arranging such a fight. It was, in fact, one of the normal annual rituals of these traditional societies. . . . Football and other similar encounters in these times were not simply accidental brawls. They constituted an equilibrating type of leisure activity woven deeply into the warp and woof of society.[116]

CONCLUSIONS

Certainly, a key theme in the sporting history of this period is the extent to which sport became a matter for legal regulation or even prohibition. Games were now seen less as harmless, local customs and more as disruptions of military duty or commercial routine. Leisure habits became subjects of national policy.

This intrusion of wealthier groups into the activities of the poor is also characterized by proscriptive measures: the commandment of archery practice. On the other side, such gambling sports as tennis and bowls were forbidden. So was football on the grounds of its disorderliness. Sometimes these prohibitions were directed expressly at servants, artificers, and the like; however, the most "modern" development of the period is the rise of property qualifications. The obligation to practice archery was couched in economic terms, and later during the period the very possession of hunting implements was set in this manner as well. The rise of towns and the reorganization of agricultural life had produced a nation of freemen. Money became the means for parsing these into categories.

Discrimination thus remained a fundamental element of sporting life. Hunting and hawking continued to be restricted by economic and social mechanisms; the tournament became even more restricted than before. However, the latter event, once so distinctive of the knightly class, was in decline. This fact, coupled with the adoption of ball play (most notably court tennis) by some of the wealthy, represents the beginning of a process of cultural unification. This movement, in which high and low shared some of the same leisure activities and interests, gathered momentum throughout the preindustrial period.

Sport also developed in terms of rules. The best example of this is the tournament, which became quite formalized by the end of the period. In this case the change was related to the social exclusivity of the event. Instead of being an opportunity for landless or disenfranchised knights to make economic and political gains, the tourney became a parade ground for a diminishing circle of notables. Vows of peace and good manners became central. Hunting and hawking also seem to have experienced a proliferation of technique and terminology. Published under the auspices of great and noble hunters, the new sporting literature succeeded in defining a courtly style even in these often small-scale endeavors. This courtly style was etched further by the medieval romances. For Tristan, Roland, and the characters of Arthurian legend, sporting ability was a substantial aspect of noble accomplishment. Such models became a unifying mechanism for the aristocracy: Life came to imitate art.

Closely tied to the themes of discrimination and formality is display. The tournament, stripped of many of its military functions, came to be devoted to the confirmation of social status. The accommodations for ladies and other spectators and the growth of peripheral activities make this plain. Likewise, events that showcased individual talents, such as the joust or *pas d'armes,* crowded out the more disorderly (and anonymous) forms of fighting. These concerns influenced the other noble sports as well. Any public gathering, such as a deer drive or the division of the carcass, demanded concessions to propriety. By performing properly, one gave evidence of his right to "gentle" status.

Lower-class sports developed in other ways for other reasons. Archery was a military exercise. The contests may well have been formal and display-oriented; however, there is no evidence of this. The street games, like the humbler forms of tennis or bowling, were likely pastimes—escapes from routine; their connection with gambling probably mitigated against the development of any clear class ethic. The mass ball games are potentially of most interest. Despite their turbulence and seeming formlessness, they may well have been vehicles for the display of group identity. Certainly, this became quite expressly the case in the period which follows.

NOTES

1. For a general treatment of this period, see George Holmes, *The Later Middle Ages: 1272-1485* (London: Nelson, 1962).

2. Bush, *The English Aristocracy: A Comparative Synthesis,* (Manchester, England: Manchester University Press, 1984), 1.

3. K. B. McFarlane, *The Nobility of Later Medieval England* (Oxford: Clarendon, 1973).

4. Bush, *The English Aristocracy,* 20.

5. Ibid., chapter 7, "Formation."

6. Annie Abram, "Chivalry," in *The Cambridge Medieval History* vol. 6 (Cambridge: Cambridge University Press, 1968), 799.

7. Bush, *The English Aristocracy,* 38.

8. McFarlane, *The Nobility of Later Medieval England.*

9. George Sitwell, "The English Gentleman," *The Ancestor 5* (April 1902): 58-102.

10. See Noel Denholm-Young, *The Country Gentry in the Fourteenth Century* (Oxford: Clarendon, 1969), chapter 1, "The Ranks of Society."

11. See Harrison, *The English Common People: A Social History from the Norman Conquest to the Present* (Totowa, N. J.: Barnes & Noble, 1984), chapter 3, "The Growth of Freedom."

12. See Rodney Hilton, *Bond Men Made Free: Medieval Peasant Movements and the English Rising of 1381* (New York: Press, 1973), 154–55.

13. See Holmes, *The Later Middle Ages,* 17.

14. Bush, *The English Aristocracy,* chapter 7, "Formation."

15. William Twiti, *The Art of Hunting,* ed. Bror Danielsson (Uppsala, Sweden: Almquist & Wikell, 1977).

16. Edward, Second Duke of York, *The Master of Game,* ed. W. A. Grohman and F. Baillie Grohman (London: Ballantine, 1904).

17. Patrick Chalmers, *The History of Hunting* (London: Seeley, Service, 1936), 194.

18. See Rachel Hands, "Juliana Berners and *The Boke of St. Albans,*" *Review of English Studies* 18 (1967): 373–86.

19. Roger Longrigg, *The English Squire and His Sport* (New York: St. Martin's, 1977), 23.

20. Marcelle Thiebaux, "The Medieval Chase," *Speculum: A Journal of Medieval Studies,* Vol. 42, no. 1 (January 1967): 260–274.

21. Edward, *The Master of Game,* 195.

22. Quoted in Michael Brander, *The Hunting Instinct,* (London: Oliver & Boyd, 1964), 60.

23. Twiti, *The Art of Hunting,* 57.

24. Erasmus, *In Praise of Folly* (1509), discussed in Roger Longrigg, *The History of Foxhunting* (London: Macmillan, 1975), 35.

25. Joseph Strutt, *The Sports and Pastimes of the People of England* (London: Metusen, 1801; reprint, ed. J. A. Cox, 1901), 19.

26. Quoted in Young, *The Royal Forests of Medieval England,* (Philadelphia: University of Pennsylvania Press, 1979), 168.

27. Roger Longrigg, *The History of Foxhunting (London: Macmillan, 1975),* 30.

28. Strutt, *The Sports and Pastimes of the People of England,* 5.

29. Chaucer, *Canterbury Tales,* 24.

30. Strutt, *The Sports and Pastimes of the People of England,* 7.

31. "Forest Chase," *Belgravia* 19 (1873): 503–510.

32. Ibid., 507.

33. Henry Knighton, *Chronicon,* ed. J. R. Lumby, Rolls Series 92, vol. 2 (1895), 127. Reproduced in W. O. Hassal, compositor, *How They Lived: An Anthology of Original Accounts Written Before 1485* (Oxford: Basil Blackwell,1962), 185.

34. Margaret Labarge, *A Baronial Household of the Thirteenth Century* (New York: Barnes & Noble), 167.

35. D. W. Robertson, *Chaucer's London* (New York: John Wiley, 1968), 117.

36. Quoted in Austin Lane Poole, "Recreations" in *Medieval England,* ed. A. L. Poole, 2 vols. (Oxford: Clarendon, 1958), 2:619.

37. 13 Richard II, ch. 13.

38. "Forest Laws," *Chambers' Journal* 43 (April 28, 1866): 262.

39. Anthony Vandervell and Charles Coles, *Game and the English Landscape: The Influence of the Chase on Sporting Art and Scenery* (New York: Viking, 1980), 29.

40. Strutt, *The Sports and Pastimes of the People of England,* 24.

41. Thomas Wright, *A History of Domestic Manners and Sebtiments in England During the Middle Ages* (London: Chapman & Hall, 1862), 305-10.

42. Ibid., 305.

43. Quoted in Longrigg, *The English Squire*, 299.

44. Strutt, *The Sports and Pastimes of the People of England.* 21.

45. Philip Glasier, *Falconry and Hawking* (London: B. T. Batsford, 1978), 12.

46. Strutt, *The Sports and Pastimes of the People of England*, 21.

47. Patent Rolls 1381-1385, quoted in Poole, "Recreations," 619.

48. 35 Edward III, ch. 22. See G. G. Coulton, *Medieval Panorama* (Cambridge: Cambridge University Press, 1939), 594.

49. Described in Strutt, *The Sports and Pastimes of the People of England,* 28.

50. Glasier, *Falconry and Hawking,* 13.

51. Quoted in Annie Abram, *Social England in the Fifteenth Century* (London: George Routledge, 1909), 230.

52. Nicholas Trivet, *F. Nicholai Triveti de ordine frat, praedictorum annales,* ed. Thomas Hog, Publications of the English Historical Society, London: English Historical Society, 1845). See Robin Oggins, "The English Kings and Their Hawks: Falconry in Medieval England to the Time of Edward I" (Ph.D. diss., University of Chicago, 1967), 223.

53. R. Coltman Clephan, *The Tournament: Its Periods and Phases* (London: Methuen, 1919), p. 20.

54. Richard Barber, *The Knight and* Chivalry (London: Butler & Tanner, 1970), 168.

55. Hilton, *Knights, Peasants, and Heretics,* 2

56. Barber, *The Knight and Chivalry,* 170

57. Noel Denholm-Young, *History and Heraldry, 1254-1310: A Study of the Historical Value of the Rolls of Arms* (Oxford: Clarendon, 1965), 5.

58. Francis Cripps-Day, *The History of the Tournament in England and France* (London: Bernard Quaritch, 1918), 62.

59. Abram, "Chivalry," 809-10.

60. See Juliet Vale, *Edward III and Chivalry: Chivalric Society and Its Context: 1270-1350* (Woodbridge, England: Boydell, 1982), chapter 5, "Foundation of the Order of the Garter." See also Richard Barber, *The Reign of Chivalry* (New York: St. Martin's, 1980), 161-173.

61. Thomas of Woodstock, "The Order of the Battel in the Court of Chivalry" (1385), quoted in Hassal, *How They Lived,* 190.

62. Jean Froissart, *The Chronicle of Froissart,* translated by Sir John Bourchier and Lord Berners, 6 vols. (London: David Nutt, 1902), 5:422-25.

63. Knighton, *Chronicon,* 2:570, quoted in Edith Rickert, comp. *Chaucer's World* (New York: Columbia University Press, 1948), 217.

64. See Barber, *The Knight and Chivalry,* 175-78.

65. Matthew Paris, *Chronica Majora,* Rolls Series, 5:318. See Poole, "Recreations," 623.

66. Cripps-Day, *History of the Tournament,* 15.

67. Poole, "Recreations," 623.

68. Clephan, *The Tournament,* 18-19.

69. Stephen Jeffreys, *Tourney and Joust* (London: Wayland, 1973), 35-44.

70. Clephan, *The Tournament,* 76-80.

71. See Barber, *The Knight and Chivalry,* 168.

72. Quoted in Holmes, *The Later Middle Ages,* 72.

73. See Arthur Ferguson, *The Indian Summer of English Chivalry: Studies in the Decline and Transformation of English Chivalric Idealism* (Durham, N.C.: Duke University Press, 1960).

74. Raymond Lull, *Book of the Ordre of Chyvalry* (1484), quoted in Cripps-Day, *The History of the Tournament,* 92–93.

75. Robert Hardy, *Longbow: A Social and Military History* (Cambridge: Patrick Steves, 1976), 69.

76. Poole, "Recreations, 158.

77. C. W. Oman, "Military Archery and the Art of War," in Francis Barnard, ed., *Companion to English History: The Middle Ages* (Oxford: Clarendon, 1902), 53–89.

78. 13 Edward I, ch. 6. See Strutt, *The Sports and Pastimes of the People of England,* 43.

79. Hardy, *Longbow,* 68.

80. 19 Henry V, ch. 9.

81. See Donald Featherstone, *The Bowmen of England* (New York: Clarkson & Potter, 1967).

82. Chalmers, *The History of Hunting,* 115.

83. Chaucer, *Canterbury Tales,* 22.

84. Coulton, *Medieval Panorama,* 596.

85. Poole, "Recreations," 625.

86. Coulton, *Medieval Panorama,* 596.

87. Charles C. Trench, *The History of Marksmanship* (London: Longman, 1972), 61.

88. W. E. Tucker, "The Archers' Guilds of Old London," *British Archer* 6 (1954–55): 147–49.

89. Strutt, *The Sports and Pastimes of the People of England,* 44.

90. Quoted in Hardy, *Longbow,* 128.

91. Ibid., 130.

92. See Strutt, *The Sports and Pastimes of the People of* England, 80–104.

93. Malcolm Whitman, *Tennis: Origins and Mysteries* (New York: Derrydale, 1932), 36.

94. Lord Aberdare, *The Story of Tennis* (London: Stanley Paul, 1959), 44.

95. Heiner Gillmeister, "The Flemish Ancestry of Early English Ball Games" in *Olympic Scientific Congress 1984, Official Report Sport History, ed.* Norbert Muller and Joachim Rühl, (Niedernhausen: Schors-Verlags Gesellschaft, 1985), 54–74. Also, Heiner Gillmeister, "The Gift of a Tennis Ball in the Secunda Pastorum: A Sport Historian's View," *Arete: The Journal of Sport Literature* 4 (1986): 105–19. The fuller treatment is found in *Aufschlag fur Walther von der Vogelweide: Tennis seit dem Mittelalter* (Munich: Droemersche Verlagsanstalt, 1986).

96. Geoffrey Chaucer, *Troilus and Criseyde,* ed. B. A. Windeatt, (London: Longman, 1984), 376 (Book 4, lines 456–62).

97. Julian Marshall, *The Annals of Tennis* (London: Horace Cox, 1878), 55.

98. 12 Richard II, ch. 46, reproduced in Marshall, *The Annals of Tennis,* 210.

99. Aberdare, *The Story of Tennis,* 44.

100. Reproduced in Marshall, *The Annals of Tennis,* 210.

101. 17 Edward IV, ch. 3, reproduced ibid.

102. Marshall, *The Annals of Tennis,* 210.

103. Ibid., 210-211.

104. Quoted in H. A. Harris, *Sport in Britain: Its Origins and Development* (London: Stanley Paul, 1975), 24.

105. Raphael Holinshed, *Chronicles,* 6 vols. (London: n.p., 1808), 3:64.

106. G. L. Gomme, *The Village Community* (London: n.p., 1890), 241. See also Francis P. Magoun, "Shrove Tuesday Football," *Harvard Studies and Notes in Philology and Literature* 12 (1931): 11.

107. Montague Shearman, *Football* (London: Longmans, Green, 1899), 3–17.

108. Reproduced in Francis P. Magoun, "Football in Medieval England in Middle English Literature," *American Historical Review* 35 (1929–1930): 36.

109. Ibid., 37.

110. A listing of football prohibitions is found in Norbert Elias and Eric Dunning, "Folk Football in Medieval and Early Modern Britain," in *Sport: Readings from a Sociological Perspective, ed. Eric Dunning* (Toronto: University of Toronto Press, 1972), 118.

111. Reproduced in Magoun, "Football in Medieval England," 41–42.

112. Reproduced ibid., 43.

113. The following account is based on E. O. James, *Seasonal Feasts and Festivities* (New York: Barnes & Noble, 1961), 298–300 and Christina Hole, *English Sports and Pastimes* (Freeport, N.Y.: Books for Libraries, 1949), 53–54.

114. James, *Seasonal Feasts and Festivities,* 299.

115. See the works of Gillmeister cited above. See also Heiner Gillmesiter, "Medieval Sport: Modern Methods of Research—Recent Results and Perspectives," *International Journal of the History of Sport* 5, no.1 (May 1988): 53–68.

116. Elias and Dunning, "Folk Football," 120.

4

SPORT IN
TUDOR ENGLAND

ENGLISH SOCIETY: 1485–1603

As Elton has put it, Henry Tudor "succeeded to a much depleted inheritance."[1] Sporadic outbreaks of plague over a century and a half had weakened the population in number and spirit. Foreign competition and protracted war had stifled export of the country's chief commodity, wool. With the market for produce in decline, agricultural activity in general was depressed. This condition was paralleled in the religious sphere, where anti-clerical feeling was becoming widespread. Finally, and perhaps most conspicuously, centralized political authority had been weakened by baronial uprisings, a fire that finally burned itself out in the War of the Roses and placed the Welshman on the throne.

The genius of the Tudors, then, was their ability to restore strong monarchy and to refashion it in line with the realities of the age. This rebalancing of power reflected primarily the diminishing political and economic scope of the aristocracy, a condition that became a "crisis" (to use Lawrence Stone's term) by century's end.[2] The era of the Tudors featured new sophistication in statecraft and court life—and the peerage was held, for the most part, within that orbit. On the other hand, the growing middle segment of society found new levels of prosperity and influence. Left at the bottom, in perhaps worse condition than before, were the poor. The ability of the Tudors to play off the aspirations of these groups against one another, while at the same time maintaining their overall loyalty, accounts for the success of the monarchy and more broadly for the vitality of the age.

The collaboration of king and Commons was expressed in a number of ways. First, there was an increased dependence on Parliament, which rose from 296 to 462 seats during the century.[3] New military needs, coupled with the inflation that marked the period after 1520, forced the king to ask the Commons for special monies. Furthermore, the actual collection of these taxes or levies required the participation of the shire and borough representatives. In each county, these administrators were the thirty to forty local gentlemen chosen as justices of the peace. They served as judges, bound apprentices, fixed wages, organized the militia, enforced church attendance, supervised the collection of the poor rate, and so on. During the reign of Elizabeth, these unpaid agents were responsible for the administration of over 300 acts;[4] they earned their nickname, "the Tudor maids of all work." In short, the property-owning classes of all levels were embedded in the political framework.

If the power of the Commons became more consolidated during this period, so did their economic standing. The Tudor age was marked by commercial expansion and economic opportunity. The trend toward social mobility begun during the later Middle Ages accelerated, and the resulting stratification system became more differentiated and fluid. A landmark in this process was Henry VIII's dissolution of the monasteries from 1536 to 1539. One-sixth of all cultivable property was thrown on the open market, and, as R. H. Tawney has demonstrated, much of it was purchased by the local gentry.[5] Likewise, the merchants of the cities were turning to country property as a source of both income and social status. In other words, rural wealth became concentrated less in the hands of the nobility.

Another key theme was the inflation of the era. By 1600 prices were five and one-half times higher than they were a century before.[6] This situation was attributable to a variety of factors: an influx of bullion from the New World, the demands of an increasing population on outmoded productive facilities, and a series of devaluations of the currency. Because prices rose much faster than wages did, the commercial classes did well; indeed John Maynard Keynes argues that the growth of business during this era was fueled by this "profit inflation".[7] On the other hand, the large landlord was among the first to experience the pinch of inflation. Despite the fact that food prices were rising sharply, the landlord could not share the benefits of this increase if his income was derived chiefly from rents that were fixed by custom or copy (that is, written contract). Some enterprising landlords therefore found ways to force their less secure tenants off the land. A part of this process was the enclosure movement, which consolidated areas formerly held under the open-strip system and often substituted pasture for cropland.

Those who could not maintain their footing in the rural world experienced a new despair. Evictions in these areas, coupled with the rising population, resulted in the problem of vagabondage, as large bands of beggars roamed the countryside.[8] Originally, the monasteries had doled out food to the poor; however, with the dissolution of the monasteries, this function fell to the state. A poor rate was collected, overseers of the poor were appointed, and poor children were bound as apprentices. Such practices, however, could not restore the old patterns of stability.

In this light, cities, especially London, were becoming huge repositories for those displaced from the rural environment. Those taking refuge included younger sons of nobles seeking their fortunes in trade or professions and various merchants, craftsmen, tradesfolk, vagabonds, mercenary soldiers, and the like. The discovery of trade routes to the East had opened new avenues for commerce, and the invention of the joint-stock venture provided the capital and limited the risk of such speculation. This entrepreneurial spirit was also growing in the craft guilds, where many masters became little more than capitalist employers of the workers in their shops. In general, cities were developing their own criteria of rank, and the arbiter of relationships increasingly was money. Indeed, Louis B. Wright has argued that this large group of merchants, trades-folk, and skilled craftsmen whose thoughts centered on business profits should be interpreted as a new "middle class"[9] At any rate, this group represented a serious challenge to the old rural order, which had been based on ascriptive status and "degree."

Other social trends begun in earlier periods continued as well. The old military ethos was supplanted by more thoroughly civilian virtues. An amateurish militia system, contrasting sharply with the standing armies of the Continent, was installed at midcentury. Emphasis was placed instead on naval development and coastal forts. The internal pacification of the country is reflected as well in architectural changes: The half-timbered Tudor mansion replaced the heavily fortified castle. Likewise, arms became more thoroughly ornamental in function; courtiers might now wear wooden swords in their scab-bards.

The new civilian ethic entailed obligations as well. The task of administer-ing the local county or borough—or even one's own property—had become complicated, and it was now necessary for the gentleman to know something of laws and judicial policy. Education at the grammar school and university levels was becoming common, and literacy was the rule rather than the exception among the upper classes. Indeed, as Stone has pointed out, more people were educated at the English universities during this time than at any other point before the 1930s.[10] The content of their education was changing as well: Stu-dies in the classics, mathematics, and philosophy came to replace the earlier em-phasis on religious subjects and canon law.

This renaissance in learning and in attitudes was extended ultimately by the adoption of the printing press, which, among other things, opened the secrets of aristocratic manners to a much wider group. The sixteenth and seventeenth centuries are famous as the great period of English courtesy literature—that is, copybooks and pamphlets giving moral advice and training in etiquette. Because of the new fortunes that were being made, status confusion—and status climbing—was rampant. "Gentle" manners became an important element in the maneuvering through London society and the court itself.

As before, sporting life was expressive of these broader changes. The rise of the gentry with its jealously guarded tangle of liberties is a theme, as are the resumption of royal authority and the linkage of crown and commoner. The spread of wealth and social mobility became preconditions for a heightened self-consciousness about status and manners in sport as well.[11] The civilizing or softening of life is felt, as is the more general influence of Renaissance Europe.

THE TUDOR COURT AND SPORT

Modern historical writing has tended to replace the earlier interest in biography and political events with descriptions of economic and social patterns, that is, with the conditions undergirding human action in general. In an important sense, however, preindustrial society was marked by the character and political predicament of its rulers. The vitality, appetites, and machinations of the monarch constituted a focus of sorts for society, and the increasingly cultivated personnas of the kings and queens became assurances of social and political stability.

The extension of this personality and the highly visible centerpiece of society was the court. Consuming one-third of the royal expenditures at its height,[12] the court became a large and complicated system of family, friends, hangers-on, advisors and administrators, guards, clerks, servants, musicians and other performers, and sportsmen. Much more than an executive branch of government, it was also, as David Loades explains, a stage and a forum, a vehicle for the dispensation of patronage, a judiciary of last resort, and a cultural center of the kingdom.[13]

The growth of the royal court—in both size and magnifcence—is a noteworthy feature of the Tudor age. It was paralleled (and, in this instance, caused) by the same phenomenon on the Continent. The dukes of Burgundy and the rivalrous monarchs of Western Europe (which, by Henry VIII's time, included Francis I of France and Charles V of Spain) were building competing courts. The function of these was, in large part, to impress each other and the constant trail of foreign emissaries. As courts were intended to radiate wealth and political stability, this purpose was also directed internally toward their subjects. Indeed, maintaining a lavish court was a royal expectation that no monarch could afford to ignore; even the financially unexpansive Henry VII understood the significance of pageantry in solidifying his newly won kingdom.

Among the chief differences between the Tudor court and modern centers of government is the mobility of the former. The court (or at least the substantial portion of it) traveled about the country, staying at not only a half dozen or so major domiciles (Whitehall, Windsor, Hampton Court, York, Greenwich, and so forth) but also at many smaller royal lodges and homes as well.[14] In addition, this "progress" included stops at the mansions of the local nobility and gentry. As the costs were borne by the often anxious hosts, the procedure shifted some of the financial burden of maintaining the court to the populace. Likewise, it reinforced the vigilance and superiority of the monarchy. Furthermore, the traveling processions gave less exalted subjects a chance to witness the spectacle of kingship.

In general, the Tudors were especially sensitive to the significance of display. The life of the royal family was a public occasion, and coronations, weddings, births, entitlements, and deaths were played out in ways that involved thousands of people. The processions and ceremonies were orchestrated with great care, for in an age given to allegory, individuals were not merely that but also embodiments of social and even mythic forces. As Michael D. Bristol explains:

> A public procession is a central and privileged objectification of what is real and essential in the social order, for it is in this act of public pedagogy that the various ranks and functions of society are fully enumerated, their order of ethical precedence given as an order of deployment in public space. The court, members of the aristocracy, and representatives of the lower orders perform as themselves and as the figural anticipation of more perfect forms to be fulfilled in the providential unfolding of history.[15]

This emphasis on the spectacular was abetted by Renaissance idealism regarding the perfect prince. As detailed in Baldassare Castiglione's classic *The Courtier* (perhaps the most influential work of the period of this subject), the ideal ruler was above all to be magnanimous, to hold festivals, games, and public shows. While Castiglione emphasized learning, political shrewdness, and eloquence as desired personal traits, he also called for physical vigor. The courtier should pursue archery, swordplay, running, dancing, horsemanship, and some of the traditional military exercises. This picture was reiterated in England three years later by the publication of Sir Thomas Elyot's *The Boke of the Gouvernor* (1531).[16] Elyot devoted several chapters to physical activity, describing the activities that were appropriate to gentry (for the most part, the ones listed above) and those that were not (such as bowling and football). Both books were part of a larger tradition that emphasized the rediscovered classical ideal: the merger of physical and mental activity. Both also justified this physicality in terms of its health-giving effects as well as its contribution to martial spirit.

In these terms the greatest Renaissance prince in England was Henry VIII. Trained from an early age in physical as well as intellectual skills, he seems in his youth to have been a paragon of physical prowess. Tall and powerfully built as a young man (he ascended the throne at seventeen), he was a fine wrestler and, by most accounts, a tremendous archer. Unlike his father, Henry was an avid patron and participant in tourneys. In addition to the hunting and hawking expected of a king, he was passionate for tennis and bowls—and had courts created for these purposes. Like the other Tudors, he was a gambler and spent large sums on pleasures. He was a patron of musical performances and a lover of disguisings and pageants. By the breadth of his passions and his physical skills, he spanned the class structure in a way that was (and remains) quite rare.

The other long-reigning Tudor bears mention here as well. Elizabeth was disqualified by gender from knightly displays and tennis, but she prominently attended both. Indeed, she restored annual tilting matches to mark her accession to the crown. She was a fine horsewoman who not only followed deer, but shot at them as well. She hawked and patronized animal baitings. These activities, which she followed into old age, were all elements in the self-styled "cult of Elizabeth" which Roy Strong has described.[17]

In general, sport was important to the court both informally and formally. In the former sense it was a way of way of amusing and otherwise working through the tensions of the members themselves.   And often the pot was sweetened by gambling.   However, sport could serve ceremonial purposes as well. Foreign dignitaries expected to be entertained in convivial and even exotic ways.   The baitings of strange animals, menageries, exhibitions of abnormal humans, disguisings, theatrical shows, and even curious sports occurred. In this light, Mary's husband, Philip of Spain, tried to introduce stick fighting (*juego de canas*) to the English, and one reads occasionally of such games as shuttlecock, pall mall, and even a form of lawn tennis.[18] Pointedly, national pride might be at stake in contests against visiting delegations; hence, expert jousters, for example, might be kept at court. If tempers ran high, they were usually cooled by the evening dances and festivities that followed. In short, the Tudors were aware of the uses of sport as a setting for both partisanship and broader good manners.

THE DECLINE OF THE TOURNAMENT

The changes in the tourney that had begun during the previous period now accelerated.   As the practical rationale diminished, the symbolic context expanded. To be sure, the events were still spirited exercise, and accidental deaths might occur; however, tourneys were now fundamentally occasions for display. Its military relevance destroyed by the arrow and shot, the Tudor tournament was a game layered in tradition, an occasion for nobles to recreate publicly the roles of their progenitors, both mythical and real.

In contrast to earlier times, the tournament was now always a background to something more important. As indicated above, the birth of a prince, a royal marriage, the reception of a foreign dignitary, or the execution of a peace treaty demanded extensive pageantry of which the tourney was merely a part. At the more successful of these pageants the conflict itself was placed within a broader mythology which embraced the balls and banquets as well. As Sydney Anglo explains:

> The element of real combat had been increasingly sacrificed to the elements of display and disguising—that is, the dressing up of combatants in fanciful and exotic costumes—and, in its most highly developed form, the tournament became an incipient drama in which the participants represented particular characters and even uttered speeches, so that the actual fighting would arise from a dramatic dispute or allegorical story.[19]

Such fanciful elements are clearly present at the tournament of 1494, when Prince Henry (later Henry VIII) was installed as Duke of York. Here, the knights rode elaborately decorated horses with whimsical mottoes on their sides; they entered the lists under pavilions carried by their servants and were preceded by ladies of the court. One of the combatants is recorded to have entered the lists on a horse decked in paper garb, "[t]hereupon peynted two men pleying at dyse, and certain othes writtyn, not worthey here to be rehearced."[20] This was done to cause the "Kyng to laugh." Whether the joke succeeded is not known; however, such practices reflect the diminishing seriousness of the event.

More elaborate was the marriage tournament for Prince Arthur (first son of Henry VII) and Catharine of Aragon in 1501, in which the emphasis was almost completely on spectacle. The lists were set up before Westminster Hall, and various stands were erected. On the south side of the field was a tilt gallery divided into two sections, one for the king and his nobles, the other for the queen and her ladies. Opposite this was another stage for the mayor of London and various dignitaries; the common folk, also, were provided with double stages all about the perimeter of the field. Furthermore, at this event there was erected a great tree of chivalry, decorated with flowers and fruits and draped with the escutcheons of the various participants. By English standards the procession of knights attained new heights of magnificence:

> On Thursday, 18 November, the entries included the Duke of Buckingham in a pavilion set with "turrets and pynacles of curyous werk;" the Marquis of Dorset preceded by a black-garbed hermit; William Courtenay in a dragon led by a giant; Guillaume de Rivers in a pavilion like a ship floating on simulated painted water; and the earl of Essex in a green mountain, with many "raggs, treis, herbys, stones, and mervelous bests upon the sidds," surmounted by a maiden clad "in her heer."[21]

For eight days the contestants sported at various events, and afterward there were great banquets at which the disguised participants were bought in on elaborate pageant cars.

More enthusiastic than his father about tourneys, Henry VIII took an active part as both promoter and participant in tournaments for over fifteen years. His reign is marked generally by a flourish of spectacles and pageants, of which his coronation tournament in 1509 is an example. The jousting itself was preceded by elaborate speeches in which the participants proclaimed themselves to be the knights of Pallas and those of Diana. This placement of the event within a mythical context, within which the players would act out their parts, was characteristic of the early tournaments of Henry's reign and represents a new stage in the transformation from practical to symbolic legitimation.

The culmination of this showy and decadent feudalism was reached in 1520. This was the meeting of Henry and Francis I at the Field of the Cloth of Gold in France. Supported at fantastic expense (and perhaps before Henry realized fully the limitations of his treasury), the event lasted three weeks. It featured a special castle created for the occasion and more than 2,000 tents for the participants. While Henry and Francis did not joust against one another (the political ramifications would have been too serious), they did wrestle—to Henry's detriment. Henry demonstrated his archery skill; and they jointly sponsored a

number of athletic, rather than specifically military, contests. As described by
Austin Lane Poole:

> This sumptuous parade of magnificent folly with its prefabricated palace, its
> towers and battlements, its decorative statuary representing classical antiquity,
> and its rich hangings of crimson and gold; with its feasting and dancing and
> fountains spouting malmsey and claret into silver cups; and with its jousting
> according to an elaborate set of rules drawn up for the event at which the two
> monarchs entered the lists against all comers, marks the approaching end of
> long-decaying chivalry.[22]

Just as the tournament itself was not an English innovation, so its development in this way in England was not original. The most sumptuous displays
were presented by the German emperor Maximilian, and it was to Germany that
Henry looked for the armor that had become specialized for tilting. Because a
barrier now restricted the range of fighting that could occur, the left (or exposed)
side of the suit was built up, and special padding for the horses was developed.
One of Henry's suits weighed 93 pounds, bringing the overall weight supported
by the horse to over 340 pounds.[23] While there remained some danger from a
bad fall or from a splintered lance penetrating the visor, the armor, for the most
part, guaranteed a gamelike quality to the event.

This quality was guaranteed in other ways as well. Scoring was now
customary, and winners were tabulated from special scoring sheets. As Anglo
has concluded, the records from such sheets suggest that the performers had lost
some of their ancestors' ability.[24] For example, during the aforementioned marriage tournament of 1501, only 4 lances were broken on the head of the
opponent, and 16 were broken by any other means. This was based on 57
courses (i.e., 114 lances). Likewise, the tournament now included other
unrelated forms of athleticism, such as those mentioned at the Field of the Cloth
of Gold. As in the previous period, the noble amateurs were protected by the
exclusivity of rank, enforced by the king-at-arms.

The tournament lapsed after Henry's reign, but Elizabeth made vigorous
efforts to revive it by an annual series of tilting matches on Accession Day, i.e.,
on the day (November 17) marking her return to London for the winter months.
The first of these (around 1570) may have been a partially spontaneous
celebration by her courtiers; however, the event was soon institutionalized by the
queen herself. The Accession Day Tilts illustrate not only the last stages of the
tourney in England but the quite conscious manipulation of popular sentiment by
the monarchy.

Strong has described these events as "an imaginative refeudalization of late
Tudor society."[25] Drawing on much older traditions, Elizabeth installed herself
as queen of beauty for the affair, and the sometimes creaking knights of her
court made supplication to her. Indeed, the entry of the participants into the lists
seems to have overshadowed their performance on the field itself. Amidst great
fanfare, the courtiers and their retinues in turn approached the queen's gallery.

Speeches were made to her, and tokens presented. Hundreds of pounds were sometimes spent for the pageant cars and livery that made each presentation distinct. Ultimately, pamphlets were prepared that listed the complete speeches and the devices used by the contestants. These were available as souvenirs.

As in the other events described above, officials were present to mark score cards, listing the courses run and lances broken. Winners were proclaimed, and some of the retired champions were charged with organizing the events once their competence waned. There were stands all about—the event was usually held at Whitehall—so that the broader London public might be a witness.

As symbolic events, the annual tilts reinforced the superiority of the monarchy amidst the factionalism of the court. Indeed, in an age turning away from Catholicism (and thereby the idealization of Mary), the events played out Elizabeth's status as a quasi-deity or Vestal Virgin. Furthermore, the symbolism connected the current ruling class to real and mythical progenitors, thereby enhancing its legitimacy. The choice of a tilting match (as opposed to other endeavors) suggested as well the underlying current of violence that could be brought to bear against challengers to that ascendancy. As Elyot put it, such activity "importeth a majestie and drede to inferiour persones, beholding him [the knight] above the common course of other men dauntyng a fierce and cruell beast."[26] Finally, the overall theme of friendship and festivity fostered a broader sense of unity among the various ranks of urban and rural life.

James I was also a supporter of this tradition. However, the events became increasingly sporadic, and the last one was held in 1621. A similar fate had already befallen the sport in France. King Henri II of France had been killed in 1559 when a member of the Scottish guard failed to drop his lance. Jousting was then outlawed. As Dennis Brailsford explains, "the elements of expense and danger were simply too great a cost for gentlemen of this time."[27]

With the decline of the tournament itself, tilting at a ring became more popular, as did elegant military riding. Both were the result of Italian influence, and Henry VIII imported horse masters from that country to instruct the English. The shift toward skill in lighter arms and horsemanship had begun.

HUNTING SPORTS

One consequence of the growing population, with its desire for fresh meat and its need for farmland and wood, was the declining quantity of game. This condition was worsened by the fact that the Tudors tended to look increasingly at their royal forests as sources of wood for buildings, ships, and charcoal.[28] Soon wild boar and wolves were no longer to be found outside Ireland and Scotland. Red deer were still hunted within the royal forests, but were quite scarce elsewhere. Fallow deer still existed in large numbers, but the number of roe deer (always a less prestigious commodity) had markedly declined. As William Harrison, in his "Description of England," explains:

> Such is the scantitye of them here in England in comparison of the plentie
> that is to be seene in other countryes and so earnestly are the inhabitants bent
> to root them out: that except that it had been to beare with the recreations of
> their superiors, it could not otherwise have been chosen, but that they should
> have been utterlie destroyed by many year agone.[29]

Likewise, of foxes, he notes that "we have some but no great store." Similar
complaints were lodged by various Parliaments regarding hares and wild fowl:

> The game of hare is declared to be now decayed and almost utterly destroyed
> by reason of diverse persons tracing in the snow and killing the same, to the
> displeasure of our sovereign lord the King and other noblemen of this realm.
> . . . It is found by our experience that the games of pheasants and partridges
> have been and still are likely to be much spoiled and destroyed by many mean
> tenants and freeholders against the will of the Lord.[30]

As in previous periods, one response was to reinforce the game laws. In
reply to frequent complaints about poaching, Henry VII made it illegal to have
in one's possession

> guns, bows, greyhounds or other dogs, ferrets, trancels [nets for taking birds],
> lowbells [bells hung on a long rope used to drive hares and other game into
> nets] or harepipes, or keep any other deer hayes or buck stalls or other snares
> and engines . . . except in his own park on pain to forfeit ten pounds.[31]

In short, the legislation served the interest of those who already owned private
hunting grounds. However, it is significant in that it is directed against poaching
by all classes and not just the lower orders. As Marcia Vale has explained, the
ordinary gentleman of the time did not have a great range of hunting opportunities.[32] He might have a warren of coneys or other small game as well as occasional privileges to hunt on the grounds of his more illustrious neighbors.
However, he was also a poacher.

In this light, a similar broad-based prohibition was produced by the Second
Parliament of Elizabeth. Anyone caught removing hawks or their eggs from
their original site is to be imprisoned:

> Whereas her majesty, as also the noblemen, gentlemen and diverse other
> persons of great dominions, and possessions, had breeding within their woods
> and grounds diverse eyries of hawks of sundry kinds, to their great pleasure
> and commodity, that if hereafter any person shall unlawfully take any hawks,
> or their eggs, out of the woods or grounds of any persons . . . he shall be
> imprisoned three months.[33]

More commonly, however, the blame for game shortages was placed specifically
on working persons who usurped the rights of gentlemen. Notable in this sense
is 33 Henry 8, ch. 6, which prohibits all who have less than 100 pounds a year
in land, tenements, fees, annuities, or offices from carrying certain species of

small arms. The fine for infraction was ten pounds. Like any system of fines, such punishment was most burdensome for the poorer classes, who would be
unable to pay and, therefore, faced other discretionary punishments.

A second response to the scarcity of game was the development of private
parks. Saxton's maps (1575–1580) show more than 700 of these, and a
contemporary, Andrew Bourde, is quoted as stating that "there be more parks
in England than in all Europe beside."[34] A foreign, and therefore less biased,
observer, the duke of Stettin, marveled that lords might have two or even three
separate parks, a device that prevented the different kinds of deer from in-
terbreeding.[35] The park was not only a source of food and entertainment for
guests but also a symbol of the prerogatives of station. As George M.
Trevelyan puts it, "after the mansion itself, the chief object of pride" for the
country gentleman was his deer park.[36]

Still another response to declining game was to extol the virtues of the
animals that remained. For example, while traditionalists like Elyot (1531) still
disdained the pursuit of the fox, by century's end it was finding some adherents.
Sir Thomas Cockaine begins his work, *A Short Treatise of Hunting* (1581) with
a discussion of the fox. By its pursuit, "men are enabled above others to the
service of Prince and Country in the Warres."[37] Likewise, the author of *The
Noble Arte of Venerie* (1575) suggests that the fox was becoming a favored
wintertime prey.[38]

Similarly, the pursuit of the hare by hounds or greyhounds, called coursing,
was growing in popularity. Again, while Elyot sniffed at it as being suitable
primarily for the less vigorous, such as scholars and ladies, the translator of *The
Noble Arte of Venerie* added some comments on hare to the original French
source. While coursing was notable for its sporting motive (the hare was
sometimes left to the hounds), it was fueled by gambling as well. In this, it was
similar to hawking which lingered—as an old aristocratic sport—throughout the
period.

Corresponding to the new restrictions in scope were changes in hunting
technique. This was particularly the case with deer hunting, which became less
strenuous than before. DeVielleville, the French ambassador to the court of
Edward IV, contrasts the English style—or at least that evident at ceremonial
occasions—with the *chase à courre,* at which the red deer might be trailed for
two or three days:

> They took me to a great park full of fallow deer and roe deer where I mount-
> ed a Sardinian horse, richly caparisoned; and in company of forty or fifty
> lords and gentlemen we hunted and killed fifteen or twenty beasts. It amused
> me to see the English ride at full tilt in this hunt, the hanger in the hand, and
> they could not have shouted louder had they been following an enemy after
> a hard-won victory.[39]

While some of this may have been intended to impress their French guest, Elyot
earlier had complained about the noise and jumble of the modern hunt. In his

view, too many hounds were used—hereby depriving the hunters themselves of much of the work of the chase.[40]

Even less vigorous—though correspondingly more ceremonial—was the practice of driving deer into enclosures and dispatching them with crossbows. For example, Elizabeth and the countess of Kildare are recorded as killing four in this manner (the queen purportedly killing three of these) at one of her visitations in 1591. She seems to have continued the practice, for at Nonesuch in 1600 (when she was 67), she rode and shot at deer every second day.[41]

As in earlier times, the hunting enthusiast was distinguished by his knowledge of an amazing welter of terms. However, there was also a growing sense (among the more educated) that this knowledge—and especially its imitation by the city classes—was perhaps a bit silly. As the contemporary John Taylor satirized:

> You must rouse a buck, start a hare, and unkennel a fox. Again, you must harbour a hart, and lodge a stag or a buck. . . . A buck is first a fawn, the second year a pricket, the third year a sorell, the fourth year a sore, the fifth a buck of the first head, and the sixth year a buck: so a hart is the first year a calf, the second a brocket, the third a spade, the fourth a staggard, the fifth a stag, and the sixth a hart. . . . Beside these ambiguous contigigrated phrases, the horns have many dogmatical epithets, as a hart hath the burrs, the pearls, the antlers, the surantlers, the royals, the surroyals, and the croches. A buck's horns are composed of burr, beam, branch, advancer, palm, and shelter. And to decline from the crown or horn to the rump or crouper: a deer, a boar, a hare, a fox, and a wolf have no more tail than a jackanapes; for it is a deer's scut, a fox's bush, and a wolf's stern. . . . Should I proceed further I should instead of an understanding wood-man, shew myself to be an ignorant made man.[42]

In contrast to earlier times, however, literacy and the printing press were making sporting language available to those who had not been reared in the traditions of the hunt. The "mushroom men" (social climbers) of the Tudor era could obtain help from a variety of sources. Among the more notable survivors of this literature are Dame Juliana Berners, *The Boke of St. Albans* (1486 and reprinted many times thereafter); *La Venerie de Jacques du Fouilloux* (1561); John Caius, *De Cannibus Brittanicus* (1570); George Turberville (or perhaps George Gascoigne), *The Noble Art of Venery* (1575 and basically a translation of Jacques du Fouilloux); and Thomas Manwood, *A Briefe Collection of the Laws of the Forest* (1592).

The appeal of such works is noted rather directly by Ben Jonson. In *Every Man to His Humour,* he has his young fashion monger ask whether his uncle

> have e'er a book of the sciences of hawking and hunting; I would fain borrow it . . . I have bought me a hawk, a hood, and bells, and all; I lack nothing but a book to keep it by. . . . Why, you know, if a man not have skill in the hawking and hunting languages nowadays, I'll not give a rush for

him; they are more studied than the Greek or the Latin. He's for no gallant's company without them.[43]

The opening of sport to the nouveau riche or the status climber is to be contrasted with conditions on the Continent, where groups without landed estates or titles generally did not hunt.

Thus, despite a bit of sniping to the contrary, hunting sports continued to grip an essentially rural populace. The anonymous *Institution of a Gentleman* (1555) went so far as to claim that "he cannot be a gentlemen whych loveth not hawking and hunting."[44] Harrison in his description of England (1577) profers with some pride that he knew of "no country that may (as I take it) compare with ours in number, excellency, and diversity of dogs."[45] Sir John Davies, in his *Epigrams* (1590), somewhat less enthusiastically describes the English country house as "stinking with dogs and muted all with hawks."[46] Indeed, so deep was the English familiarity with hunting life that Shakespeare could use some of its most arcane terminology as metaphors in his plays.

ARCHERY

Archery, which had accounted in large part for the English military victories of the fourteenth and early fifteenth centuries, experienced its final popularity as a military sport during the Tudor era. Firearms had been introduced during the latter part of the fifteenth century; and although the complete superiority of muskets was not to be acknowledged for another 200 years, archery was in sharp decline by 1600.[47] The longbow had played such an important role in the mythology of England that officials were very reluctant to abandon it. In addition, the longbow remained a very cheap weapon and had the further advantage of rapidity of fire. Furthermore, archery practice on Sundays was one way of monitoring the lower classes and otherwise keeping them, in the official view of things, out of trouble. The history of archery during the Tudor era, then, is marked by the series of royal acts promoting its practice. It is also marked, as Brailsford has emphasized, by the extent to which shooting cut across a number of social classes.[48] The monarch most emphatic in his attempts to sustain archery was Henry VIII. An accomplished archer, his exploits at the Field of the Cloth of Gold have already been noted. His favorite pageant disguise was Robin Hood or forest garb more generally (as he wore at the Field of the Cloth of Gold); and he attempted to encourage other members of his court, including Anne Boleyn, in the sport. Such leadership by example was not without its purposes. In 1512 Henry reissued an earlier proclamation of his father that required all subjects between the ages of seventeen and sixty who were not "laim, decrepit, or maimed" (excluding clergy, justices, and barons) to practice archery.[49] Furthermore, parents were to provide for every boy between the ages of seven and seventeen a bow with two arrows; after that, he was to maintain four arrows. Also, Henry forbade to anyone with less than 300 marks (100 pounds) in land the possession or use of a crossbow—again in recognition of the latter's uses in poaching. Any ineligible person found in possession of such an implement was to pay a fine of ten pounds. This legislation was reissued periodically throughout the reign, as in 1541 when An Acte for the Maytanance of Artyllarie and Debarringe of Unlawful Games promoted archery at the expense of other pastimes.

By such acts the bulk of the populace was ordered to continue the medieval practice of shooting at butts or marks in the open areas about the towns and villages. Again, Sundays and holidays after church services seem to have been the prescribed time. Interestingly, the 1541 act forbade anyone under the age of twenty-four to shoot at a standing mark—that is, at a stationary distance—or to shoot at distances closer than eleven score (or 220) yards.

Clearly, there were concerns even at this date about the declining quality of archery, particularly among the young. Bishop Latimer, preaching before Henry VIII (who was pleased enough with the sermon to grant him five pounds) decried the general neglect:

> The art of shooting hath been in times past much esteemed in this realme, it is a gift of God, that he hath gyven us to excell all other nations withal. It hath been Goddes instrumente whereby he hath given victories agayneste our enemyes. But now we have taken up horynge in towns instead of shutynge in the fyldes.[50]

The bishop, who was himself a yeoman's son, went on to remember his own training in the bow—the long hours during which he learned to draw it with his body and not his arms. After the mid-sixteenth century, the decline becomes even more precipitous. In studying the muster rolls of the Elizabethan period, J. C. Cox notes that the record for March 1559 in Derbyshire shows that this small county put 292 archers into the field as compared to 918 billmen (that is, carriers of pikes).[51] By 1587, out of 400 soldiers pressed for service, 160 were for shot, 160 were billmen, and only 80 were archers. In other words, the proportion of archers dropped from one-fourth to one-fifth, and Cox argues that the decline was even steeper in other counties. At any rate, in 1604 the trades of fletcher and bowyer petitioned James I that their occupations were suffering from lack of interest.[52] In 1627 the bowyers complained that there were only four of their number left and that they could find no new apprentices to teach.[53]

Despite the decline in military significance and the waning interest of the lower classes, archery was supported by a number of literary works attempting to fan enthusiasm among gentlemen—and ladies. As noted above, Castiglione listed archery as one of the accomplishments of the successful courtier, and Elyot praised it as the "principal of all other exercises."[54] In 1545 the classic work on archery, Roger Ascham's *Toxophilus,* was presented to Henry VIII. While the book contains the first descriptions of the sport in England, it was offered fundamentally as a propaganda piece: Archery was to be the solace of the gentleman. This work was followed ultimately by other books and pamphlets, including Sir Thomas Smythe, *Certain Discourses* (1590); William Neade, *The Double-Armed Man* (1625); and Gervaise Markham, *The Art of Archery* (1634). Combined with the testimony to archery's military value was an emphasis on its physiological benefits. Thus, Dr. Jones, the Buxton physician during Elizabeth's reign, recommends the following to his patients: "Shootings at Garden Butts to them whom it agreeth and pleaseth, in place of Noblest exercise standeth, and that rather wythe Longe bowe than with Tyller, Stone bowe, or Crosse bowe."[55]

For such reasons, various archery societies for gentlemen were established. In 1539 Henry VIII granted letters patent to several members of his court for the establishment of a society termed the Fraternity of St. George. The group was authorized "for pastimes sake to practice shooting at all kinds of marks" in certain open areas about London.[56] The weapons of the group, which was also known as the Honourable Artillery Company, included the longbow, crossbow, and handgun. In 1590, after the bow had become more or less retired for military purposes, certain of these gentlemen formed a new group called the Finsbury Archers, who emphasized sociability and mild recreation.

Another group organized by Henry was the "Ancient Order, Societies and Unitie Laudable of Prince Arthur's Knights and his Knightlie Armory of the Round Table."[57] The original company was composed of fifty-six gentlemen, each of whom assumed the name and bearing of an illustrious member of that legendary group. Following Henry's lead, archery was one focus of the group. And, as in the case of the Tudor tournaments, the emphasis in Prince Arthur's shows was on pageantry and display. However, gambling was also an element of the group's activities, and privy purse expenditures indicate Henry lost as well as won.

The proclivity for elaborate costumes and ceremony was also a central part of the "silver arrow" contests at Harrow School, which began around the end of this period and continued until 1771. Originally, six (though later twelve) boys, attired in fancy costumes of green and white spangled satin, contended for the silver arrow. Whenever a shot fell within the three circles surrounding the bull's eye, the achievement was noted by a concert of French horns. As in the previous cases, sociability was a key theme, and the event was followed by a ball which the families attended.

THE DEVELOPMENT OF FENCING

As the assizes of 1181 and 1252 had granted to each freeman the right to certain arms according to his station, it was the common man generally who relied on the short sword for protection. Swordplay found its early adherents among the dwellers of towns, and originally this activity, like fighting with quarterstaffs, was a rather rude and impromptu affair.[58] The contestants fought with short broad swords and defended themselves with small round shields termed bucklers. The bucklers were at times manufactured with sharp spikes

which were used to ram an opponent, and wrestling skill was a attribute useful
to the practice. This form of fighting remained popular throughout the sixteenth
century. J. D. Aylward reports that every haberdasher in mid-sixteenth century England sold bucklers, and sword and buckler play was a regular part of the
early Cotswold Games.[59]

Skill with a sword or dagger was necessitated by the uncertainties of the
age. Without an effective police the citizen was left, for the most part, to his
own resources for personal protection. Because an attack on the open highway
or on city streets after dark was a constant concern, it was considered important
that each man carry a weapon and learn to use it. Thus, the sword, as a weapon
that could be used effectively at a moment's notice, became a customary
accoutrement to the dress of the period. Harrison, writing in 1586, attests to
this practice:

> Seldom shall you see one of my countrymen above 18 or 20 years old go
> without a dagger at his backe or his side, although they are aged burgesses
> or magistrates of a citie, who in appearance are most exempt from brabbling
> and contention. Our nobility weare commonly swords or rapier or these
> daggers, as doth everie common serving man that follows his master. . . .
> Finally, no man traveleth by the waie without his sword or some such weapon
> except the minister, who commonly weareth none at all unless it is a dagger
> or hanger at his side.[60]

Under such conditions, there was a market for instruction in personal
defense; and various "schools of fence" arose in medieval towns. While little
is known of these organizations, Egerton Castle, the nineteenth-century authority
on fencing, has made the following observations: "The earliest masters of fence
seem in all countries seem to have been a somewhat objectionable gentry, sword-
dancers in play and gladiators in earnest, professional champions more or less
openly recognized, or 'bravos' of perfectly unscrupulous character."[61] At any
rate, as early as 1285 Edward I, in his Statute for the City of London, forbade
the teaching of fencing: "As fools who delight in their folly do learn to fence
with buckler and thereby be encouraged in their follies, it is provided that none
shall keep school for, nor teach the art of fence within the city of London under
pain of imprisonment for forty days."[62]

The prototype for later fencing schools was the Brotherhood of St. Marcus
of Lowenberg, which was established in Frankfurt during the fourteenth
century.[63] The Marxbruder was originally a group of enterprising swordsmen
who, like the members of other medieval guilds, banded together to monopolize
a certain trade, instruction in swordplay. Throughout Europe, schools on this
model instructed primarily middle-class citizens in the use of arms. By 1545,
Roger Ascham in *Toxophilus* might claim:

> For of fence, all mooste in everye towne there is not onely Masters to teache it,
> wyth his Provostes, Ushers, Scholars and other names of arte and Schole, but there

hath not fayld also whyche hathe diligently and favouredly written it, and is set out in Printe that every man maye rede it.[64]

This circumstance came about largely because Henry VIII issued letters patent in 1540 to a group of swordsmen to monopolize instruction. Patterned on the Marxbruder, the Masters of Defense established formal controls for the training process and for the general conduct of its members. No person of disreputable character was to be taught, and serious students were to advance by a series of public exams termed prizes. The students advanced through a series of levels: scholar, free scholar, provost, and master. Each required competence in additional weapons and competition against the local holders of that rank. For example, for the free scholar rank, one competed against at least six others with long sword and backsword. Higher levels required competition with the quarter-staff, pike, and dagger.

However, if gentlemen were to patronize schools of fence, certain difficulties had to be overcome. First, sword and buckler play (and the use of pike, dagger, and so forth) was traditionally an activity of the commoner, rather than the elite.[65] The second was the fundamental difference between sword and buckler play and the classical swordsmanship of the knight. The great two-edged sword of knightly fame was primarily a battering instrument. With the development of plate armor, these sword fights basically were tests of endurance, each knight hacking away at the other in hopes of exhausting him or severing a joint in his armor. The activity bore little resemblance to the subterfuge and decoy required by a man whose only defense might be a small shield. Hence, fencing was suspected by some members of the elite as being a trade which derogated from true, meaning chivalric, value.[66] Finally, the masters of defense in England were decidedly not gentlemen. Typically then, the gentlemen did not merely accommodate themselves to a lower- or middle-class activity; instead they transformed it in terms of their own interests.

The solution of the gentlemanly class to the above issues was simple enough. If fencing with sword and buckler was a commoner's pursuit, the gentleman would find (as before) his own distinctive weapon. If the English masters of defense were in some ways unsuitable, he would find or import those who were gentlemen. Finally, if fencing was thought to oppose the chivalric ideal, he would transform the activity until it was the very epitome of that ideal.

To accomplish these objectives, the English elite turned to fencing masters from the Continent. Instruction in swordplay became part of the young gentleman's continental travels. In this light, there were two basic approaches to the art: the Spanish and the Italian.[67] The Spanish school was sometimes called the geometrical or Euclidian school, for it was based on theories of geometry. By this method the fencers stood at the boundaries of a circle formed by the diameter of their extended swords. Around this wheel they turned and then entered in prescribed ways. One might attack by the *pasada* (a step of twenty-four inches), the *pasada simple* (thirty inches), or the *pasada doble* (two *pasadas*).

The Spanish method was a beautiful one, well suited to the elegance and courtliness of the times. However, the English turned increasingly to the Italian masters. This was due in part to the English antipathy toward Spain. More practically, however, it was because the Italians methods were deemed superior to the Spanish in actually killing a man. The Italians were the acknowledged authorities on the Continent; and their appeal was doubled by the fact that they were gentlemen. During this period, then, the Italians Marozze, Agrippa, Grassi, and Viggiani popularized fencing. England imported its own crop of Italian masters, including Rocco Bonetti, Jeronimo, and Saviolo, creating through their teaching and manuals an aura of respectability for the craft.

The new weapon, introduced from Spain during the reign of Mary and dominant by the time of Elizabeth, was the rapier. To be sure, there was some resistance to this long slashing blade. The Englishman George Silver in his *Paradoxes of Defense* (1599) attacked the Italian fencing masters on the grounds that there was something underhanded about the rapier. He warned his fellow countrymen to beware:

> how they forsake their own naturall fight, that they may be casting off these Italianated weake, fantastical and most divellish and imperfect fights and by exercising of their own ancient weapons be restored, or achieve unto their naturall and most manly victorious fight againe.[68]

Likewise, in a contemporary play, *The Angry Women of Abingdon* (1599), a character offers this:

> sword and buckler fight begins to grow out of use. I am sorry for it. I shall never see good manhood again. If it be once gone, this poking fight of rapier and dagger will come up. Then, the tall man, that is a courageous man and a good sword and buckler man, will be spitted, like a cat or rabbit.[69]

Such views notwithstanding, the rapier deposed the short sword, as it did the old two-handed sword (which was too cumbersome for wear). The appeal of the new weapon is described well by Castle:

> The rapier was decidedly a foreigner; yet it suited the Elizabethan Age. It was ornamental as well as practical. Its play was decidedly picturesque, indeed fantastic, in comparison with the unimaginative hanger of home production. The phraseology attached to it had a quaint, southern smack which recalled outlandish experience, and gave those conversant with its intricate distinctions that curious character at once so euphuistic and "ruffling," which was so highly appreciated by the gilded youth of the time.[70]

Thus, the English gentle class managed to redefine its relationship to the common man at home and to reassert its connection to an aristocracy abroad.

TENNIS AND BOWLING

As Lord Aberdare has put it, "the accession of Henry VII to the throne . . . marks the start of the great days of tennis in England."[71] Through the efforts of that king and his son, tennis was accorded full legitimacy. For the young nobleman as for the social climber, skill at tennis was still another expectation, and "public" courts and tennis masters proliferated to fill the need.

From the records of the royal accounts it is clear that Henry VII was a tennis enthusiast who gambled at the game (at least his losses are recorded). They also list some of his courts—at Woodstock, Wycombe, Westminster, Sheen, and Windsor. Tennis play became—along with hunting, hawking, animal baiting, and the other pastimes mentioned above—a way of entertaining foreign dignitaries. In this light, one such meeting between Philip of Castile and the marquess of Dorset has been recorded.[72] Philip played with a racket and, therefore, gave his barehanded opponent fifteen points. The incident says less about the development of sportsmanship than about the rudimentary status of the racket at that time (1506).

Following his father, Henry VIII was an accomplished player. As Giustiana, the Venetian ambassador, recorded in 1519, "He is extremely fond of tennis, at which game it is the prettiest thing in the world to see him play, his fair skin glowing through a shirt of finest texture."[73] Henry erected courts at Hampton Court (where the court may be visited still), the Palace of Whitehall, and St. James Place.

There is no evidence that Elizabeth played, although she was a spectator and planned (but did not finish) a new court at Windsor. Members of the court played before her with some passion, as the following anecdote suggests:

> Latlye the Dukes G. [of Norfolk] and my L. of L. [Leicester] were playing at tennes the Q. beholdinge of them, and L. Rob. being verie hotte and swetinge tooke the Q. napken owte of her hands and wyped his face, which the Duke seinge saide that he was too sawcie and swhore that he wolde laye his racket upon his face. Here upon rose a great troble and the Q. offendid sore with the Duke.[74]

Furthermore, the practice was finding its literary apologists. The reception begins coolly enough with Elyot's (1531) admission that "tenyse seldome used, and for a lyttel space, is a good exercise for young men, but it is more violente than shootinge, by reason that two menne do play. Wherefore, neither of them is at his own libertie to measure the exercise."[75] A more spirited defense is provided by Castiglione: "Also, it is a noble exercise, and meete for one living in court to play at tenise, where the disposition of the bodie, the quickness and nimbleness of everie member is much perceived, and almost whatsoever a man can see is all other exercises."[76]

The educational reformer Richard Mulcaster in 1591 praised the "little hand ball whether it be of some softer stuffe and used by hand or some harder used with the rakette," which he argued is "one of the best exercises and the greatest preservations of health."[77] Roger Ascham in *The Scholemaster* (1570) lists tennis among the gentleman's proper pursuits, and James I recommended the game as part of the education of his son Henry.[78] Even Erasmus speaks of tennis: "Let's leave the net-covered instrument to the fishermen; it's more elegant to use the hand."[79]

Such acceptance by educated people was perhaps as much a recognition of tennis's popularity as an advertisement for the game. Tennis was already a fad at the universities (where official support was withheld) and, more generally, in the towns. Here, entrepreneurs erected enclosed courts and extracted a fee for playing privileges. The admission of anyone with money in his pocket did not sit well with the proclivities of the age, however, and attempts to restrict the activity were made. Acts of 1535–1536 and 1541–1542 imposed fines for every day that these public courts were kept open, and no one, except those with incomes over 100 pounds, was to have a private court.

As has been seen in other cases, such legislation was sometimes the prelude to the granting of special privileges. In this light, Joseph Strutt records the apparently successful application of Thomas Bedingfield for a license to keep all such houses (where bowls, cards, and dice might be played as well) within London and Westminster.[80] Bedingfield argued that such houses had in the past been frequented by disorderly persons and proposed that only "noblemen, gentlemen, and merchants or such as shall be entered in the Book of Subsidies at ten pounds in land or goods" be allowed to continue playing. As he petitioned:

> By these means deceitful playing be suppressed, many young men kept from spoil, many poor men driven from unlawful exercises to live upon lawful labor, much other wickedness reformed, and the ancient exercise of shooting, now greatly decayed, be revived.[81]

A similar development is exhibited by bowling, two varieties of which were popular during the period.[82] Lawn bowling or bowls was practiced on a square grass plot where the turf was smooth and level. This bowling green was an important part of the gentleman's garden during the sixteenth and seventeenth centuries. It was also played on specially constructed wooden alleys—as was the second variety of bowling, ninepins or skittles. These alleys were often attached to inns and taverns, where they were much patronized by common folk.

Because bowling alleys were characterized by gambling and rowdiness and because they were thought to draw the populace away from archery practice, Henry VIII in 1541 ordered that the keeping of such alleys for "gain, lucre or living" cease.[83] Furthermore, he ordered that "no manner of artificer or craftsman of any handicraft or occupation, husbandman, apprentice, labourer, servant at husbandry, journeyman or servant of artificer, mariner, fisherman, waterman, or any serving man" be permitted to bowl. The only exception might be play in their master's houses and then only during the twelve days of Christmas. On the other hand, noblemen and others worth 100 pounds could have their own bowling greens, though no one was to play in "open places out of his garden or orchard." The fine for infraction was 20 shillings for each game played by a member of the lower class and 6 shillings 8 pence for others. This legislation was not countermanded until 1845.

As has been shown frequently before, such proclamations are better interpreted as expressions of problems perceived by the ruling group than as successful corrections of the practice. At any rate, bowling continued to grow in popularity during the following reigns. By 1579 Stephen Gosson could complain that "common bowling alleys are privy moths that eat up the credit of many idle citizens."[84] Twenty-five years later, John Stow lamented the closing of the old common grounds, an act which, he says, drove London citizens "into bowling alleys and ordinarie diceing houses near home, where they have room enough to hazard their money at unlawful games."[85]

In summary, both tennis and bowling reflect the efforts to preserve social distance in a socially mobile society. However, they also illustrate such broader themes as the shrinking of playing areas around towns, the growth of purely artificial amusements, and the softening of the gentlemenly ideal itself. As Gosson put it: "Our wrestling at arms is turning to wallowyng in ladies' laps, our courage to cowardice, our running to ryot, our bowes into belles, and our darts to dishes."[86]

FOOTBALL

If the poorer person might pursue tennis and bowling only with some jeopardy, a host of other diversions could claim his attention. Trap-ball, stool-ball, tipcat, nur and spell, and nine men's morris were typical pastimes. Likewise, mass ball games continued to be played, both informally and on festive occasions. Alexander Barclay in 1514 provides this charming account:

> They get the bladder and blowe it great and thin
> With many beanes and peason put within;
> It ratleth, soundeth, and shineth clere and fayre
> While it is throwen and caste up in the ayre.
> Each one contendeth and hath a great delite
> With foote and hande the bladder for to smite
> If it fall to the ground, they lift it up again,
> This wise to labour they count it for on paine;
> The sturdie plowman, lustie, strong, and bold
> Overcometh the winter with driving the foote-ball
> Forgetting labour and many a grievous fall.[87]

As Barclay's comments indicate, football was still a winter sport, played by the laboring classes. Regulations regarding the use of hands and feet were still not clearly specified, though (as will be shown in the next period) more specialized games like hurling and knappan were arising.

Predictably, such bumptious play by people who should be practicing archery found its opponents. Indeed, football and its variants incited a special invective from the property holders and moralists of the period. We can by now expect the following comments from Elyot:

> likewise foot balle, wherin is nothinge but beastly furie and exstreme violence, whereof procedeth hurte and consequently rancour and malice do remain with them that be wounded; whereof it is to be put in perpetuall silence.[88]

Of course, it would not be silenced; and fifty years later we find this even more stirring assault by the Puritan Philip Stubbes: "A develishe pastime . . . and hereof groweth envy, rancour, and malice and sometimes brawling murther, homicide, and great effusion of blood, as experience daily techeth."[89]

This attitude is consistent with the attitudes of the monarchy. Football was classified with the other, sometimes illegal sports cited previously. However, less predictably, there is no record that the rulers indulged in the pastime themselves. Football was a rough sport even by the standards of the age. As the future James I explained to his son in 1599, it was "meeter for laming than making able the users thereof."[90] Furthermore, for an elite that glorified the capacities of the individual, mass sports had little appeal.

This hostility of the upper-class groups was also reflected in the policies of educational institutions. For example, Oxford, during the reign of Elizabeth, issued the following warning:

> If any Master of Arts, Bachelor of Arts or Scholer being above the age of eighteen years shall use anie plaieing at Football in New Parke or elsewhere within the precincts of the universitie . . . for the first offence he shall pay 20 s. and suffer imprisonment.[91]

The second offense carried a forty-shilling fine; and the third brought expulsion from the university.

During the Tudor period one finds the first explicit connections between football and the occupational associations. Such references express both the relationship of mass games to the Shrovetide holiday and the use of such events to articulate collective identity. The earliest of these comes from Chester, where in 1533 it was decreed by the town council that the custom of guild football should cease:

> that the said occupacions of shoumacres which alwayes tyme out of man's remembrance have geven and delyvered yerlye upon Teuesday commonly caulyd Shroft Teuesday, otherwyse Goteddesday, at afternoune of the same unto drapers afore the mayre of the cities at the Cros uon the Rood Dee one ball of lether, caulyd a fout baule, of the value of iii s iiii d. or about to play

at from thens to the Common Haule of the said cities and further at pleasure
of evill disposed persons wherfore hath grete inconvenynce.[92]

Henceforth, the drapers and shoemakers were to express their relationship by a
footrace.

The connection between football and guilds is also found in records from
Dorset from about this time. At Dorset the game was organized by the
quarriers:

On Shrove Tuesday which is the great day of the company the officers are
nominated by the outgoing ones . . . on Candlemas Day . . . all persons who
wish to take out their freedom of the company assembled, and with a band
. . . used to parade the streets of Corfe and Swanage . . . the Neophytes go
by the name of "free boys" . . . the qualification of a "free boy" is that he
must be the son of a free man. . . . At the same meeting on Shrove Tuesday,
a foot-ball is to be provided by the last married man who thereupon is freed
from the payment of the marriage shilling. . . . It is carried on Ash Wednes-
day, together with a pound of pepper, the acknowledgent to the lord of the
Manor in respect of the right of way to Owre, by the steward of each body
down to that place.[93]

Clearly, football was part of a complex of ceremonies that dramatized the status
of various members of the company. The presentation of the football itself was
affiliated with marriage and, thus, adulthood; and the pound of pepper suggests
the sanctioning of the event by authorities.

More generally, Shrove Tuesday festivities featured special license for the
apprentices of the period. As Wlater Besant explains, the "prentice in that
century arrived at the height of his power and importance, chiefly as a disturber
of the peace."[94] The town wards were too thickly populated and forces of
control too haphazard to provide strong, continuous checks on the behavior of
youth and apprentices. Thus, Shrove Tuesday represented a more or less
institutionalized period when the apprentices could take the law into their own
hands. In London the vast number of apprentices considered it their right to
disrupt the bawdy houses, theatres, cockpits, and foreign ministries. Among
these disruptions were mass football games.

Football was, at this point, too entrenched as a lower-class custom to be removed. Recognizing this, the educational reformer Mulcaster in 1581 sounded
a solitary note in its behalf. Football, he argued, could not have "groune to the
greatness that it is now at . . . if it had not great helpes, both to health and
strength." He therefore recommends "a trayning maister" and a "smaller
number of players sorted into sides and standings, not meeting with their bodies
so bositerously to trie their strength."[95]

Sound advice surely, but offered two centuries too soon. Football in Tudor
England was still too clearly a collective ritual. What the game offered was not
a replication of orderly social routine, but an escape from it. In the swirling

mass on a winter's afternoon there was freedom—and that urge still defied
regulation.

CONCLUSIONS

It is no coincidence that the dawn of the great era in English sport should
be associated with the destruction of monastic life. Though not, of course,
tangibly connected, the two events signal the deeper transformation in ideals and
attitudes that differentiate the medieval and modern worlds. Monastic life made
visible such themes as order, tradition, duty, deference, self-denial, cor-
poratism, contemplation, and faith. Fundamentally, the monk was a living
symbol of a world that stood above and beyond the hurly-burly of everyday life.
Sport, on the other hand, is the public celebration of carnality. Activity
substitutes for contemplation; the language of the senses supersedes faith.
Disorder, novelty, hedonism, partisanship, individualism—these are hallmarks of
the sporting age.

As E. M. Tillyard has argued, the Tudor period was still a deeply religious
and hierarchical one.[96] Society was possessed of a profound sense of order.
Similarly, the preceding chapters of this book have tried to communicate the
liveliness and tension of the Middle Ages. Sport was an important part of this.
Nevertheless, it does seem that sport acquired a new kind of legitimacy during
this period. The hunters, hawkers, archers, and tourneyers of earlier times
could convince themselves that they were doing something socially useful
—gathering food for the household or refining needed military skills. Art and
praxis combined.

By the Tudor era, however, the military and economic rationales were
wearing a bit thin. To be sure, hunting still provided food; but other sports—
especially the various kinds of ball play—had only the loosest connections to the
earlier motives. In keeping with the spirit of the Renaissance, sports were
interpreted increasingly as benefactors of the health and well-being of the individual. Sport also came to be recognized as a social accoutrement for the
upwardly mobile—a skill or language that facilitated communication with others.
In other words, sporting accomplishment became a significant badge of ability
for those emulating the Renaissance ideal.

Historians have argued that the Tudor court played a major role in this
shift. Geared as it was toward entertaining and impressing, the court fostered
experimentation in sport and other dramatic forms. Indeed, it was a receptacle
and channel for foreign ideas. Furthermore, the court possessed the leisure
time to cultivate sports and the social visibility and centrality to enable its habits
to be disseminated. It was small enough and stable enough to allow the development of more or less standardized manners, ideals, and fashions.

Setting the tone for the whole production was the monarchy. The Tudors,
on the whole, were a vigorous crew who labored to meet both the princely ideals

of their times and the more customary appetites of their people. Sports (and other theatrical shows) were found to be this common ground.

It would be wrong, however, to conclude that the interest in sport was somehow imposed from the top down. Quite the opposite, the ruling class patronized a range of activities that were already the province of commoners—archery, swordplay, and the broader category of ball games. In so doing they reached across the class system; sporting participation and spectatorship became a cultural unifier for a wide assortment of status groups.

The reasons for the closing of social distance between the upper and middle classes and between city and country dwellers are several. First, with the decline in military participation, the aristocracy lost some of its mystique (and, indeed, its essence) as a special caste. Second, new types of property and property holders had become important. While the large rural landowner maintained his dominant position, his power relative to king and Commons diminished. The diversification of the stratification system (and the mobility within it) confused the old categories of privilege. Third, money itself disrupted the previous patterns. Within the city, money, and not status, was commonly the criterion for admission to the pleasure domes—a trend that was stoutly resisted by those who were already socially established. Finally, the printing press and literacy opened the secrets of aristocratic habits and manners to middling groups. The status climber could now ape his social superiors more effectively than before.

Still, the age was not democratic in either its inclinations or its results. The fact that gentlemen were dipping into the habits of poorer groups only meant that new, more refined measures of discrimination emerged. The upper-class fencer found his own weapon and his own teachers. The archer swathed his efforts in pageantry. The tennis player and bowler created refined playing courts not easily imitated by those below. The hunter safeguarded his prerogatives by the palisades of his park. The middle class could not afford such lavish private preserves; still, they endeavored to keep their playgrounds—the more or less "public" tennis courts, bowling alleys, and such—away from the various servants and artificers mentioned in the ordinances of the times.

The poorer classes of the country were little influenced by all this wrangling. Largely unrecorded, their play seems to have followed the folk models of earlier times. On occasion, they were forced into archery practice; however, such common village recreations as dancing, wrestling, casting the barre, running, quoits, and simple stick and ball games were the norm. In other words, while the local variations in pastimes existed as cultural possibilities to be picked up and developed later by wealthier groups, the rural poor themselves cannot be considered agents of change.

One does find a somewhat clearer picture of the ceremonial uses of sport by the lower classes during this period. Mass games, especially football, were sociopolitical events as well as festivity. They were used to articulate not only horizontal social distance between guilds, villages, and so on, but also more personal status passage (for example, marriage and apprenticeship). Furthermore, the association of mass games with holiday license and disruption indicates a recognition of the tensions that'the stratification system generated. Most interestingly, football illustrates the continuing commitment of poorer people to corporate life, while the rich pursued sports that showcased their individual talents.

NOTES

1. G. R. Elton, *England Under the Tudors* (London: Methuen, 1955), 9.

2. Lawrence Stone, *The Crisis of the Aristocracy, 1558-1641* (Oxford: Oxford University Press, 1965).

3. F. Smith Fussner, *Tudor History and the Historians* (New York: Basic, 1970), 188.

4. Fritz Caspari, *Humanism and the Social Order in Tudor England* (Chicago: University of Chicago Press, 1954), 4-5.

5. R. H. Tawney, *The Agrarian Problem in the Sixteenth Century* (New York: Harper and Row, 1967).

6. A. L. Rowse, *The England of Elizabeth* (New York: Macmillan, 1951), 81-82.

7. John Maynard Keynes, *A Treatise on Money, 2* vols. (New York: Harcourt Brace, 1930), 2:154.

8. R. Liddesdale Palmer, *English Social History in the Making: The Tudor Revolution* (London: Longmans, 1934), chapter 2, "Ruffling and Beggarly."

9. Louis B. Wright, *Middle Class Culture in Elizabethan England* (Ithaca, N. Y.: Cornell University Press, 1958), 2.

10. Lawrence Stone, "The Educational Revolution in England: 1560-1640," *Past and Present* 28 (July 1964): 41-80.

11. See Dennis Brailsford, "Sport and Class Structure in Elizabethan England," *Stadion* 5, no. 2 (1979): 244-52.

12. David Loades, *The Tudor Court* (London: B. T. Batsford, 1986), 8.

13. Ibid., 6-7.

14. See Ralph Dutton, *English Court Life: From Henry VII to George II* (London: B. T. Batsford, 1963).

15. Michael D. Bristol, *Carnival and Theater: Plebian Culture and the Structure of Authority in Renaissance England* (New York: Methuen, 1985), 59.

16. See Dennis Brailsford. *Sport and Society: Elizabeth to Anne* (London: Routledge and Kegan Paul, 1969), 15-25.

17. Roy Strong, *The Cult of Elizabeth: Elizabethan Portraiture and Pageantry* (London: Thames & Hudson, 1977).

18. See Loades, *The Tudor Court,* 96-113.

19. Sydney Anglo, *Spectacle, Pageantry and Early Tudor Policy* (Oxford: Clarendon, 1969), 98.

20. Annie Abram, *English Life and Manners in the Middle Ages* (London: George Routledge and Sons, 1913), 233.

21. Anglo, *Spectacle, Pageantry, and Early Tudor Policy,* 100.

22. Austin Lane Poole, "Recreations" in *Medieval England,* ed. Austin Lane Poole, 2 vols. (Oxford: Clarendon, 1958), 624.

23. R. Coltman Clephan, *The Tournament: Its Periods and Phases* (London: Methuen, 1919), vi.

24. Sydney Anglo, *The Great Tournament Roll of Westminster* (Oxford: Clarendon, 1968), 38. See also Joachim Rühl, "Who Is the Best Jouster?" in *Proceedings of the 1987 HISPA Congress* (Gublio, Italy, 1987).

25. Strong, *The Cult of Elizabeth,* 129.

26. Sir Thomas Elyot, *The Boke named the Gouvernor* (London: n.p., 1531), 68.

27. Brailsford, "Sport and Class Structure in Elizabethan England," 249.

28. Michael Brander, *The Hunting Instinct* (London: Oliver & Boyd, 1964), 66.

29. William Harrison, "A Description of England," in Raphael Holinshed, *Chronicles,* 6 vols. (London: n.p., 1808), 1:380.

30. 14 and 15 Henry VIII, ch. 10. See also 23 Elizabeth I, ch. 10.

31. 11 Henry VII, ch. 17.

32. Marcia Vale, *The Gentleman's Recreations: Accomplishments and Pastimes of the English Gentleman 1580–1630* (Totowa, N.J.: Rowman & Littlefield, 1977), 30.

33. Quoted in Patrick Chalmers, *The History of Hunting* (London: Seeley, Service, 1936), 286.

34. "English Deer Parks," *Edinburgh Review* 49 (March 1829): 68.

35. Philip Julius, Duke of Stettin-Pomerania, *Diary of Philip Julius, Duke of Stettin-Pomerania, Through England in the Year 1602,* ed. and trans. Gottfried von Bulow, Transactions of the Royal Historical Society, vol. VI (London, 1892), 45. See Vale, *The Gentleman's Recreations,* 29.

36. George M. Trevelyan, *England Under the Stuarts* (New York: G. P. Putnam's Sons, 1926), 6.

37. Thomas Cockaine, *A Short Treatise of Hunting* (1581), discussed in Chalmers, *The History of Hunting,* 292.

38. See Vale, *The Gentleman's Recreations,* 33.

39. Quoted in W. A. Grohman, "Sports in the Seventeenth Century," *Century* 54 (July, 1897): 390.

40. Quoted in W. A. Grohman, "The Early History of British Hunting," in, *British Hunting: A Complete History of the National Sport of Great Britain and Ireland,* ed. Arthur Coaten (London: Sampson, Low, Marston, 1909), 3–11.

41. Elizabeth Burton, *The Elizabethans at Home* (London: Secker & Warburg, 1963), 190.

42. Quoted in "Elizabethan Sport," *Quarterly Review* 192 (October 1900): 391.

43. Ben Jonson, *Every Man to His Humour,* 1601 (Louvain: Bang & Gregg, 1905), I:1.

44. See Brander, *The Hunting Instinct,* 11.

45. Harrison, "A Description of England," in Holinshed, *Chronicles* 1.

46. Quoted in Burton, *The Elizabethans at Home,* 190.

47. See C. J. Longman and H. Walrond, *Archery* (New York: Frederick Ungar Publishing Co., 1894), 137–38.

48. Brailsford, "Sport and Class Structure in Elizabethan England," 251-252.

49. The former act was 19 Henry VII, ch. 17. It was reissued 3 Henry VIII, ch. 3. See Daines Barrington, "Some Observations on the Practice of Archery," *Archaeologia* 7 (1785): 46–68 for a listing of Tudor archery legislation.

50. Quoted in Joseph Strutt, *The Sports and Pastimes of the People of England* (London: Metusen, 1801; reprint, edited by J. C. Cox, 1901), 46.

51. Ibid., 55 (footnote, 1901 ed.).

52. L. A. Govett, *The King's Book of Sports* (n.p., n.d.) 51.

53. Ibid.

54. Elyot, *The Boke Named The Gouvernor,* 115.

55. Strutt, *Sports and Pastimes of the People of England,* 53.

56. *Victoria History of the Counties of England: Middlesex,* 2 vols. (London: Constable, 1911), 2:285.

57. George Hansard, *The Book of Archery* (London: Henry G. Bohn, 1841), 261–62.

58. Egerton Castle, *Schools and Masters of Fence from the Middle Ages to the End of the Eighteenth Century* (London: Arms & Armour, 1885; reprint, 1969), 13–15.

59. J. D. Aylward, *The English Master of Arms: From the Twelfth to the Twentieth Century* (London: Routledge and Kegan Paul, 1956), 17.

60. Harrison, "A Description of England," 1:335.

61. Egerton Castle, "The Story of Swordsmanship," *National Review* 17 (May 1891): 315.

62. Quoted in Aylward, *The English Master of Arms,* 8.

63. See "The Development of Fencing," *Antiquary* 15 (February 1887): 55–61.

64. Quoted in A. Forbes Sieveking, "Fencing and Duelling," in *Shakespeare's England: An Account of the Life and Manner of His Age,* ed. Sir Sidney Lee, 2 vols. (Oxford: Clarendon, 1916), 2:389.

65. See Walter Pollock, *Fencing* (London: Longmans Green and Co., 1901), p. 5. Also see Julius Palffy-Alpar, *Sword and Masque* (Philadelphia: F. A. Davis, 1967), chapter 1.

66. Aylward, *The English Master of Arms,* 8.

67. See Sieveking, "Fencing and Duelling," 395–99.

68. Quoted ibid., 395.

69. Quoted in Castle, "The Story of Swordsmanship," 319.

70. Ibid., 318.

71. Lord Aberdare, *The Story of Tennis* (London: Stanley Paul, 1959), 47.

72. Ibid., 48–49.

73. Ibid., 50.

74. Ibid., p. 57.

75. Elyot, *The Boke Named The Gouvernor,* 82.

76. Baldassare Castiglione, *The Book of the Courtier,* trans. Thomas Hoby (London: J. M. Dent, 1928), 42.

77. Richard Mulcaster, *Positions,* 1581 (London: n.p., 1581; reprint, Longmans, Green, 1888), 103.

78. James I, *His Majesties Instruction to His Dearest Son, Henry the Prince* (n.p., 1603), 120.

79. Desiderius Erasmus, *Colloquia Familiarica Ulmae,* as quoted in Malcolm Whitman, *Tennis: Origins and Mysteries* (New York: Derrydale, 1932), 51.

80. Strutt, *The Sports and Pastimes of the People of England,* 87.

81. Quoted in Julian Marshall, *The Annals of Tennis* (London: Horace Cox, 1878), 71.

82. See Robert MacGregor, "The Game of Bowls," *Belgravia* 36 (September 1878): 352–59.

83. 33 Henry VIII, ch. 16.

84. Stephen Gosson, *School of Abuse,* as quoted in MacGregor, "The Game of Bowls," 353.

85. John Stow, *Survey of London* (Oxford: Clarendon, 1808) 97.

86. Gosson, *School of Abuse,* as quoted in Christina Hole, *English Sports and Pastimes* (Freeport, N.Y.: Books for Libraries, 1949), 44.

87. Alexander Barclay, *Amintus and Faustus,* as quoted in Francis P. Magoun, "Football in Medieval England and in Middle English Literature," *American Historical Review* 35 (1929–1930): 44.

88. Elyot, *The Boke Named The Gouvernor,* 113.

89. Philip Stubbes, *Anatomy of Abuses in England in Shakespeare's Youth,* ed. Frederick Furnivall (London: N. Trubner, 1879), 137.

90. James I, *Basilicon Doron,* as quoted in Strutt, *The Sports and Pastimes of the People of England,* 98.

91. *Statuta Antiqua Universitatus Oxoniensis,* as quoted in Poole, "Recreations," 626.

92. Quoted in Francis P. Magoun, "Shrove Tuesday Football," *Harvard Studies and Notes in Philology and Literature* 12 (1931):13.

93. Ibid., 14.

94. Walter Besant, *London in the Time of the Tudors* (London: Adam & Charles Beck, 1904), 323.

95. Richard Mulcaster, *Positions,* (1581), reproduced in A. Forbes Sieveking, "Games," in *Shakespeare's England: An Account of the Life and Manners of His Age,* ed. Sir Sidney Lee, 2 vols. (Oxford: Clarendon, 1916), 2:463.

96. E. M. Tillyard, *The Elizabethan World Picture* (N. Y.: Macmillan, 1944).

5

SPORT IN STUART ENGLAND

ENGLISH SOCIETY: 1603-1714

The European Renaissance of the preceding period was in large measure a celebration of the individual and a protest against some of the structures that had traditionally channeled human energy. In the realm of thought, secular philosophy grew while the Christian church splintered. In the economy a small elite of rural landowners found itself joined in its privileges by a growing group of professionals and merchants. The base of the polity expanded, as did the number of citizens enjoying social respect. Such changes were the beginnings of a movement that continues still. Thus, the seventeenth century may be seen as a maturing or refinement of these themes.

To be sure, such changes were not always a gradual affair. Indeed, the seventeenth century is remembered as a time of political and religious revolution.[1] The new House of Stuart wished to establish in England the patterns of absolute royal authority that flourished in France. That effort led to opposition and ultimately to civil war and regicide. More than in earlier centuries, people found themselves torn between rival political and religious ideals. The royalists and traditionalists were supplanted at midcentury by a Puritan Commonwealth (1649). This, in turn, was replaced by a restored monarchy (1660) which found itself deposed in 1689 by a constitutional monarchy with a new branch of the royal family on the throne.

As Lawrence Stone has argued, the destruction of the Stuart dynasty resulted from events that occurred during the Tudor era.[2] The Tudors were proponents of a strong monarchy, yet they did not create the agencies (that is, a centralized bureaucracy and a standing army) that could enforce its will. To enlarge their power the Tudors created a number of prerogative courts outside the jurisdiction of the common law. These were increasingly seen as instruments of royal tyranny. In addition, the Tudors consolidated the power of middling groups at the expense of the aristocracy. By the time of the Stuarts the aristocrats were no longer able to hold the lower groups in place. That Tudor creation, the Anglican church, drifted from firm state control and became inhabited by clerics of indifferent ability. This prepared the way for a resurgence of the Protestant groups that had been persecuted under Mary.

The Tudors had maintained their authority by their appeals to English patriotism, their skillful manipulation of the middle class, their ability to capture diverse aristocrats within the court, and their own personal charisma. The Stuarts lacked these gifts. James I (who brought the Scottish crown with him) was in mood and outlook a foreigner. He distrusted the Commons and the more democratically oriented Protestants he had already encountered in Scotland. His insistence on the doctrine of the divine right of kings did not sit well with a country accustomed to parliamentary involvement in government. He allowed the source of Tudor strength—sea power—to fade, thereby alienating some of the commercial classes. His court was narrow in its favoritism, a fact that diminished his aristocratic base. His personal habits were the subject of widespread criticism. While personally more inspiring, his son Charles (who inherited the uneasy crown in 1625) continued many of these habits. For eleven years before 1640 he kept Parliament out of session. Ultimately, he had to reassemble them for financial reasons; fairly soon thereafter they engineered his demise.

The famous Civil War of 1642–1649 was caused by many factors and defies simple explanation. Nobility and gentry seem to have been divided in their loyalties, as were merchants.[3] The poorest elements of both town and country were not prominent in the dispute. However, middling elements—artisans, apprentices, shopkeepers, and yeomen—were usually found in the opposition. The economically more progressive south and east tended to support the rebellion, the more traditional north and west were a base of royal support. Many counties were divided in their loyalties.

Amidst the great variety of motives is the theme of religion.[4] If the English Revolution was a protest against political absolutism, it was also a struggle against religious authority. Again, the context of this dispute was established by the Tudors. Henry VIII's dissolution of the monasteries was motivated more by administrative and financial concerns than by doctrinal ones. By the sale of these lands he was able to finance among other things an abortive war with France. However, this "English Reformation" set in motion broader questions about church leadership and the role of the church in mediating salvation. To fill the vacuum, an official state church with a uniform prayer book was established. Suffering from such a policy were the English Catholics (who maintained their allegiance to the Church of Rome) and several new Protestant groups (who de-emphasized the role of the church and clergy). These positions were, furthermore, kept alive at the English universities.

By its simplicity and the assurance that it granted to adherents, Puritanism turned out to be a revolutionary force. Protestantism in general had prospered because of the spread of literacy, the printing of Bibles, and the emphasis on individual judgment and personal conscience. In its Calvinist version these ideas were combined with a belief in predestination. God had elected certain Christians as his chosen few and, furthermore, "called" them to glorify him through their work in the world. This self-assurance allowed them to oppose even kings and bishops; as God's Englishmen, they would create a New Jerusalem. Moreover, Puritan simplicity was opposed to the hierarchical and ritualistic complexity of Anglicanism (and its Catholic antecedents). Such labyrinths of power, it was thought by the Puritans, could be settings only for corruption, favoritism, and subtlety. This critical mentality extended to the king's court as well. Here, so the reasoning went, was a most conspicuous (and unapologetic) example of indolence, moral dissolution, and popish tendencies.

As a moral scheme, Puritanism emphasized the coming industrial values of discipline, frugality, asceticism, rational calculation, and upward mobility. It was an ethic for individuals who wished to advance in a world made complicated by commerce and money relations. For this task the virtues of thrift and independence were necessities. Conspicuous waste, including the waste of time, was a cardinal sin. Leisure fell into disrepute, while work was glorified. In its more radical expressions Puritanism was committed to social and political equalitarianism as well. Along those lines, Puritans might refuse to remove their hats before authorities or to take oaths. Similarly, visible symbols of wealth were to be avoided, as it was the individual relationship to God that mattered.

The Civil War briefly polarized people of all shades of belief. When it was over, the victorious Puritans eliminated not only the institution of monarchy itself, but also the positions of the Anglican bishops, the prerogative courts, taxation without consent, and the intermission of Parliament. However, the short-lived Commonwealth of Oliver Cromwell could not last without the support of the army he created. When he died, his government quickly crumbled.

Having experienced more systematic government, many Englishmen longed for the administrative and moral flexibility of a royal regime. When the Stuarts were restored, Charles II exhumed Cromwell's corpse, killed a number of regicides, and restored his bishops and prayer books. The courtly or "cavalier" values of conspicuous display and graceful leisure were once again popularized. Ideological fervor had died; moral complacency reigned. Charles's court was brilliant and dissolute and much given to French fashion. Meanwhile, the Cavalier Parliament took measures to restore the rural landowner to his former prominence as well. It was the beginning of what has been termed a conservative or neoclassical age in England. When James II's Catholic connections proved his undoing in 1688, a new constitutional monarchy with William and Mary only formalized the power of the landed interests. A modern state, with the monarch as executive and Parliament in power, had been established.

As social and economic conditions had prompted the changes in government, so they responded to it. By the end of the century the mechanism of modern credit had been established. Mortgages made it possible to borrow money on the basis of land, a central bank was established, stock prices were published, and a national debt developed. In particular, the bank's financing of the government meant that business and politics were firmly conjoined. Under such conditions London reached a population of over 500,000 and became a center of world trade. Likewise, industry—aided by the rise of coal mining and primitive machines—began to grow. Buoyed by this new wealth, London was becoming a cosmopolitan center of coffeehouses, fancy shops, and theatres.

The rural areas changed more slowly. Gregory King's calculations for 1688 reveal a population of around 5.5 million.[5] Of these, over 4 million still lived in the country. Nearly three-quarters of England and Wales was now in agricultural use. Each county continued to be dominated by a few local families who held their position on the basis of wealth and tradition. Arrayed below them was the rest of the hierarchy, each family holding its designated spot.

In keeping with the growth of population and of commerce, the stratification system both thickened and became more complicated.[6] A landed estate was still the basis of highest prestige and power, and the broad distinction between gentility and the other classes remained the chief division. However, such differences as title, degree and source of wealth, occupation, political office, education, and type of tenure supplemented family of origin and introduced subtle, but important, distinctions. Sir Thomas Wilson's five categories at the start of the period (higher nobility, lesser nobility, citizens, yeomen, and artisans and laborers) could yield to King's somewhat more detailed depiction of occupational types by century's end.[7]

Some groups did well during the period. The peerage rose from 60 to 161 by King's time. A slightly less honorific title, the baronet, was created in 1611; and 800 families received that. Before the Civil War, the number of squires increased from 800 to over 3,000, and the overall gentry rose from 5,000 to 15,000.[8] Professionals, lesser gentry, and even some merchants were elevated in this way. The proliferation of honors reflected the financial weakness of the monarchy; it also contributed to status consciousness among the titleholders themselves. More important than prestige was the ability of the landed classes to raise rents during the period. Combined with the restoration of the local system of governance (with officials appointed by the prominent families), this factor solidified the status of this group.

However, the middle forty percent of the country—the prosperous tradesmen, artisans, larger tenant farmers, and lesser officials—increased their standard of living as well.[9] Indeed, the century is sometimes referred to as the century of the middling sort. Left at the bottom were the remaining fifty percent—the landless laborers, servants, and paupers. In an era of increasing population, their position before their employers was very weak indeed.

What the sporting life of the period exhibits, then, in this broad contrast between old and new. The rural areas maintained their time-honored pursuits, while the emerging city culture and court sponsored new developments. More clearly than before, sport became a moral issue. In this regard, the excesses of Cavalier and Puritan were played out in alternating regimes. While some of the sobriety of Puritanism survived, the return of the Stuarts in 1660 guaranteed the ascendancy of the former—and older—view through the close of the period.

PURITANISM AND SPORT

A society still dominated largely by the rhythms of the agricultural year offered many opportunities for sport and other forms of festivity. Robert Burton, in his *Anatomy of Melancholy* (1621), enumerates the now familiar list of pleasures: wrestling, pitching the bar, leaping, running, fencing, swimming, and quintain.[10] To these, he added three species of ball play: hurling, football, and balloon ball (in which an inflated bladder was struck with flat pieces of wood attached to the players'arms). This vision of a "merrie England" with its cakes and ales and simple festivities, like dancing on the village green, was the publicly supported myth of English country life. However, criticism of this ideal of rustic comfort and social stability was growing.[11]

It has been commonplace to picture the sixteenth- and seventeenth-century Puritan as an officious spoilsport, who condemned bear baiting not for the pain it caused the bear, but for the joy it caused the spectators. However, it is important to place this antipathy toward play in its proper context. That context was the religious legitimation of individual work. The Puritan labored in the world not only to advance his station, but also to convince himself that he was truly among God's elect. In other words, work and worship were the center-pieces of life; play was merely that which drew people away from their proper duty. As Dennis Brailsford explains, the Puritan emphasized only two ends of the spectrum of physical effort, hard work and complete rest.[12] In between was a vast gray area of idleness, which was to be avoided. The Puritan ethic was, then, not only a reaction to the excesses of courtly life but also a challenge to the morality of a rural order that promised festive release instead of steady accumulation for the lower orders.

On the other hand, for the rural landowner, leisure was an art to be refined. As George M. Trevelyan has explained, the seventeenth-century cavalier saw himself as the descendant of the knightly class and the purveyor of chivalric tradition.[13] Occupying the upper echelons of a hierarchically organized locality, he maintained the old beliefs in the qualititative differences among ranks and in the obligations of station. In this sense he adhered to the traditions of con-spicuous display and generosity and spent his own life in decorous leisure.

Predictably, Puritans such as Robert Burton were sharply critical of this view:

> But amongst us the badge of gentry is idleness: to be of no calling, not to labour, for that's derogatory to their birth, to be a mere spectator, a drone, *fruger consumer natus* (born only to consume his food), to have no necessary employment (some few governors exempted), "but to rise to eat," etc. to spend his days in hawking, hunting, etc. and such-like disports and recreation . . . are the sole exercises almost, and ordinary actions of our nobility, and in which they are too immoderate.[14]

While the Puritan accepted the value of physical fitness for the maintenance of health, such fitness typically was to be acquired not by play, but by work. Based on a study of Puritan theologians, Joachim Rühl has concluded that this disapproval of sports was not a blanket condemnation.[15] Rather an athletic activity might be acceptable if:

1. The sport is useful (especially in its military application) and not played primarily for pleasure.
2. The sport is practiced by "men of renown," meaning people who have good breeding and advanced social standing.
3. The sport has some classical heritage, as did discus throwing, running, and others.
4. The sport is played in moderation, in order that the players avoid excesses of time and expense.

While theoretically plausible, such stipulations were clearly at odds with the gaming instincts of the times.

One issue expressing the opposition between Cavalier and Puritan idealism was Sabbatarianism. While Catholics and Anglicans emphasized the importance of the Sabbath, their primary concern was church attendance. The rest of the day was left more or less to the discretion of their parishioners. Thus, Sunday recreations were customary. However, if recreations were tolerated, it is also true that some work might be expected from the laboring classes on Sundays. Puritanism sought to discontinue both kinds of Sabbath activity. Instead, Sundays were to be devoted to spiritual contemplation.

This issue of Sunday observance precipitated the issuance of a celebrated *King's Book of Sports* by James I in 1617.[16] The specific setting for the debate was Lancashire, a county divided between Catholic and Puritan. Two years previously the Puritan justices of the peace had issued a series of orders regarding Sabbath observance and instructed clergy to read these from the pulpit quarterly. The Catholic members of the community then appealed to James, who responded by listing the various recreations that were permissible. Dancing, leaping, archery, vaulting, and other "harmless recreations" were allowed, as were such traditional rites as morris dancing, May games, Whitsun ales, and Maypoles. Again, as Christopher Hill explains, this siding with the Catholic and traditional elements at the expense of the "industrious sort of people" was not without its political motivations, for the former groups provided much of the monarchy's support in the Civil War to come.[17] This issue was also addressed by Charles I, who in 1633 reissued the declaration along with the requirement that every clergyman read it from the pulpit.

This issue may also have been behind a more organized expression of village games. In 1604 James authorized a Scottish supporter, Robert Dover, to revive a yearly festival known as the Cotswold Games. In a 1636 book of poems dedicated to Dover, there are indications of the sports included (wrestling, leaping, running, pitching the bar, throwing the sledge, hare and hounds, and horsemanship). For female contestants there were May games, masques and rounds, and races for a smock.[18] To sanctify the proceedings the writers drew parallels to the ancient Olympic Games.

Between 1642 and 1660 the Puritans had an opportunity to enact their views concerning sport. As Brailsford has emphasized, this period is remarkable for it represents the first instance of governmental pressure toward sport that was exercised in an entirely negative direction.[19] While earlier rulers had sought to curtail certain sports among lower status groups, usually this was done to promote other types of physical exercise. Now all sports, as examples of idleness, became objects of suspicion.

While early ordinances of the Puritan era touched on "the wicked profanation of the Lord's day, by sports and gamings, formerly encouraged even by authority," the spirit of Puritanism is reflected most clearly in legislation of 8 April 1644. Parliament ordered that the earlier proclamations regarding Sunday observance be put into practice. One focus of the ordinance was work; the second was play:

> That no person or persons shall hereafter upon the Lord's Day use, exercise, keep, maintain, or be present at any wrestlings, shootings, bowling, ringing of bells for pleasure or pastime, masque, wake, otherwise called feasts, Church-ale, dancing, games, sport, or pastime whatsoever.[20]

The penalty was five shillings for those over fourteen and twelve pence for the parents of those under that age. The ordinance continues:

> And because the profanation of the Lord's day hath been heretofore greatly occasioned by May-poles (a heathenish vanity, generally abused by superstition and wickedness) the Lords and Commons do further order and ordain That all singular May-poles that are, or shall be erected, shall be taken down and removed. . . . It is further ordained that "the King's Declaration concerning lawful Sports to be used" and all other books and pamphlets that have been or shall be written, printed or published, against the morality of the fourth commandment . . . be called in, seized, suppressed, and publicly burnt. . . .

As indicated previously, the effectiveness of governmental policies depended on the cooperation of the local justices of the peace. In the Puritan strongholds of the south and east there were much enforcement and less in the north and west. Somewhat surprisingly, London maintained most of its Sunday pleasures. In response to such laxity an ordinance of October 1645 provided a new punishment, suspension from the sacrament of the Lord's Supper.

In June 1647, when Parliament banned the traditional church festivals of Christmas, Easter, and Whitsuntide, the population was compensated for the loss of this recreational time. Henceforth, "scholars, apprentices, and other servants" were to have special recreational days on the second Tuesday of every month. In essence, recreation was to be taken from work time and not holy days.[21]

Sabbath violation was one theme of Puritanism; however, sports were considered dangerous for other reasons as well. Sporting events, especially those that drew large crowds, were seen as occasions for rebellion. In this regard, the Dorset Standing Committee in 1647 complained to Parliament:

> . . . knowing what small beginnings have formerly come to, we think ourselves in duty bound to give you an account the distempers of these parts, where under pretence of football matches and cudgel playing and the like, have been lately suspicious meetings and assemblies at several places made up of very disaffected persons, and more such are appointed.[22]

As the resistance to the regime mounted, the most intensive efforts to prohibit such meetings occurred during the time of the Protectorate, when England was partitioned into eleven military districts under Cromwell's leadership. In 1654 all hunting, hawking, horse racing, bull baiting, and football were prohibited for such reasons. This ban was released in 1659.

As might be expected, there was much resistance to this legislation. One specific symbol of resistance was the Maypole. As Hill explains, the "maypole was for the rural lower classes almost a symbol of independence of their betters."[23] Its erection was a clearly understood affront to authority. He goes on to cite a number of examples of this, including some festivities that were instigated by the local gentry. Upon the restoration of the Stuarts, Maypoles were an important element of local celebrations.

In conclusion, it seems that the moral rigor of Puritanism was simply too strenuous for what was essentially an agricultural society. As Rühl has shown through his study of diaries, many sports continued almost unabated during the Commonwealth, and the remainder burst forth upon its completion.[24] In 1676 Edward Chamberlayne compiled a list of sports that resembled those of fifty years before. The upper groups had their hunting, hawking, horse racing, bowls, and tennis.

> The citizens and peasants have hard-ball, football, skittles, or nine-pins, shovelboard, stow-ball, goffe, trol-madam, cudgels, bear-baiting, bull-baiting, bow and arrow, quoits, leaping, wrestling, pitching the bar, and ringing of bells, a recreation used in no other country of the world.[25]

Thus, in 1660 not only was a set of activities restored to former prominence, but also, in more general terms, an attitude toward life was legitimized.

HORSEMANSHIP

Among the great transformations of the modern era is the relative absence of the horse. In its wake have come the sights and sounds and smells of machines. However, the horse of the preindustrial period was much more than a source of transportation and a beast of burden. It was also a companion, a coparticipant in a range of field sports, and, perhaps most significantly, a moving pedestal for the self. In an age when the judgment of horses was a common topic of conversation, one was marked by the quality and carriage of the horse he rode. Likewise, men and women were judged by their own carriage and deportment as riders.

Because the horse presents a very public display of the self (in contrast to the coach) and because the possibilities for indignity are spectacular, noble youth were trained in horsemanship from an early age. The great houses had their riding masters, and instruction in this matter might also be part of one's travels abroad. Indeed, Marcia Vale concludes that mastery of the horse was "perhaps the single most important accomplishment for the gentleman."[26]

There were fundamentally two types of horsemanship that bear noting here.[27] The first, the *manège* or "scientific" horsemanship, was introduced into England by Henry VIII and is attributable to Italian influence. Basically, the manège was the successor of the tournament and, more recently, the practice of tilting at a ring. The manege itself involved commanding a large horse suitable for battle at different gaits (for example, pacing, trotting, galloping), making complicated turns, and leaping. This kind of maneuverability in warfare was certainly important; however, the artifice and precision of the manege suggest that qualities of display had become the major consideration.[28]

Both the manege and tilting at the ring were popular within the court during the latter part of the sixteenth and the early years of the seventeenth centuries. However, they were shortly outmoded by another form of equitation touching a far great portion of the population—racing.

Racing has, of course, been popular to every age. However, during the late Tudor and early Stuart eras, it was put on a more organized footing. Furthermore, after the Restoration, Charles II sanctioned the sport in a hitherto unprecedented way.

As Wray Vamplew has explained, match races between rivalrous horse owners were a common feature of the preindustrial era.[29] Similarly, "sale races" (indicating quality to prospective buyers) were a long-standing tradition. However, the Tudor and Stuart eras saw the establishment of municipal racing. City corporations, wishing to attract trade, would sponsor races by offering silver or gold artifacts to the victors. Such races were part of wider festivals which included beer tents, musical and theatrical entertainments, games, and dancing. The first indication of this seems to be at Chester during the reign of Henry VIII. As an expression of the relationship between the saddlers and the drapers, the former sponsored a horse race and offered a prize of a silver bell. During the reign of Elizabeth the number of towns offering regular races increased, and by the end of the century there were a dozen or more.[30] During the seventeenth century many others were added. As at Chester, the typical prizes now were silver cups for the first, second, and third finishers. Other changes included grandstands, marked-off courses, and railings for finishing straights. No admission was charged to spectators, so the events attracted a wide range of people; however, money might be charged for admission to the stands.

The races were long (four miles being the usual distance) and were run in several heats. Clearly, stamina was valued as much as speed; however, the number of heats was also an indication of the smaller number of horses that could be assembled.[31]   Requiring the ultimate victor to win at least two heats was a way of spacing out a day's pleasure for the spectators as well.   There might be races for horses of different caliber, and owners, as well as grooms, rode at this time.

The interest of the Stuart court in racing was given its great impetus by the development of Newmarket by James I.[32]   James was originally attracted to this area because of the quality of its terrain for field sports and its prevalence of hares.   He had a house built there and had the grounds stocked with partridge and hares to facilitate his passion.   While James himself was not a great rider or particular patron of racing, in 1622 one finds the first match between horses (for 100 pounds) there.   His successor Charles was more of a horseman.   Racing between members of the court became quite common, and the first stands for viewing these races were erected at Newmarket.   Indeed, the identification of Newmarket with dissolute court life was strong enough that the Puritans had the heath plowed upon their ascendancy.

However, it is after 1660 that Newmarket emerged as the racing center or, as some put it, the "second capital" of England during its spring and fall meetings.   Charles II was a fine rider, and in 1664 he established an annual race, "the Plate" (referring to the silver prize), which he himself won seven years later.   Charles established other races and even took the nickname "Old Rowley" after a favorite racehorse.   Under his patronage Newmarket became the fashion center of England.   Unlike the municipal meetings, it was restricted exclusively to the upper class.   This pattern was continued by William III (who, though not much of a horseman, was a gambler) and by Anne, who founded the Ascot races.   She is also credited with establishing a system of "thoroughbred" breeding by which selected horses with Arabian ancestry would serve as the only breeding stock.   This practice, however, did not become widely adopted until later in the eighteenth century.

As today, gambling was central to racing.   Gentlemen wagered hundreds of pounds among themselves, a pattern that became much more prevalent after the Restoration.   Bets were sometimes placed on a rider and horse's ability to traverse a certain distance within a predetermined time; more commonly they were the result of matches made between owners.   Under such conditions, regulations encouraging fairness (and thereby facilitating the exchange of money) were established.   The earliest and best known of these were Kiplingcote's Rules, set forth in 1619.   These established riders' weights, types of fouls, disqualifications, and the subscription of prize money.[33]   At Newmarket the king himself was the arbiter of the disputes which still arose.

In general terms the different kinds of races express different kinds of social relationship.   The match races were the result (and sometimes a continuing source) of interpersonal rivalry.   Like dueling, challenges to race were assaults on self-confidence; the level of the bet indicated the depths of this confidence. Such races between rivalrous local gentlemen and free-spending courtiers remained important throughout the preindustrial period.   However, group races represent a somewhat more diluted form of competition. Significantly, these were first developed not by courtiers, but by the municipalities. Rules proliferated; subscriptions were charged; spectators of all types abounded. Such changes are antecedents of modern times.

FENCING AND DUELING

During the seventeenth century, Italian influences on court life gave way to French ones. During their exile the Stuarts naturally became familiar with the games and diversions of the French court; some of these were imported to England upon their return. Among the changes in fashion was the adoption of the small sword, popularized in France during the 1650s.[34] Much shorter than the rapier, the small sword featured a triangular blade and was used primarily for thrusting. The new style in fencing, then, demanded a quickness of wrist, a refined motion that was much in contrast to the slashing quality of rapier play.

The rapier, and after it the small sword, became arbiters in the duel of honor, which developed during the late Tudor and early Stuart eras. Dueling, or single combat, had been given some legal sanction during the feudal period in the form of trial by battle between accuser and accused. However, the judicial duel fell off during the later Middle Ages, particularly the fifteenth century, when disposing of one's enemies by henchmen became common. The sixteenth- and seventeenth-century duel of honor, thus, was a reclamation of the chivalric ideal, for it was based on the idea of two men opposing each other openly and with equal weapons. While prohibited officially, such duels did represent an ethical advance over the earlier "killing afray." Furthermore, they corresponded to the new individualistic emphasis of the Renaissance. As John Selden in *The Duello or Single Combat* (1610) writes:

> Truth, honor, freedome, and curtesie being as incident to perfit chivalry upon the eye given, fame impeached, body wronged, or curtesie taxed, a custom hath bin among the French, English, Burguignons, Italians, Almans, and the Northern people (which as Ptolemy notes are always inclined to liberty) to seek revenge of their wrongs on the body of the accuser, and that by private combat *seul à seul*, without judicial lists appointed them.[35]

Endemic to the duel of honor was the belief that certain crimes are so heinous that for them the law makes no adequate retribution. Among these are the insult to gentlewomen, the slap or blow, and that slur on fame or reputation termed "giving the lie." As explained in *A Discourse of Civil Life* (1606), no assault is considered worse than

> to be accounted lyer, that any other injury is cancelled by giving the lie, and he that receiveth it standeth so charged in his honour and reputation that he can not disburden himself of that imputation, but by striking of him that hath given it, or by challenging him the combat.[36]

Books of the times recounted the kinds of lies which might be incident to a challenge.

Seen in these terms, dueling appears as a kind of identity play in which the participants try to regain the dignity of station. Judicial-legal reprimands are replaced by social-personal ones. What the single combat expressed as much as anything was the sphere of worth that had grown up around the individual during the Renaissance. The duel became an extralegal mechanism for rectifying (and perhaps preventing) assaults on the self-concept. While such activity cannot be considered sport in any strict sense, the duel of honor represents the context into which elite sword play was cast.

For those whose social position did not permit them to wear "the sword" (meaning the small sword), there was the backsword, a straight, thirty-two inch blade with one sharp edge, a dull point, and a basket hilt. For practice, wooden cudgels with basket hilts were used instead. During the seventeenth century, cudgeling or singlestick play was replacing swordplay at country gatherings. The object was to split the head of the opponent, the streak of blood signaling victory.

Such contests were given inspiration by the public exhibitions termed "playing a prize." Fynes Moryson in 1617 speaks of "frequent spectacles in London exhibited to the people by fencers, by walkers on ropes, and like men of activity."[37] His comments reflect the decline in status of the English fencing masters. During the early seventeenth century the guild established by Henry VII (the Masters of Defense) deteriorated; by the Civil War, it had lapsed completely. After the war, disbanded soldiers assumed this title and staged exhibitions before the public with many of the traditional weapons, such as the two-handed sword, sword and buckler, backsword, and singlestick. In contrast to the earlier public "exams," swords were sharp, and a bit of blood became an expected part of the show.

It is this scene that Samuel Pepys came across in 1667:

> Abroad, and stopped at the Bear-garden stairs, there to see a prize fought. But the house so full there was no getting in there, so forced to go through an alehouse into the pit, where the bears are baited; and upon a stool did see them fight, which they did very furiously, a butcher and a waterman. The former had the better all along, till by and by the latter dropped his sword out of his hand, and the butcher, whether or not seeing his sword dropped I know not, but did give him a cut over the wrist, so as he was disabled to fight any longer. But Lord! to see in a minute how the whole stage was full of watermen to revenge the foul play, and the butchers to defend their fellow, though most blamed him; and there they all fell to it knocking down and cutting many on each side. It was pleasant to see, but that I stood in the pit, and feared that in the tumult I might get some hurt.[38]

Such fights typically were held in theatres or fair booths where entrance money could be collected. In addition to providing spectators like Pepys with a seemingly death-defying confrontation, they also provided (again) an occasion to gamble on the outcome.

The matches were promoted by a series of public challenges attesting to the hostility and determination of the contestants. The following advertisement at the end of this period is typical:

> At the Bear Garden in Hockley in the Hole A Tryal of Skill to be Performed between two Profound Masters of the nobel Science of Defense on Wednesday next, being the 13th of the instant July, 1709, at Two of the Clock precisely.
>
> I, George Gray, born in the City of Norwick, who has Fought in most parts of the West Indies, viz., Jamaica, Barbadoes, and several other Parts of the World; in all Twenty-five times, upon a Stage, and was never yet worsted, and now come lately to London, do invite James Harris, to meet and exercise at these following Weapons, viz.:
> Back Sword
> Sword and Dagger
> Sword and Buckler
> Single Falchon and
> Case of Falchons
> I, James Harris, Master of the Noble Science of Defence, who formerly rid in the Horse guards, and hath fought a hundred and ten Prizes, and never left a stage to any Man; will not fail (God Willing) to meet this brave and bold Inviter at the Time and Place appointed, desiring Sharp Swords and from him no Favour.
> Note: No person to be upon the Stage but the Seconds. Vivat Regina.[39]

Interestingly, such spectacles of backsword fighting possess aspects of both rude country matches and formalized duels. While there is no pretense that the performers are gentlemen, there is clear attention to civility, proper form (as evidenced, for example, by the presence of seconds and the listing of licit weapons), and personal honor. No mention of money is made. In this sense the challenges evoke memories of the later tournament. Indeed, these stage plays were in some sense a residue of feudal culture, with ordinary people now dramatizing the proud tradition of the fighting man.

COCKFIGHTING AND ANIMAL BAITING

Animal fights were another instance of the passion for blood and battle that could be found in most segments of society. Indeed, few activities better distinguish the character of preindustrial life from that of today than the public tormenting of animals. The modern belief that humans (and, to a lesser degree, animals) have rights and deserve compassion simply because of their categorical status as living beings still was not widespread. As Johan Huizinga has argued, the preindustrial world was not unsympathetic and, in fact, indulged itself publicly in great ranges of emotion.[40] However, the perception of a great chain of being with profound differences between the various categories of life was still a prevalent one. In an age accustomed to physical pain and early death, public executions, torture, and the exhumation and display of corpses, the circle of compassion was not widely drawn.

For most of the population the public death of an animal occasioned even less concern. As humans were created to serve God, so animals were created to serve people. However, it should be noted that animal fighting was high on the list of activities forbidden by the Puritans. For the most part, these objections were based not on the essence of the activity, but on the activities that seemed to surround it—that is, drinking, gaming, swearing, quarreling, and profaning the Sabbath. Occasionally, the objection was more fundamental, as noted in these comments by Philip Stubbes:

> What Christian hearte can take pleasure to see one poore beaste to rent, teare, and kill an other, and all for his foolish pleasure? An although they be bloudie beasts to mankynd, and seeke his destruction, yet wee are not to abuse them, for his sake who made them, and whose creatures they are. For not-withstanding that they be evill to us, and thirst after our own bloud, yeat are they good creatures in their own nature and kind, and made to set forthe the glorie, power, and magnificence of our God, and for our use, and therefore . . . we ought not to abuse them.[41]

While cockfighting and bear and bull baiting are mentioned by William Fitzstephen as early as the twelfth century, they seem to have grown in popularity during the sixteenth and seventeenth centuries. Every town (and many villages) had their pits and rings for this purpose. As with other sports, a major influence on this process was the legitimacy provided by the sovereigns, including the establishment of regular locations for the sports.[42] Henry VIII made the masterships of bear and bull baiting a court office and that king was also responsible for the erection of an amphitheatre in Southwark, near London, for this purpose. This amphitheatre was maintained and even expanded by Elizabeth and then the Stuarts. Indeed, when theatres south of the Thames began to draw patrons from the bear garden in the 1590s, Elizabeth ordered the theaters closed on Thursdays so that the baitings would survive. James some-times attended the baitings twice a week when he was in London, and Charles was a vigorous patron as well.[43]

The pattern was reproduced in cockfighting. Henry VIII instituted a royal cockpit near London, and during Elizabeth's reign several other cockpits arose there. For his part James I appointed a cockmaster who was responsible for training the king's birds. This level of royal support was continued by Charles II who oversaw the creation of some Rules and Orders for Cocking, which attempted to standardize matches and eliminate the worst gambling abuses.

Cockfighting involved a series of contests between individual birds.[44] Once released by their handlers within the specially constructed circular pit, the birds would flail at each other until one was rendered senseless by the opponent's beak or spurs. Although an older method had been to sharpen their natural spurs with a knife, by the late seventeenth century some had elaborately engraved spurs of steel or silver attached. The battle might be over in an instant, or it might go on for an hour. Under specific conditions the handlers were allowed to enter the ring and prop up their proteges for further fighting. The battle continued until one or the other was dead or could no longer fight. Individual contests were often organized into bigger tournaments, called mains. The ultimate champion might be produced, then, by a battle royal (featuring several birds in the ring at once) or by an elimination tournament (a Welsh main). Mains could last four days and were, predictably, centers of rabid gambling.

The cocks themselves were selected while young and were subjected to special diets and training. Normally, a cock was two years old before he fought, and he was matched against others of similar weight and size. He was presented for battle by trimming his excess plumage and cutting his comb and wattle. Furthermore, he was prepared by sparring (with his spurs covered) and by sweating in a straw-filled basket or bag. Charles Cotton, in *The Compleat Gamester* (1674), then recommends the following:

> Towards four or five a clock in the evening take them out of their stoves, and having lickt their eyes and head with your tongue, put them into their pens, and having filled their troughs with square manchet, piss therein, and let them feed whilst the urine is hot; for this will cause their scouring to work, and will wonderfully cleanse both head and body.[45]

This process of feeding, resting, sparring, stoving, and chasing (allowing the cock to chase a bird held in one's arms) continued, with variations, for six weeks. What makes it striking to the modern reader is the intimacy between man and beast.

Even more spectacular was bear baiting. The baiting itself was often preceded by a parade through the streets headed by the bear ward and his animals. At the bigger amphitheaters there was an admission charge of a penny (two, for the better seats), and attendance might reach 1000.[46] The bear would be chained to a stake and then expected to fend off several large dogs unleashed on it. As one dog was killed, another would be set forth. When the bear was worn down (or even killed), he was replaced by another. As many as a dozen bears would be baited in this way. A variation was the baiting of bulls by bull dogs. A bull tied to a fifteen-foot rope would defend himself from the dogs with his horns. As he tossed the dogs into the air, attendants with long poles would scurry about trying to break their fall. For alternatives, men with whips would set upon a blinded bear, or a more exotic animal like a lion could be tested.

Two related activities might be mentioned here as well.[47] Cockshying featured attempts by men and boys to throw a broomstick at a tethered bird. If they succeeded in hitting the bird and could race in and claim it before it regained its footing, the bird was theirs. Experienced birds became adept at dodging the stick and became lucrative for their owners. In gooseriding, a greased goose was hung by the legs from a bough. The bird was won by the contestant who, riding fast below, could reach up and pull its head off.

Such games are cruel by modern standards. Yet this cruelty was tinged with a certain fascination and respect for the animals involved. As the French visitor Saussure described a cockfight early in the eighteenth century, "It is surprising to see the ardour, the strength, and the courage of these little animals, for they rarely give up till one of them is dead."[48] Thus, the more established animals were personified by names and carefully attended by their owners. They were cheered or spared when they showed special valor.

In an age when death was an often unpredictable and inexplicable event, animal fighting allowed people to experience vicariously the precariousness of life. Through a combination of effort, luck, and courage, an animal might triumph over almost insurmountable odds. By gambling, the spectators invested themselves in the success of those in the pit. For such reasons, cockfighting was seen not as base, but rather, as Cotton claimed, as a "noble recreation" which "hath gain'd so great an estimation among the gentry."[49]

BALL GAMES

At all social levels ball games were played. There were field games in which the ball was directed or carried toward some goal, as in balloon ball, hurling, and football. Others relied on some barrier such as a wall or net, as in the various forms of handball and tennis. Some games involved rolling a ball toward a target (bowls, ninepins, and cloish) or directing it toward some target by means of a club (pall mall and golf). Finally, there were games in which the ball was hit away from a center of activity into an open field (soot ball, tipcat, and, in its earliest glimmerings, cricket). As the reader will have already gathered, some of these pastimes (and others not mentioned) were bound for obscurity. Others, for a number of reasons, became the ancestors of modern forms.

The sport best illustrating the popularization process is bowling. Indeed, bowling, in its various forms, is generally considered to have been the most widely played ball game of the age. The reasons for this are instructive.

First, bowling was well suited to the proclivities of the age: It was a gambling sport. The invective of such opponents as Bishop Earle in 1628 only argue its success:

A bowl-alley is the place where there are three things thrown away besides bowls, to wit, time, money, and curses, and the last ten for one. The best sport in it is the gamester's, and he enjoys it that looks on and bets not. It is the school of wrangling and worse than the schools, for men will cavil here for an hair's breadth, and make a stir where a straw would end the controversy. No antic screws men's bodies into such strange flexures, and you would think them here senseless, to speak sense to their bowl, and put their trust in entreaties for a good cast. The betters are the factious noise of the alley, or the gamesters' beadsmen that pray for them.[50]

Likewise, it was successful as a spectator sport for a limited audience. Because it is a confined and relatively uncomplicated game, a small group of observers could follow the action and the scoring. Furthermore, bowling, in contrast to most ball games, requires little space. Thus, it was particularly suited for the taverns and gaming houses in the population centers.

Another point in bowling's favor was its appeal to women.[51] The bowling ground became a place for social mingling, a point made several times by Pepys. Finally, bowling to a limited degree carried the stamp of royal approval. James I appointed one Clement Cotterell in 1620 to license persons to "keep several numbers of Bowling Allies, Tennis Courts, and Such Like Places of Honest Recreation."[52] In this light, Robert Ashton records the licensing of thirty-one bowling alleys (as well as fourteen tennis courts and forty gaming houses) in London and Westminster during this time.[53] While James himself was not an avid players, Charles I was, wagering large sums on his play. This patronage was resumed after the Restoration, and the bowling ground remained a requisite part of the great house.

While associated with similar vices and virtues, tennis was more exclusively an aristocratic sport. More than bowling, it received the favor of the Stuart kings. James' sons Henry (who died at eighteen in 1622) and Charles were enthusiasts, having been instructed by the king's master of tennis plays. Charles continued to play after his accession and saw to the instruction of his sons, later Charles II and James II. During the early years of this reign, Charles II would take his "usual physicks at tennis," a regimen of an hour or two of play at five o'clock in the morning.[54] Several times Pepys went to watch him play, though he comments that the king's play, while exuberant, was overpraised.[55]

Tennis remained a passion at the universities as well. In his *Microcosmographie* of 1628, J. Earle characterizes the scholar: "the two marks of his Senioritie, is the bare Velvet of his gowne, and his proficiencie at Tennis, where when hee can once play a set, he is a Fresh-man no more."[56] Tennis seems especially to have been a younger person's game, and it was, like the other gambling sports, a scene of much wrangling. Among the casualties of the age was the nineteen-year-old son of the bishop of Bristol who reputedly killed himself rather than confront his mother about his tennis debts.[57]

However, after the accession of William and Mary, tennis faltered dramatically. Without an example of royal patronage, the game became less fashionable. Furthermore, the size and expense of tennis facilities (recall the architectural encumbrances) mitigated against continued growth. In 1615 there were fourteen courts in London. By the time of the London fire (1665), that number was six, and this was reduced by two.[58] The royal courts remained, but the other public courts fell into disuse. By the eighteenth century those remaining were being used as theatres or places of other entertainment.

Royal patronage was a key element in the diffusion of a game, but it could not guarantee it. Two particular games, golf and pall mall, were introduced by the Stuarts; neither achieved any marked success. Golf was brought south by James' Scottish courtiers. In 1608 a course was laid out on Blackheath Common near Greenwich, and play continued there for some time. North of the border, golf was quite popular, and in 1618 James granted a monopoly to Scotsman James Melville for the production of balls (and the seizure of illegal ones). However, aside from a few stray comments, there is little indication that golf was becoming very popular in England. Geoffrey Cousins has attributed this to the problems of adequate equipment.[59] Feather-stuffed balls were expensive (perhaps five shillings), and wooden clubs were difficult to manufacture with any precision. Further refinements in the late eighteenth century only took the sophisticated versions farther away from the humbler forms.

Pall mall was brought over from France after the Restoration. A cross between golf and croquet, the game was played along huge alleys, sometimes 800 yards in length.[60] A small boxwood ball was driven by a mall or mallet along an avenue of (in some cases) powdered cockleshells over sand. As in croquet, the object was to hit the ball through a series of iron wickets, and for this purpose a smaller ball and mallet were substituted. To restrict errant shots, the course was sometimes enclosed with a low wooden railing. The best known ground was "the Mall," laid out by Charles II in St. James's Park.

In general, tennis, golf, and pall mall probably faltered because of technical considerations (that is, large, elaborate playing grounds and complicated, expensive equipment). Such elements constituted status advantages for the possessor; however, a bowling establishment could also provide these. Furthermore, the former games were somehow foreign in their inspiration. After the Glorious Revolution of 1688 and the installation of the landed oligarchy, there was a growing sense of Englishness that fitted better with other sports. In particular, such historic pastimes as horse racing and field sports were revamped as centers of status consciousness. With bowling (and soon archery) fulfilling the functions of cross-sex mingling and limited physical opportunities for women, racing, hunting, and fencing provided more praiseworthy options for male rivalry.

MASS SPORTS AND PUBLIC DISORDER

The mass ball games of earlier periods continued as activities of common people and students. Indeed, no record of any high-status adult's playing exists, and when Oswald in Shakespeare's *King Lear* is called a "base foot-ball player," the insult is clear.[61] Students of gentle status seem to be the only exceptions—though their participation frequently drew moral rebuke. The common origins of mass sports, their collective theme, and the ready possibilities for injury were simply at odds with an elite bent on individual display. As James

I counseled his eldest son, football was "meeter for laming than making able the users thereof."[62]

Another continuing element was the association of mass games with festive release, public disorder, and even politically motivated disruptions. As in centuries past, gangs of apprentices and students wandered the streets on Shrove Tuesday, accosting passersby, vandalizing property, and disrupting, among other businesses, bawdy houses. In London there were as many as 20,000 apprentices who might wander the generally unsupervised streets.[63] It is not surprising, then, that the bellmen in towns such as Bristol went about decrying the usual customs of cock throwing, dog tossing, and football on that day.[64] However, football could become a pretext for other kinds of violence as well. In Lincolnshire in the 1640s, for example, the assembly of a football game several times resulted in the destruction of property built on recently drained fen land.[65]

It is worthwhile placing such events in perspective. As noted previously, lower-class people had little economic leverage and no political power as individuals. Hence, they resorted to the traditional strategies of the powerless—public disruption (in the form of riots, looting, and such) and private theft. As Buchanan Sharp has explained, such disturbances were usually perpetrated by nonagricultural wage earners, meaning those trapped by rising prices.[66] The two central causes were food shortages and the enclosure or "improvement" of common land or waste areas. In the former instance, shipments of grain might be detained or confiscated; with regard to the latter, new fences and property would be destroyed. Typically, such lawlessness was placed within the context of long-standing local traditions (for example, the customary use of wood or browsing from an unenclosed area). Likewise, the events were not usually an assault on the principal of authority itself but were instead targeted against specific property owners or officials deemed especially greedy or unjust. While foreigners and Catholics were sometimes the victims of mob action, the highest authorities were rarely challenged. A ball in the streets, then, was not only a pretext for general misadventure, but also an occasion for more focused social complaint.

The role of mass sports in articulating rivalries between local groups also is prominent in this period. For example, Richard Steele in his *Spectator* for 11 July 1712, writes: "In Parishes and Schools the Thirst of Glory still obtains. At the seasons of Football and Cockfighting, these little republics reassume their national hatred to each other. My tenant in the country is verily persuaded that the Parish of the enemy hath not one honest man in it."[67] Steele's comments suggest not only the continued association of the events with the pre-Lenten period, but also a sort of bemused and paternalistic tolerance on the part of the landowner. However, there is evidence that the connections of gentlemen to mass sports could be much closer than this. Richard Carew, writing about hurling in Cornwall during the first part of the seventeenth century, indicates that matches commonly were sponsored by landowners.[68] Two or three parishes might be assembled on each side, and the manor houses of the sponsors sometimes served as goals.

We do not know if gambling was behind the sponsorship described above; however, it was certainly the inspiration for a football match between the servants of Charles II and those of the duke of Albemarle in 1681.[69] The king's men having lost to the duke's at fencing and wrestling, a game of football was proposed. Such an event was part of an older pattern involving various sports. For example, in 1667 representatives of the west and north wrestled before Charles.[70] The stakes were 1,000 pounds, and great sums were wagered on both sides. This role of the gentleman, as sponsor and organizer of common people's pursuits, became more prominent in the period that followed.

Another quality that becomes clearer now is the existence of rules for mass games. In his description Carew distinguishes two forms of hurling. "Hurling to the countrie" was more like the mass fights of earlier times. Teams were of no set size, and men on horseback got into the act as well. However, "hurling to goales" took a more complicated form. A field approximately 200 feet long was marked out with two goals, eight to ten feet wide, at its ends. As Carew explains, clear rules of play had evolved:

> The Hurlers are bound to the observation of many lawes, as that they must hurle man to man, and not two set upon one man at once: that the Hurler against the ball, must not *but,* nor hand-fast under the girdle: that he who hath the ball, must *but* onely in the others brest: that he must deale no Fore-ball, viz., he may not throw it to any of his mates, standing neerer the goale, than himselfe. Lastly, in dealing the ball, if any of the other part can catch it flying, between, or e're the other have it fast, he thereby winneth the same to his side, which straightway of defendant becometh assailant, as the other, of assailant falls to be defendant. The lest breach of these lawes, the Hurlers take for a just cause of going together by the eares, but with their fists onely; neighter doth among them seek revenge for such wrong or hurts, but at the like play againe.[71]

Significantly, no judges appear, but self-regulation (prized as a trait of later gentlemanly sport) is clearly there. In short, what one finds in this period is a broader picture of the settings and circumstances of mass play.

HUNTING

Still preeminent in the sporting imagination was hunting. Speaking of hawking and hunting, Moryson in 1617 opines that that "no nation so frequently useth these sports as the English."[72] Surveying the court of James I in 1621, Burton pronounces hunting as "the sole almost and ordinary sport of all our noblemen . . . tis all their study, their exercise, ordinary business, all their talk, and indeed some dote too much on it; they can do nothing else, discourse of nought else."[73]

However, forces first active in the previous century continued to change the sport. The growing human population, the conversion of wooded areas to cropland and pasture, and the use of the forests for lumber and charcoal all diminished animal life. Also threatening was the gun, which, when combined with the growing market for game in the cities, constituted a real poaching menace. The early Stuarts had played a part in this process by their sale of royal forest lands to agricultural and commercial interests. Likewise in need of money, the governments of the Commonwealth and the Protectorate accelerated the disafforestation.

Most threatened by these changes was deer hunting. When James I wished to revive the custom of the forest stag hunt, he had to ask Henri IV of France for a huntsman to instruct the court in the practice, and he even had to import the deer themselves from France.[74] Charles I kept up the royal hunt; however, during the Civil War there was widespread destruction of royal game. Upon the Restoration it was necessary to once again import deer from the Continent. Outside the parks of wealthy gentlemen, even fallow deer were scarce.

In recognition of this decline (and of the poaching menace constituted by the large number of cottagers living within forest lands), the Stuarts turned quickly to game restrictions. In the first year of his reign James reanimated (with modifications) the property qualifications of 1389.[75] By these it was illegal for any person to keep greyhounds, nets, or other hunting implements unless they possessed a landed estate worth 10 pounds, a copyhold to the value of 30 pounds, or goods worth 200 pounds. Sons of esquires or ranks above that could hunt as well. Two years later, James's attention was directed more specifically to deer and rabbits. The taking of these was restricted to those persons with lands worth 40 pounds or goods worth 200 pounds. Furthermore, as in Henry VIII's time, the possession of guns, bows, and crossbows, and so on was limited to the above group. Furthermore, he outlawed the sale of venison.

However, the most enthusiastic restrictions appear after the Restoration. As part of the conservative backlash regarding rural property rights, the hunting of "game" (defined initially as hares, partridges, pheasants, and moor fowl) was restricted to four categories of persons:[76] (1) those having inherited estates worth 100 pounds a year; (2) those with leases of 99 years or more at 150 pounds a year; (3) the eldest sons of esquires, knights, and nobles; and (4) the game-keepers of the above. In essence, this change meant that the large property holders of the country, titled gentlemen, and their designates could hunt such beasts. Others could not hunt these, even on their own ground. On the other hand, the hunting of deer and rabbits was restricted to those with private preserves, for the selling of rabbit skins and meat had become a substantial business. In summary, the hunting of truly wild animals such as game birds was restricted to certain categories of gentlemen and their designates; the hunting of more confined beasts such as deer and rabbits was placed within the growing tradition of private property rights. Henceforth, game illegally taken was "poached"; deer and rabbits were "stolen."

As P. B. Munsche has argued, the spirit behind this legislation seems to have been an animosity toward those groups that had provided much of the opposition to the royalists in the Civil War.[77] The policies of James had allowed the middling property holder of the country (over 40 pounds in land) and the wealthier citizens of the towns (over 200 pounds in goods) to hunt. Now these groups were pointedly excluded. In essence, hunting was restricted by the 1671 act to perhaps 20,000 in a population of more than 5 million.[78] It was reinforced by 5 Anne, ch. 14, whereupon innkeepers were fined five pounds for the sale of game fowl, and by 4 William and Mary, ch. 23, the so-called "Second Game Law." By this act new categories of birds were added to those already restricted.

If the development of the gun as a poaching device was in part responsible for the new restrictions, it also effected the virtual death of a time-honored pastime, hawking. During the early years of the Stuart reign there was still much interest in the activity, and Joseph Strutt records payments of between 40 and 100 pounds for hawks at this time.[79] Likewise, there were several new books, including *The Falcon's Lure and Cure* by Simon Latham (1615) and Edmund Bert's *A Treatise on Hawks and Hawking* (1619). However, by 1624 James found it necessary to ask Louis XIII of France for a falcon and sixteen casts (with generally two birds in a cast) of hawks as a way of sustaining interest at court. The remainder of the Stuarts were not proponents of the art, and after the Civil War it became more common to take birds with fowling pieces.

With the decline in deer hunting, the hunting of smaller game continued to rise in prominence. As George Turberville put the case for the hare, "Hare-hunting is not a privilege confined, like that of the buck, to great noblemen, but a sport easilie and equalie distributed to the wealthy farmer as to the great gentleman."[80] Wealthy farmers did not have enclosed parks, but they did have their packs of hounds, and hare hunting remained (for the eligible) fairly good sport. Indeed, Richard Blome in his *Gentleman's Recreation* (1686) continued to praise it as the best of hunts.

An offshoot of hare hunting was the development of public coursing matches, popularized by Charles I.[81] Coursing is the chasing of the hare by greyhounds, which hunt by sight rather than smell. After the game was started, the dogs were slipped from their leash (which usually connected three hounds). The twists and turns of the resulting chase provided great amusement to the spectators. In public coursing matches individual greyhounds were paired against one another. It was an elaborate contest with rules framed by Thomas, duke of Norfolk, late in Elizabeth's time. By these Laws of the Leash, the hare was given a start of 240 yards. Points were awarded for certain maneuvers, so that the dog who did the most toward capture would be judged the winner. Once again, the motivation behind these rules was the prevention of gambling disputes, and several of the laws are devoted explicitly to this subject. The Laws of the Leash served as guidelines for the sport for nearly 200 years.

The other hunt that gained favor was the fox hunt.[82] Before the Civil War there was still limited support for this. Gervase Markham, in *Country Content-ments* (1615) complained that fox and badger hunting were of "less use" than other forms and noted that it was hard to get dogs to chase them. However, after the war, isolated gentry were finding the pleasures of fox hunting, especially during the winter months. The famed Charlton hunt is traced to packs of hounds owned by the duke of Monmouth and Lord Grey during the 1660s.[83] Likewise, the Burton and Brocklesby hunts claim origins from the packs of this period. Still there is little praise of fox hunting in sporting literature at this time.

With deer, hare, and most kinds of game birds denied to the great majority of the population, one may well wonder what legal sport remained. One activity that experienced a new popularity during this period is fishing. To be sure, the stocking of ponds and the taking of fish had been important throughout the Middle Ages, especially during Lent or other times when meat was not available. In this regard, Richard Hoffman has argued that sport fishing emerged in England during the early part of the fifteenth century.[84] Still there was little celebration of the activity before Elizabethan times.

The major exception to this conclusion occurs in 1496, when "A Treatisse of Fishing with an Angle" was added to the discussions of hunting and hawking in the *Boke of St. Albans*. In this edition the author extols the virtues of fishing over hunting and hawking. Indeed, the fisherman

> . . . shall have his wholesome walk and merry at his own ease, and also many
> sweet airs of diverse herbs and flowers that shall make him hungry and well
> disposed of his body. He shall hear the melodious melodies of the harmony
> of birds . . . which meseemeth better than all the noise of hounds and blasts
> of horns and other games that falconers and hunters can make.[85]

The Tudor era was still too vigorous to embrace such an ideal. However, the time of the Stuarts was a less active and more contemplative age. In particular, city dwellers and lesser gentry who were denied other pleassures turned to the pursuit. They were encouraged by a fresh crop of books, including John Taverner's *Certain Experiments Concerning Fish and Fruit* (1600), John Dennys's *Secrets of Angling* (1606), Gervase Markham's *Country Contentments* (1611), and William Lawson's *The Secrets of Angling* (1620).

Fishing was an activity closer to Puritan, rather than Cavalier, sensibility. It is instructive, then, that while other sports were being restricted during the Commonwealth, fishing was promoted. The sudden collection of works included Thomas Barker's *Art of Angling* (1651), Izaak Walton's *The Compleat Angler* (1653), Richard Franck's *Northern Memoirs* (1658), and Robert Vanable's *The Experienced Angler* (1662). As in fowling or hunting, many practices no longer considered good sportsmanship were encouraged. Netting and spearing were common, as were such techniques as baiting the leg of a goose. Perhaps because fishing was fundamentally a private activity, it yielded to the code of gentility more slowly than did public sports.

Of the various works of the period, Walton's is, of course, the one that is remembered.[86] Although the book borrows passages from Thomas Barker and earlier treatises and is, as a technical manual, inferior to Richard Franck's volume, it went through five editions in Walton's lifetime and was subsequently repopularized by Samuel Johnson in the eighteenth century. As a well-placed

London tradesman, Walton spoke to that milieu. A royalist in a Puritan setting, he understood social climbing and the anxieties of the self-made man. In addition to the comments on the philosophical and spiritual advantages of fishing (in contrast to hawking and hunting), the book embodies the desire to escape a politically charged society, to wander walkways along riverbanks, to escape into reflection. For such reasons, he subtitled his work, "The Contemplative Man's Recreation."

CONCLUSIONS

It is the ambition of every ruling dynasty to cast a spell over its age. For the most part, the Tudors, if headstrong, were a vigorous and expansive lot, reaching out to and accommodating their subjects in various ways. The Stuarts were rather more restricted in scope: doctrinaire in their policies, self-involved to the point of extravagance in their personal habits. Their century was a more contemplative and divisive era in English history. Ideology led to warfare—and warfare to the self-serving policies of victors. Such themes were played out in sporting life.

The Puritan sensibility—which found a brief moment for legislative expression—is remarkable for its contrast with the broader preindustrial tradition that has heretofore been cited. Before, play had been a central occasion for communal and self-expression, a situation that was most pronounced in those classes that defined themselves as nonworking. During the Puritan regime the status of work was elevated. It became less the curse of Adam and more an opportunity to glorify God. Playful activity (including sport) was moved forcibly out of the spotlight, and a more calculating, enterprising mentality prevailed. Visions of steady accumulation replaced the agriculturally based patterns of labor and festivity. Like the characters in Aesop's famous fable, the Puritans were the ants of the world, come to wreak vengeance on indolent, fiddling grasshoppers.

At complete odds with this viewpoint was the Stuart court. As in previous centuries, the court provided a public (though excessively dramatic and elaborate) model of what the great landowner might aspire to. Like their Tudor counterparts, they were assiduous sportsmen. They nursed such pastimes as tennis and bowls, and brought in new ones, including pall mall and golf. They elevated the status of horse breeding and racing; they popularized coursing matches. They attended animal baitings and cockfights; they attempted to sustain royal hunting traditions and redefined the game laws.

Furthermore, they publicly supported the old village amusements against Puritan restrictions. The non-aristocratic diversions, including Maypoles, morris dancing, leaping, wrestling, quintain, and casting the bar were maintained by such vehicles as *The King's Book of Sports* and the Cotswold Games. With the old rationale of military preparedness now stripped away, sport emerged quite clearly as a protected right of both ordinary people and princes.

What the Restoration accomplished in large part was a resurgence of traditional, rural ideals. The careless valor of the prerevolutionary cavalier became almost a compulsive gaiety afterward. However, some changes longer in progress could not be reversed. The gentlemanly ideal continued to soften and grow more "civilized." Fishing and bowling attained broader popularity. The slashing style of rapier play was replaced by more refined French maneuvers. Card and table games became fashionable. Stag hunting lost out to the pursuit of the gentle hare. As in the hunting of the hare and fox, the gentleman was becoming increasingly a spectator to killing and violence rather than a perpetrator of it himself.

This development of spectatorship during the seventeenth century deserves special mention here. As indicated previously, horse racing and coursing matches became popular during this time. Furthermore, such blood sports as cockfighting, animal baiting, and public backsword matches were prevalent, particularly in the towns where one could gather an audience with money enough to pay admittance and gamble. Such matches tended to be organized along two separate lines. The first was the event sponsored by a benevolent patron, whether a collection of city fathers, gentleman gamblers, or a noble host. In contrast to this setting (which was usually free and open to all within the vicinity) were events sponsored by enterprising theatre owners, tavern keepers, and license holders. Here money was king. While social distinctions were still preserved, the various classes were united by their gambling habits and the often bloody show. Such habits appear most clearly in the century that follows.

What is special about this age is the nascent development of relatively fixed times and places for events. Likewise, the late sixteenth and seventeenth centuries are marked by the first publicly proclaimed, written regulations for such activities as horse racing, cockfighting, and coursing. Before the end of the eighteenth century other sports would be included within this pattern.

Much of this development was fueled by gambling. While there is little indication of gambling's being connected to village pastimes and communal games, few other sports (especially those sponsored by wealthier people) were untouched by the urge. In what is sometimes considered an age of possessive individualism, horses, dogs, cocks, and even servants were fairly intimate extensions of the self. These substitutes carried on for their owners and supporters, who indicated their own courage and character by the depth of their wagers.

After the Restoration, gambling became a rage at court, and this influence trickled down through society. Pepys, in his travels about London, could marvel at the mingling and commotion it caused:

> To Shoe Lane to see a cock-fighting at a new pit there, a spot I was never at in my life: But Lord! to see the strange variety of people, from Parliament man, by name Wilder . . . to the poorest prentices, bakers, brewers, butchers, draymen, and what not; and all these fellows with one another cursing and betting. I soon had enough of it. It is strange to see how people of this poor

rank, who look as if they had not bread to put in their mouths, shall bet three or four pounds at a time, and lose it; and yet bet as much the next battle; so that one of them will lose 10 1. or 20 1. at a meeting.[87]

At court the monarch set the style. Charles II, whose courtiers reputedly gambled at his death bed, and William III were heavy betters. Indeed, it is during this period that the gamester, an expert who exploits the financial opportunities of cards and other betting games, became a social type.[88]

Significantly, Restoration legislation regarding gambling was concerned not with any inherent evils of gambling, but with its excesses and the failure to pay for one's losses. For example, An Acte against deceitfull, disorderly, and excessive Gaming (16 Car. II, ch. 7) is, as the title implies, especially directed against fraudulent play and stakes of more than 100 pounds—not gambling itself.[89] By the time of Anne (9 Anne, ch. 19), the amount considered excessive had dropped to ten pounds; however, the concern the was primarily about play by those without ready money. After the Stuarts, gambling at court became more subdued; however, the urge for speculation in both economic enterprise and sport continued strongly throughout eighteenth-century society.

NOTES

1. For a useful general introduction, see Roger Lockyear, *Tudor and Stuart Britain* (London: Longmans, 1964).
2. Lawrence Stone, *The Causes of the English Revolution* (London: Routledge and Kegan Paul, 1972), chapter 3, "Causes."
3. Ibid.
4. See Christopher Hill, *Society and Puritanism in Pre-Revolutionary England,* 2d ed. (New York: Schocken, 1967).
5. Gregory King's calculations are discussed in K. B. Smellie, *Great Britain Since 1688* (Ann Arbor: University of Michigan Press, 1962).
6. See Keith Wrightson, *English Society: 1580-1680* (New Brunswick, N. J.: Rutgers University Press, 1982), chapter 1, "Degrees of People."
7. See J. Thirsk and J. P. Cooper, eds., *Seventeenth Century English Documents* (Oxford: Oxford University Press, 1972), 751–57 (Wilson) and 780–81 (King).
8. Stone, *The Causes of the English Revolution,* 70.
9. Ibid. See also Barry Reay, "Popular Culture in Early Modern England," in *Popular Culture in Seventeenth Century England,* ed. Barry Reay (New York: St. Martin's, 1985), 1–30.
10. Robert Burton, *Anatomy of Melancholy,* ed. Floyd Dell and P. Jordan-Smith (New York: Tudor, 1927), 443.
11. The Puritan reaction during Tudor times is traced by Joachim Rühl, "Religion and Amusements in Sixteenth and Seventeenth Century England: 'Time might be better bestowed, and besides we see sin acted,'" *British Journal of Sports History* 1, no. 2 (September 1984): 125–65.
12. Dennis Brailsford, *Sport and Society: Elizabeth to Anne* (London: Routledge and Kegan Paul, 1969), 128.

13. George M. Trevelyan, *History of England,* 4 vols. (New York: Doubleday Anchor, 1956), 2:185ff.

14. Robert Burton, *Anatomy of Melancholy,* 3 vols. (New York: E. P. Dutton, 1932), 2:70.

15. Rühl, "Religion and Amusements," 148.

16. James' work is reproduced and discussed in L. A. Govett, *The King's Book of Sports* (n.p., 1808).

17. Hill, *Society and Puritanism,* 165.

18. *Annalia Dubrensia* (n. p., 1636).

19. Brailsford, *Sport and Society,* 135.

20. Quoted in W. B. Whitaker, *Sunday in Tudor and Stuart Times* (London: Houghton, 1933), 147.

21. Ibid., 155–56.

22. Brailsford, *Sport and Society,* 135.

23. Hill, *Society and Puritanism,* 184.

24. See Rühl, "Religion and Amusements," pp. 148–59.

25. Edward Chamberlayne, *Angliae Notitia or the Present State of England* (1676), quoted in Molly Harrison and O. M. Royston, eds., *How They Lived: An Anthology of Original Writings from 1485 to 1700,* 2 vols. (Oxford: Basil Blackwell, 1963), 2:88.

26. Marcia Vale, *The Gentleman's Recreations: Accomplishments and Pastimes of the English Gentleman, 1580–1630* (Totowa, N. J.: Rowen & Littlefield, 1977), 19.

27. Roger Longrigg, *The History of Foxhunting* (London: Macmillan, 1976), 69.

28. See A. Forbes Sieveking, "Horsemanship with Farriery," in *Shakespeare's England: An Account of the Life and Manners of His Age,* ed. Sir Sidney Lee, 2 vols. (Oxford: Clarendon, 1916), 2:408–27.

29. Wray Vamplew, *The Turf: A Social and Economic History* (London: Allen Lane, 1976), chapter 1, "Racing Before 1840."

30. Roger Longrigg, *The History of Horse Racing* (London: Macmillan, 1972), 39.

31. See Vamplew, *The Turf,* 17–18.

32. See Richard Onslow, *Headquarters: A History of Newmarket and Its Racing* (Cambridge, England: Great Ouse, 1983).

33. Roger Longrigg, *The English Squire and His Sport* (New York: St. Martin's, 1977), 84.

34. Egerton Castle, *Schools and Masters of Fence from the Middle Ages to the End of the Eighteenth Century* (London: Arms & Armour, 1885; reprint, 1969) 238.

35. Quoted in Robert Baldick, *The Duel: A History of Duelling* (London: Chapman & Hall, 1965), 30.

36. Ibid., 33.

37. Fynes Moryson, *Itinerary* (1617), reproduced in R. B. Morgan, ed. *Readings in English Social History* (Cambridge: Cambridge University Press, 1923), 368.

38. Quoted in Molly Harrison and O. M. Royston, eds., *How They Lived,* 90.

39. Quoted in Castle, *Schools and Masters of Fence,* 202.

40. Johan Huizinga, *The Waning of the Middle Ages* (Garden City, N. Y.: Doubleday, 1954), chapter 1.

41. Philip Stubbes, *Anatomie of Abuses* (1585), quoted in Harrison and Royston, ed., *How They Lived,* 83.

42. See Sidney Lee, "Bearbaiting, Bull-Baiting, and Cockfighting," in *Shakespeare's England: An Account of the Life and Manners of His Age,* 2 vols., (Oxford: Clarendon, 1916), 2: 428–36.

43. Vale, *The Gentleman's Recreations,* 130.

44. See Norman Wymer, *Sport in England* (London: George Harrap, 1949), 90–93.

45. Charles Cotton, *The Complete Gamester* (1674), in *Games and Gamesters of the Restoration,* ed. J. Issacs (London: Routledge, 1930), 107–08.

46. Lee, "Bearbaiting, Bull-Baiting, and Cockfighting," 428.

47. See E. D. Cuming, "Sports and Games" in A. S. Turberville, ed., *Johnson's England,* 2 vols. (Oxford: Clarendon, 1933), 2:373.

48. *Ibid.,* 2:372.

49. Cotton, *The Compleat Gamester,* 101.

50. J. Earle, *Microcosmographie* (1628), quoted in Harrison and Royston, *How They Lived,* 2:87–88.

51. See William Conor Sydney, *Social Life in England from the Restoration to the Revolution 1660–1690* (New York: Macmillan, 1892), 339.

52. Thomas Rymer, *Foedera,* 3 vols. (Farnborough, England: Gregg, 1967), vol. 3, pt. 3, 158.

53. Robert Ashton, "Popular Entertainment and Social Control in Later Elizabethan and Early Stuart London, *London Journal* 9, no.1 (1983), 8.

54. Lord Aberdare, *The Story of Tennis* (London: Stanley Paul, 1959), 172.

55. 4 January 1664, in Pepys's diary. For a discussion of Pepys's tennis experiences, see Julian Marshall, *Annals of Tennis* (London: Horace Cox, 1878), chapter 2, "Tennis in England."

56. Marshall, *Annals of Tennis,* 81.

57. Aberdare, *The Story of Tennis,* 65.

58. Marshall, *Annals of Tennis,* 79.

59. Geoffrey Cousins, *Golf in Britain: A Social History from the Beginnings to the Present Day* (London: Routledge & Kegan Paul, 1975), 2–5.

60. See Wymer, *Sport in England,* 85–86.

61. Act I, Scene 4, vv. 85–95.

62. James I, *Basilicon Doron,* quoted in Joseph Strutt, *Sports and Pastimes of the People of England* (London: Metusen, 1801; reprint, edited by J C. Cox, 1901), 98.

63. Peter Burke, "Popular Culture in Seventeenth Century London," in *Popular Culture in Seventeenth Century England,* ed. Barry Reay (New York: St. Martin's, 1985), 33.

64. Francis P. Magoun, *The History of Football—From the Beginnings to 1871* (Bochum-Langendreer, Germany: Verlag Heinrich-Poppinghaus, 1938), 17.

65. Barry Reay, "Popular Culture in Early Modern England," in *Popular Culture in Seventeenth Century England,* ed. Barry Reay (New York: St. Martin's, 1985), 21.

66. Buchanan Sharp, "Popular Protest in Seventeenth Century England," in *Popular Culture in Seventeenth Century* England (New York: St. Martin's, 1985), 271–308.

67. No. 432, quoted in Magoun, *The History of Football,* 18.

68. Richard Carew, *A Survey of Cornwall* (London: n.p., 1602), 73–75.

69. Montague Shearman, *Athletics and Football* (London: Badminton Library, 1887), 263.

70. Sydney, *Social Life in England,* 341–42.

71. Carew, *A Survey of Cornwall,* 75.

72. Moryson, *Itinerary,* 369.

73. Burton, *Anatomy of Melancholy,* 441.

74. W. A. Baillie Grohman, "Sports in the Seventeenth Century," *Century* 54 (July 1897): 390.

75. See Charles C. Trench, *The Poacher and the Squire: A Preservation in England* (London: Longmans, Green, 1967), 122.

76. 22 and 23 Charles II, ch. 25.

77. P. B. Munsche, *Gentlemen and Poachers: The English Gam* (Cambridge: Cambridge University Press, 1981), 15–19.

78. Longrigg, *The English Squire and His* Sport, 72–73..

79. Strutt, *The Sports and Pastimes of the People of England,* 27–29.

80. George Turberville, *The Noble Art of Venery* (1575) quoted in Longrigg, *The History of Foxhunting,* 26.

81. See Harding Cox and Gerald Lascelles, *Coursing and Falconry* (London: Longmans, Green, 1892).

82. See Raymond Carr, *English Foxhunting: A History* (London: Weidenfeld & Nicolson, 1976), 26.

83. Patrick Chalmers, *The History of Hunting* (London: Seeley, Service, 1936), 316.

84. Richard Hoffman, "Fishing for Sport in Medieval Europe: New Evidence," *Speculum* 60: 4 (1985): 877-902. See also Henry Hall, *Idylls of Fishermen* (New York: Columbia University Press, 1912).

85. Quoted in Michael Brander, *The Hunting Instinct (London: Oliver & Boyd, 1964),* 72.

86. See John Lowerson, "Izaak Walton: Father of a Dream," *History Today* 33 (December 1983): 28–32.

87. 21 December 1663, in Pepys's Diary.

88. See J. Isaacs, *Games and Gamesters of the Restoration* (London: Routledge, 1930.)

89. See Marshall, *Annals of Tennis,* 214, for discussion of Stuart gambling legislation.

6

SPORT IN
GEORGIAN ENGLAND

ENGLISH SOCIETY: 1714–1830

By the eighteenth century the changes of earlier times coalesced and gathered speed. Individual rights, especially the right to property, became firmly etched. Money relations were overwhelming the personal bonds between employer and employee. Parochialism was being destroyed by the geographical mobility of human populations and by the development of cheap publications and entertainments. The middle classes continued to grow, and status consciousness, expressed through an explosion in consumer goods, prevailed. Law extended its sway over the country; commerce and industry grew at unprecedented rates. As if history had rounded a bend, the modern world was coming into view.

It is commonplace to speak of this period as "an age of revolutions."[1] Developments in farming techniques and land use burst forward in an agricultural revolution. The enclosure movement of Tudor and Stuart times continued as common land and waste were put to private use. Corresponding to this discovery of the economic advantages of bigger productive units were new theories of intensive cultivation, crop rotation, and soil management. Inventions such as Tull's horse hoe and seed drill speeded the work, and scientific principles of stock breeding maximized outputs. During the century the average weight of sheep increased from twenty-eight to eighty pounds.[2] Such changes led to an increased standard of living; however, they were not without casualties. Smaller landowners could not compete with larger ones. As the former disappeared, a tripartite pattern of wealthy landowner, substantial tenant farmer, and landless laborer became established.

Corresponding to this movement was the growth of commerce and industrialization. The economic inventions of the late seventeenth century (such as the central bank and the modern mortgage) had given confidence to a new breed of investor, and his enthusiasm was hardly dampened by such debacles as the bursting of the South Sea Bubble in 1721.[3] Feeding this speculative mentality was the availability of credit. In 1700 the prevailing rate of interest was seven to eight percent; by 1750 it was three percent.

The expansion of national and even international trade was enhanced by a series of military victories in the continuing hostility toward France. By the treaty of Utrecht in 1713 England gained Newfoundland, Nova Scotia, Hudson Bay, and St. Christopher in the West Indies. From Spain it took the gates of the Mediterranean, Gibraltar and Minorca. Fifty years later the conclusion of the Seven Years' War added Canada, India, and much of the West Indies to Britain's American colonies. A great empire was being fashioned. Within the British Isles the union with Scotland in 1707 opened further channels of trade and provided added manpower for global expansion. By the last quarter of the century, then, such economists as Adam Smith could preach a gospel of free trade and envision an unimagined increase in British wealth.

Perhaps the most profound change of the last 300 years, the Industrial Revolution, is usually assigned a beginning within this period as well. It was attributable not only to the policies of free trade and easy credit, but also to the proximity of coal and mineral deposits, the relative absence of guilds in certain key industries, and the congeniality of the royal scientific society. Fundamentally, human and animal energy was being replaced by steam power. The larger economic units that had revolutionized farming were being applied to other kinds of production. During the last quarter of the century industrial output doubled. A "working class" of wage earners was accumulating within a host of true cities. London was by now the largest city in Europe and more than ten times the size of any other British town. However, Bristol and Norwich were approaching 50,000, and Manchester, Liverpool, Sheffield, Leeds, Halifax, Birmingham, and Coventry had become substantial cities as well.[4] These latter communities had developed about a distinctive industry or industries; unlike London they had little sophistication or elegance to relieve the sight of their burgeoning slums. By the census of 1801 England had reached a population of 9 million; twenty-two percent of these were now classified as "urban."[5]

As the agricultural revolution expanded the production of food and wool for distant markets, so the Industrial Revolution increased the availability of consumer goods. In addition, it fueled the continued rise of such middling groups as shopkeepers, tradesmen, and professionals as well as farmers. By their expenditures on houses, domestic furnishings, clothing, entertainments, and even coaches and servants, this group expressed its separation from those below.[6] Indeed, Lawrence and Jeanne Stone describe the consolidation of this group, which accounted for perhaps fifty percent of the national income, as "the most important social feature of the age."[7]

With such rewards for property owners, the gulf between rich and poor widened. By compounding the urban population, the Industrial Revolution made public the consequences of poverty and dislocation. Crime and violence were common; gambling and drunkenness (especially from gin) reached epidemic proportions. New religious movements such as Methodism and Evangelicalism made moral appeals to the poor, and the Poor Laws attempted to restrict their mobility. However, the governing class would not (and, perhaps, could not) abrogate the broader conditions causing their plight.

Amidst such massive changes, the political system remained remarkably stable. England had experienced its political and religious revolutions during the preceding century. The memory (and later the mythology) of these acted as a break on further experiments. By the Glorious Revolution of 1688, the principles of divine right and royal prerogative had been destroyed. Government was now in the hands of a small minority of wealthy estate owners who ruled in collusion with the urban capitalists. The new royal family, the German Hanovers, acted officially only with the advice of their ministers, who in turn depended on the support of Parliament. After two minor and abortive attempts to restore the Stuart line (in 1715 and 1745), the power of this oligarchy was never substantially challenged. For most of the century the party that had flirted with royalism (the Tories) was kept from highest office; however, this group was only modestly different from its victorious opponent, the Whigs. Both were united by the belief that the protection of private property was the basis of social order and the aim of good government.

For the most part, then, Parliament was an expression of the self-interest of its members. The characteristic ambition of the member of Parliament was simply the entrenchment of his own political and economic fortune, for membership in that body opened the gates to a broad range of jobs within the government, armed forces, and church. From this treasure chest, the upper class subsidized its members and created obligations among the recipients of these favors. However, in addition to voting supplies and private bills, Parliament added a host of new laws extending and reinforcing the principle of property ownership. Indeed, the number of crimes punishable by death rose from 50 in 1688 to over 200 by 1820; most were breaches of property law.[8] By 1740 children could be hanged for the theft of a spoon. In part, the justification for such repressive measures was the specter of mob violence which loomed over the eighteenth century. In J. H. Plumb's view, no nation rioted more easily or savagely.[9] The property owner's fears in this regard can be better appreciated when it is remembered that there was no regular police force until 1829. Local constables were helpless in the face of large crowds, and this threat seemed even more pronounced after the French Revolution, when the specifically political consequences of crowd action were made apparent.

In summary, England was ruled by the "richest landed elite in the world."[10] This privileged two or three percent controlled access to positions of governmental, military, and religious leadership, and maintained congenial (and even familial) relations with professionals and businessmen. By its dominance of county government and the court system, it regulated local and even private life as well as public affairs. By its representation within Parliament and its gathering in London during the winter months, it became a more or less cosmopolitan, unified, self-conscious class—aware of its interests and the threats to it. Within the rural areas, at least, it expected and, for the most part, was granted deference by the inhabitants of the increasingly articulated layers below.

However, as Edward P. Thompson has maintained, this control was far from complete.[11] The paternalistic assurance and personal intimacy of earlier times had been eroded by a psychology of free labor and by the interposition of a variety of working groups no longer directly dependent on the aristocrat. Furthermore, plebian traditions and, indeed, a whole mythology of the common man were still fiercely alive. What was sought, then, was a series of vehicles to impress, cajole, and pacify a rapidly growing, unruly populace. The majesty of law (with its powdered wigs and hanging tree) was one device; the spectacle of material substance was another. Still a third was the patronage of public sporting events.

In sport, as in industry and agriculture, the property-owning classes were emerging more clearly as the organizers and sponsors of common people's pursuits. In the case of sport, much was made of the relative openness between classes in the audience and of the democratic nature of the contest itself. Foreign observers marveled at the mingling that occurred at boxing and cricket matches, horse races, and animal baitings; they were astonished by the sight of upper-class individuals fighting with commoners in the street or participating with them on the cricket field. In fox hunting, too, the English came to mythologize the farmer on his plough horse clamboring after the gentlemen in pursuit of the prize. Amidst these egalitarian flirtations was the powerful theme of class protectionism. Hunting laws were strengthened; elite clubs were formed; costume and etiquette took on special significance. To appreciate the ways in which these contradictory themes were interwoven is to understand much about the social structure of that time.

HUNTERS: QUALIFIED AND UNQUALIFIED

As seen in the previous chapter, the game qualification law of 1671 was a specific act of class protectionism. By it the members of the landed elite not only separated themselves from the upcoming professionals and merchants, but also took on the prerogative of kings. Heretofore, only monarchs could wander the realm of England taking game more or less at will; now this license was to be shared. As P. B. Munsche has argued, hunting privileges were a keystone in the social identity of the squirearchy.[12] This lower level of the privileged class might be ridiculed by urban types for rusticity and boorishness. Poorer squires could not afford the continental travels and London seasons of their more sophisticated superiors. However, the privilege of field sports (and coats of arms) was what united them with aristocrats above and divided them from other contending groups. Hunting was a part of a larger portrait that included defiant localism, traditional values, staunch Anglicanism, and scorn for fashion. Effete city types who wished to hunt would have to do it by the good graces of this squirearchy or not at all.

Significantly, the legislation of 1671 did not specify penalties. Apparently the threats laid out in 1609 (three months in jail or a small fine for each bird or hare taken) were considered adequate. By 1707 the fine had been increased to five pounds or three months and this remained the common punishment throughout the eighteenth century. However, during this century hunting legislation took several new directions. Of most significance was the connection of hunting with the sharp defense of rural property rights. Not only deer and rabbits, but increasingly pheasants and partridges were being bred in enclosed circumstances by landowners. The illegal taking of game was equated with stealing, and the penalties mounted. Following the act of 1671, five more statutes addressing hunting had been added by the close of the century.[13] Between 1700 and 1750 there were nine more. However, in the last half of the century, there were seventeen, and then nineteen in the thirty-year period before reforms came.

Some of the laws concerned the sale of game. Poaching was a serious problem in large part because there was then a ready market for game in the cities. The sale of game by innkeepers and other venders was made illegal by 5 Anne, ch. 14 (1707). However, until 1818 the purchaser was free to buy. Hence, a vigorous black market flourished. Furthermore, "gifts" of game from qualified to unqualified people were legal. Thus, it was very difficult to determine which of a cartload of birds might be contraband.

Another approach was to increase the penalties for trespass. By an act of 1692 trespass in a gentleman's park occasioned a fine of twenty pounds, and the killing of deer a penalty of thirty pounds.[14] In effect, this consigned the unlucky poacher to a year in debtor's prison. In 1719 the penalty was increased to seven years' transportation to the colonies. Still, the new severity did not produce the desired effect. Perhaps the most notorious law was the Black Act, passed in 1723.[15] In response to the sterner penalties (and egged on by the lucrative possibilities of the enterprise), poachers had become both more organized and more desperate. Particularly in the areas accessible to London, armed gangs would set off from the towns at night, ready to defend themselves should they meet resistance. In one particular instance, a large group raided the royal forest at Windsor and the bishop of Winchester's forests in Hampshire and Surrey. Because these men blackened their faces in disguise and were composed partially of men from the village of Waltham, they became known as the Waltham Blacks. The resulting Black Act (9 George I, ch. 22) made it a felony, punishable by death, to poach deer or hare while armed with weapons or in disguise. Furthermore, other activities of the gang, such as robbing fishponds and burning haystacks (as acts of reprisal or terror), were made felonies. What is significant here is that the death penalty could now be invoked for poaching, a situation that had not prevailed since the Forest Charter of 1217.

Thompson has argued that the activities of the Blacks were not simple acts of criminality, but rather a more complicated expression of the social and political tensions in the forest areas. What made this particular example of poaching an emergency was

> . . . the repeated humiliation of the authorities; the simultaneous attacks upon
> royal and private property; the sense of a confederated movement which was
> enlarging its social demands, especially under "King John" (their self-styled

leader); the symptoms of something close to class warfare, with the loyalist
gentry in the disturbed areas objects of attack and pitifully isolated in their
attempts to enforce order. It was a sorry state of affairs when the King . . .
could not prevent his own park from being driven for deer.[16]

He argues then that the poachers had, at least to some degree, the support of the
local population, and that their number included a few substantial farmers and
even gentry. Furthermore, the act had broad political implications, for it
corresponded to the rise of the Whigs and Robert Walpole after the embarrassment (and corruption) entailed in the South Sea scandals of 1721. As the act
was an expression of support for a hunting king and conservative gentry, so it
set the stage for a broad use of the law to control the lower classes throughout
the century. Now fifty specific offenses could be punished by death.

Predictably, such legislation was unpopular with the great majority of the
rural population. And local justices were reticent to sentence a person to death
or transportation for poaching. Correspondingly, the qualified landowner sought
other means of deterrence. Spring guns and mantraps (legal until 1828) were
concealed in the undergrowth to catch the unwary prowler. Larger estates had
paid "watchers" and armed gamekeepers who patrolled the grounds and set out
poison for the poacher's dog. Likewise, landowners banded together to reward
informers and pay for prosecutions. In 1752 a wider Society of Noblemen and
Gentlemen for the Preservation of Game was established. Its special charge
was to prosecute and otherwise stop the sale of game in southern England, and
it continued this work throughout the century.[17]

Yet another measure involved taxation. By an act of 1784 two guineas
were to be paid by each qualified person for the purchase of a stamp; game-
keepers were to pay half a guinea. This was raised in 1791 to three guineas,
and a tax on dogs was added in 1796. As Chester Kirby has explained, this not
only set the stamp office against the poacher, but also posed a hardship for the
farmer who barely qualified economically.[18]

Conditions for the farmer who did not qualify were more difficult. Not
only was he expected to stand by while birds and hares fed on his crops, but
sometimes he was instructed by his landlord to let his hedges grow into immense
jungles to support the game. Furthermore, the quantity of game was increased
during the latter part of the eighteenth century by such artificial methods of
preservation as the semidomestication of pheasants. A large quantity of game
was needed for the new pleasure of the qualified, the battue.

By the 1770s refinements in the gun made shooting on the wing easier,[19]
and in the battue the birds were driven in front of the gun by beaters. By this
process dozens of birds could be taken at once. In short, the unqualified farmer
provided (at his own expense) food and sport for his economic superior.
Munsche has argued that the game preservation movement and the resulting
battue changed the nature of hunting.[20] Before, hunting had been mostly a
private, or at least a small-scale, affair. Now it developed into something more
public and elaborate, often with as many spectators as participants. Lunches

were provided, paths were cut, and servants prepared the guns. Perhaps even more important, the competition now shifted from the basic struggle between man and beast to a competition between hunters. The quantity of game shot within an afternoon became something to brag about and, indeed, a symbol of the success of the whole affair.

As can be readily imagined, such excesses did not sit well with the excluded public, especially those who were forced to confront their lack of privilege daily. The taking of small game from unsupervised areas was a tradition long enjoyed among the poorer classes. Such a view contrasted directly with the reconstitution of wild life as private property. The *Edinburgh Review* describes the situation in 1819:

> The experiment was tried of increased severity; and a law passed to punish poachers with transportation who were caught poaching in the night time with arms. What has the consequence been? Not a cessation of poaching, but a succession of village guerillas; — an internecine war between gamekeepers and marauders of game; the whole country flung into brawls and convulsions, for the unjust and exorbitant pleasures of country gentlemen. The poacher hardly believes he is doing any wrong in taking partridges and pheasants. He would admit the justice of being transported for stealing sheep and his courage in such a transaction would be impaired by the knowledge he is doing wrong. But he has no such feeling in taking game; and the preposterous punishment of transportation makes him desperate and not timid. Single poachers are gathered into large companies for their mutual protection, and go out, not only with the intention of taking game, but of defending what they take with their lives. Such feelings soon produce a rivalry of courage and a thirst for revenge between the villagers and the agents of power.[21]

The old poacher whom the authorities knew about, but could not convict, became a rural hero, and evenings in the alehouses were filled with accounts of his escapades.

Sometimes these escapades took on a darker and more political tone. An example is this anonymous circular letter responding to increases in the night poaching penalties in 1816:

> Take notice — We have lately heard and seen that there is an act passed that whatever poacher is caught destroying the game is to be transported for seven years. — *This is English liberty!*
> Now we do swear to each other that the first of our company that this law is inflicted on, that there shall not one gentleman's seat in our country that shall escape the rage of fire. We are nine in number and will burn every gentleman's house of note. The first that impeaches shall be shot. We have sworn not to impeach. You may think it a threat, but they will find it reality. The game laws were too severe before. The Lord of all men sent these animals for for the peasants as well as for the prince. God will not let his people be oppressed. He will assist us in our undertaking, and we will execute it with caution.[22]

The reader may wonder how such severe policies were justified. The proponents of the hunting laws argued that the large property holder was performing a service to the nation by remaining in the country where he provided economic, moral, intellectual, and political leadership. Indeed, he was touted as a pillar of civility within a primitive rural world. Shooting privileges were an important inducement for him to remain in the country to perform these vital functions.

Surprisingly, the great increase in capital crimes during the eighteenth century did not result in a dramatic increase in executions. Indeed, fewer people were executed than in 1600. As Douglas Hay has argued, law was as much a theatrical and ideological device as a process of punishment.[23] In the case of hunting the apprehended poacher was at the mercy of the justice and of the offended person prosecuting the case. Usually, both were gentlemen. They could select from a wide variety of infractions (violations of qualification, hunting seasons, licenses, nighttime activity, kinds of beasts stolen, and so forth). In addition, a host of fines, suits for triple damages, and even legal costs could be applied. Except when an example of punishment was thought to be needed, the gentry typically exercised a merciful, or at least moderating, posture. Thus, they could appear (or be) beneficent personally despite the ferocious legality issuing from Westminster. More pertinently, they could smooth over relations in their own locality.

Ultimately, however, the social criticisms overwhelmed them. The Game Laws Amendment Act of 1831 finally abolished all class distinctions, legalized the sale of game, and redefined poaching within the older (and more moderate) traditions of trespassing. Thus, all landowners regained the right to wildlife crossing their property. The rights of tenants to game became part of the lease they signed. With this act, hunting shed its connection with hereditary title and quality of estate; correspondingly, it marks the close of the preindustrial period in English sport.

FOX HUNTING: NEW FORMS OF DISTINCTION

Fox hunting took a quite different path of development from shooting. Indeed, two factors ensured that this would be the case. The first is simply that fox hunting, unlike shooting, was never restricted by law to any class of qualified property owners. Thus, instead of being categorized with other protected game, the fox was considered a species of vermin, like the badger or the otter. Since medieval times, whenever foxes became numerous enough to threaten domestic fowl, the local farmers would band together to drive the beasts from their dens. The commonest method was to place nets over the entrance to the earth, smoke out the inhabitants, and then kill them with clubs. Dogs were used primarily to chase the fox from one hole to another. Such was the status of the pest that villages might offer a reward for each brush (tail) nailed to the church door. Thus, despite the later association of fox hunting with the life style of the gentry, the origin of the activity is humble indeed.

The second factor is the amount of space that the sport came to require. Shooting, as we have seen, was closely connected with private property rights. For the most part, the qualified landowner confined his hunting to his own woods and fields, and he could take serious measures to see that others did not encroach on that domain. However, riding to hounds was a venture that required the cooperation of others in the locality. When the fox bolted from its cover, the chase might entail twenty miles of hard riding. This meant that a number of different properties might be crossed. As the horses might damage the hedges or fences that they encountered, it was important that the riders have the good will of the local farmers. Specifically, this meant obtaining the permission of the very people who might be denied shooting privileges.[24] Thus, the requirement that all properties in the locale be available for the hunt created a public context for the sport. Not only did the hunt dramatize the cooperation of large and small property owners in a venture (purportedly) for community welfare, but also it offered a setting in which the farmer might participate with his social superiors.

As the Stones have pointed out, England was the perfect soil for fox hunting.[25] Large portions of the countryside were pasture; and the land itself was apportioned among a relatively small number of great landowners and large tenant farmers (who themselves might profit from the good will of their landlord). The remaining small freeholders could usually be brought along with a bit of encouragement from the powerful. Had the country been divided into many smaller plots, the process of obtaining permissions would have been much more onerous.

In the seventeenth century, riding to hounds typically meant the hunting of the hare, the great joy of which was watching the hounds puzzle out the scent. However, the hounds of that period were not bred to follow the scent of the hare alone, and if a fox's trail was uncovered, it would be followed. Hares were more numerous, and the hunt itself was less time onsuming. While many hunters continued to concentrate on the hare, more came to prefer the longer, straighter runs of the fox.

The earliest packs were made up of the few trencher-fed hounds kept around the house by individual farmers.[26] Hunting foxes exclusively, which seems to have begun about the beginning of eighteenth century, was at first dependent upon the "drag"—the line of scent left by the fox as he returned to his kennel after a night's foraging. As the drag tends to disappear after sunrise, the hunt had to start at dawn. A fox gorged with a night's meal is slower; thus, the relatively unspecialized horses and hounds had a better chance of keeping up with their prey.

By the middle of the eighteenth century broad changes were occurring. Now a typical hunt began at eleven o'clock, rather than at dawn. In consequence, the fox, having had time to digest his food, was much faster. The riders would wait impatiently while the hounds, assisted by the huntsman, earth stoppers, and whippers-in, "worked the cover" until the fox finally broke into the open and began his flight across the open countryside. Although most of the riders lost sight of the pack after a few miles, there were always some who followed the new fashion of hard riding and attempted to leap the various hedges and ditches that stood in the way.

This transformation in hunting technique was effected by a number of factors. First, the continued shrinking of the English woodland created the open fields that the sport required. With this change of the hunt into a sort of footrace came the desire for faster horses and hounds. Carefully bred packs—fast and steady and hunting by eye as well as nose—became an English trademark. Before the eighteenth century, dogs had been imported from France; afterward they were exported to that country.[27]

These changes in breeding and pack management were, in turn, the result of social changes in the sport. By the mid-eighteenth century, certain wealthy gentlemen began to maintain their own packs of hounds bred specifically for this purpose. Included in the expenses of such an establishment were not only the provisions for the dogs themselves, but also the salaries of a huntsman and other hunt servants and the cost of maintaining several horses for these and for guests.[28] The most lavish stables and kennels were showplaces in themselves, with paved floors for the animals and attics for the servants sleeping above.

While a few of the most prominent packs continued to be maintained by rich families, this substantial expense was in many other cases defrayed by subscriptions from other gentlemen. For example, the Pytchley Hunt Club in 1777 was limited to a membership of forty, each paying ten guineas a year.[29] Such clubs were themselves headed by a master of fox hounds, who managed the kennels and stables, plotted the areas to be hunted, and autocratically supervised the participants. By the close of the eighteenth century there were perhaps 200 packs in England, each hunting an average of three days a week from November to March.[30]

In some aspects, then, the development of fox hunting parallels the rise of the battue in shooting. Both were fairly elaborate events staged by one or more gentlemen for themselves and guests. Both transformed the confrontation between man and beast into a kind of competition between participants. Both made important concessions to leisureliness—later starting times, hunting breakfasts, attending servants, and so on. Both became spectacles of human endeavor.

In the hunt itself the competition among the riders consisted in being the first on the scene when the hounds finally caught up with the fox. The custom, then, was to take the fox from the hounds and divide the trophy among those who followed to the site. After holding up the fox by the neck and giving the "view-halloo," the first in cut off the brush and kept it as the honor of the day. The next rider received the mask (the head) and the next four, the pads (the feet). The remainder was then thrown to the dogs who tore it to pieces. This division of the prey according to meritocratic principles stands in sharp opposition to the older traditions of the stag hunt, where the highest ranking member of the party killed or designated the kill of the beast and then supervised the division of the carcass.

In theory, the fox hunt was based on the equal opportunity of each participant to win the trophy, and the tale of the farmer who rode his old plug to victory was a cherished one. Even "foot followers" sometimes ran in pursuit of the prize.[31] However, the speed and distance of the hunt now meant that in practice the gentlemen, who possessed the best mount or mounts, would claim the prize. Indeed, serious participants were no longer riding their hunter to the hunt itself. Furthermore, the more competitive riders instructed their servants to station substitute mounts at various points along a prospective route. Thus, by virtue of their superior resources the gentlemen could stage a public event that proclaimed the equal opportunity of each rider and yet effectively limited the real competition to a select few. Through sport the gentle class could seem to emerge as the "natural" as well as the social leaders of the community.

If fox hunting integrated to some degree the different levels of a community, it was also a lubricant for rural-urban differences.[32] As a guest at a meet, the Londoner was the recipient of the hospitality of the old rural establishment. Conversely, it gave members of the landed gentry an opportunity to cultivate the new money in their own rural setting. The center for such interchange was the "Shires" (Leicestershire, Rutland, Northamptonshire) to the north of London. Here the local towns were transformed every winter by a predominantly male society of fox-hunting guests of the three great hunts that ruled the region.

When fox hunting came under fire for being boorish or cruel, this theme of social mixing was a keystone in its defense. An exuberant version of this was produced by John Hawkes in 1808:

> The field is a most agreeable coffee-house, and there is more real society to be met with there than in any other situation of life. It links all classes together from the Peer to the Peasant. It is the Englishman's peculiar privilege. It is not to be found in any other part of the globe than in England's true land of liberty—and may it flourish to the end of time.[33]

However, fox hunting was equally the most aristocratic of sports. The outsider who did compete was woven into the fabric of the meet in certain specified ways.

As indicated previously, many of the hunts were organized by social clubs. Their membership was typically quite restricted, with one or two black balls being enough to exclude the unwelcome applicant. While the club might invite local farmers to their hunt breakfasts, the hunt dinners and balls were limited to members and their wives.

The centrality of the gentlemen-members was expressed visually in distinctive uniforms. For example, the Tarporley Hunt Club in Chesire, founded in 1762, insisted that its members wear a blue frock coat, scarlet cape, waist-coat, and buckskin breeches.[34] By century's end the most popular attire for a

gentleman was a scarlet coat, black waistcoat, and white cord breeches. During
the first decade of the nineteenth century pants and coat fitted so snugly that the
occupant sometimes had to put his horse into a ditch to mount.[35] This attention
to fashion was most pronounced among the more socially prominent clubs. As
the *Quarterly Review* explains:

> The style of your Meltonian fox hunter has long distinguished him above his
> brethren of what we call the provincial class. When turned out in the hands
> of his valet, he presents the very beau-ideal of his caste. The exact stulze-
> like fit of his coat, his superlatively well-cleaned leather breeches and boots
> and the generally apparent high breeding of the man can seldom be matched
> anywhere.[36]

In contrast to such finery was the black coat of the sporting minister, while
prosperous farmers, smaller squires, and professional men became differentiated
by blue or brown coats.[37] Hunt servants dressed in the manner of club members
except for some distinguishing device, such as a soft cap or a specially colored
bridle. Thus, status within the field itself was marked clearly enough, and, as
David Itzkowitz insists, deference was an expected part of any mingling before
or after the run.[38] In short, the level of intimacy was managed by the gentle-
men-hosts. The temporariness of the guests was neither forgotten nor mini-
mized.

ARCHERY CLUBS

Fox hunting offers one glimpse into club life during the eighteenth century;
archery provides another. While archery as military exercise had lapsed during
the early seventeenth century (replaced in the main by firearms), archery as sport
experienced a boom in popularity at the end of the eighteenth century. This
flourish of activity says much about the social aspects of the club, the importance
of patronage, and the attitudes of the gentry toward sport during this period.

It is significant that the varying interest of the upper class in archery seems
directly attributable to periods of royal patronage. In other words, information
about gentlemanly archery is recorded primarily within three eras: the reign of
Henry VIII, the reign of Charles II, and the long tenure of George IV as prince
of Wales, regent, and king. As noted previously, Henry VIII was instrumental
in the formation of the societies of St. George and Prince Arthur. Charles II,
while not establishing any societies directly, had taken to the sport during his
exile in France and patronized various public meetings and processions upon his
return. Finally, George IV, as patron and participant, was responsible in large
part for the proliferation of groups at the close of the eighteenth century.

The most popular account of the rebirth of archery during this period points
to a Mr. Waring, who, suffering from an "oppression upon his chest," was
encouraged by his host, Sir Ashton Lever, to take up archery.[39] As a result of

this happy experience, Lever, Waring, and a few friends formed the Toxophilite Society in 1780. In 1784, when the club requested to use the old Artillery Grounds in London for its practice area, there were about twenty-four members.[40] However, in 1787 the prince of Wales accepted the position of patron to the society and gave it the privilege of affixing "Royal" to its name; suddenly its ranks shot up to 168 members. In the same manner the prince became patron to the Kentish Bowman in 1789. By 1790 their membership had increased enough to lay out a new field and to build a clubhouse.[41] The interest in archery was not confined to these clubs alone. As George Hansard notes, "Soon after the Royal Toxophilites were established, almost every city in the kingdom possessed its bow meeting."[42] In this light, E. Hargrove has recorded twenty-nine societies that existed during the last decade of the eighteenth century.[43]

The prince also lent his authority to new regulations for shooting. Earlier meets had featured shooting at successive distances of 120, 90, 60, and 30 yards. This was altered to 100, 80, and 60 yards, and the new measurements were known as the "Prince's Lengths." The count of the target rings was fixed at nine, seven, five, three, and one, a system known as the "Prince's Reckoning." Finally, an end of arrows, which had been two at each target, was changed to three. In deference to the prince, these changes were quickly incorporated by nearly all the existing societies.[44] To understand this connection between patronage and sporting appetites, it is important to remove from one's mind any preconceived notions about a modern cult of athleticism with its sober emphasis on record keeping, rational improvement, supervised training, and the like. Archery for gentlefolk during the late eighteenth and early nineteenth centuries was essentially a pretext for the association of influentials. Here the gentleman or lady might exchange bits of gossip, local news, or information about investments, while at the same time obtaining a modicum of exercise.[45]

A picture of one such society is provided by records of the Woodmen of Arden.[46] This group was founded in 1785 by the earl of Aylesford and five other gentlemen. It is clear that the earl was patron for the group, as he was quickly named perpetual warden (a post that passed to his son in 1813); furthermore, he provided the shooting grounds. The membership grew to forty-two in 1786, and in 1788 (after the expression of interest by the prince of Wales) it was necessary to restrict membership to seventy-five. Originally, the Woodmen met at a local tavern, but within a year or two a clubhouse was erected where dinners and dances were held. By 1789 women were allowed to shoot, although they (and strangers) shot at different targets and for different prizes.

In such groups, social exclusiveness was paramount. An early list of thirty-four members of the Woodmen reveals that four were lords, three knights, twenty-one esquires, three reverends, and three mere "gentlemen." This emphasis on gentility is quite explicit in one group, the Royal Foresters, instituted in 1674 and revived in 1812:

A candidate for admission shall prove the gentility of his descent on his father's side for at least three generations, for which purpose he shall transmit his pedigree of three descents to the registrar, which must be verified on oath together with the following certificate of the respectability of his character . . . signed by a beneficed clergyman, a barrister-at-law, and a field or flag officer, who must name the benefice, inn of court, and regiment or ship to which they respectively belong.[47]

The meetings of these societies seem to have focused as much on pageantry and spectacle as competition. Each group had special uniforms, and members were levied a substantial fine (in one case, ten guineas) if they appeared without these. Likewise, there were strict adjurations against gambling—with the punishment that all wagers be forfeited to the society.[48] In short, the archery societies offer a view of early "amateur" sports, in which exclusiveness, good form, and sociability were central (and interrelated) elements.

THE RISE OF CRICKET

Still another sport owing its formal development to the influence of noble or royal patrons is cricket. While most authorities trace the origin of cricket to the late sixteenth or early seventeenth century, very little is known about the game until the mid-eighteenth century. However, it is generally believed that cricket first gained popularity among the villagers of southern England and that the first organized matches were between local villages in Kent and Sussex. The first reliable reference to cricket in English literature is in Edward Philipp's "Mysteries of Love and Eloquence" (1685), and the first public announcement of a cricket match comes from the *Foreign Post* of 1697, which proclaims a "great cricket match in Sussex, eleven a side for fifty guineas."[49]

It is this connection of early cricket with gambling that is the keynote of the game's development as a spectator sport. The eighteenth-century mania for gambling—which extended to all major spectator sports—seems to have been indigenous to cricket. As H. S. Altham explains:

In reading the "announcements" of cricket matches of the eighteenth century, no one could fail to remark the extent to which the game went hand-in-hand with wagering. The very first match recorded was, as we have seen already, played for 50 a side, and wherever we turn in the contemporary press we find stakes of 100 or 200 guineas the rule rather than the exception. Even matches between women, first organized in 1745, involved heavy sums, though it is only fair to say that here and there we find a game played for more homely stakes, such as a whole lamb, a plumb cake, and a barrel of ale, eleven good hats and one for the umpire on the winning side. The Earl of Sandwich's Old Etonians v. England matches at Newmarket in 1751 were played for 1500, and in side-bets, it was said at the time that near 20,000 is depending.[50]

Gambling remained a central fact of the public matches well into the nineteenth century and was the instigation behind a variety of curious contests. R. MacGregor has collected references to such events, including a 1794 match between gentlemen on horseback for one guinea a man, matches of two gentlemen versus a commoner and a dog (the man with the dog invariably won), and the battles between the one-armed and one-legged pensioners of Greenwich Hospital for 1,000 guineas a side.[51]

Just as gentlemen gamesters were behind these curiosities, so wealthy patrons were originally instrumental in organizing the various local teams into representative county sides.[52] To this end, they arranged the matches, provided the site, gathered the teams, and arranged transportation and lodging. The first Sussex teams of the 1730s were organized by Sir William Gage and the second duke of Richmond, while their archrival Kent was under the patronage of Edwin Stead. Surrey was headed by its great patron and captain, Frederick Louis, oldest son of George II and prince of Wales. After Frederick's death in 1751 (popularly reported to be from complications of an old cricket injury), Surrey was championed by the fourth earl of Tankerville. Perhaps the most influential patrons, however, were the Sackvilles of Knole—the Earl of Middlesex, his brother Lord John Sackville, and Lord John's son, the third duke of Dorset.

These patrons began the practice of guaranteeing the participation of expert cricketeers on their sides by employing them on their estates. As we have seen, the stakes of the public matches might be quite high, and sponsors were interested in fielding the strongest teams possible. Thus, in cricket matches of the 1740s we find the curious phenomenon of gentlemen performing publicly with commoners (and even servants) on a level of apparent equality. Particularly cherished by lovers of the democratic myth of cricket play is the match of Kent versus All-England in 1744. The victorious Kent team was captained by Lord John Sackville's gardener, and the decisive catch was made by Lord John himself.

The propriety of such exhibitions did not go unchallenged, particularly by those who felt that the spectators should be spending their time elsewhere:

> Cricket is certainly a very innocent and wholesome exercise, yet, it may be abused, if either great or little People make it their business. It is grossly abused when it is made the subject of publick amusements to draw together great Crowds of people, who ought all of them to be somewhere else. Noblemen, gentlemen, and Clergymen have certainly a right to divert themselves in what Manner they think fit; nor do I dispute their privilege of making Butchers, Cobblers, or Tinkers their Companions provided these are qualified to keep them company. But I very much doubt whether they have any Right to invite thousands of people to be Spectators of their agility at the expense of their Duty and Honesty.[53]

To be sure, the behavior of these spectators was not above reproach. Indeed, the cricket crowd, its passions fed by gambling, is a good example of the public disorderliness of the eighteenth century. With some regularity spectators attacked each other or the opposing team or even the home team if they seemed to give less than a worthy effort.[54]

If gambling contributed to disorder, it was also responsible for the written rules of cricket. Because of the level of the stakes, the participants could not be counted on to adjudicate disputes as they arose. Thus, "articles of agreement" were drawn up beforehand and umpires (typically gentlemen representing each side) chosen. These articles covered such matters as the date and place of play, whether or not the match would be played out, stakes, penalties, qualifications of the players, handicaps, and so forth.[55] The first such agreement was created for a match between the teams of the duke of Richmond and Mr. Broderick in 1727. This was followed in 1744 by the first issue of the Laws of Cricket, which were formalized by the London club (whose president was the prince of Wales).

The gentlemen's club figured importantly in the previous discussions of fox hunting and archery; it was at least as significant to the rise of cricket. The earliest of these clubs was the Hambledon Club, which played near the village of Hambledon in Hampshire after 1767. This club, which was founded by several former Westminster boys, was the dominant force in cricket during the following decade. The Hambledon men wore dark breeches and snowy vests, with the gentlemen players being distinguished by their silk stockings.[56] For the gentlemen (that is, the members) there was a lodge erected on the grounds. This club, then, was a prototype for others that emerged in the last quarter of the century. Sometimes these clubs (generally composed of "old boys" who had learned to play informally in school) might have trouble fielding the requisite twenty-two players; then they would advertise in the press—with the stipulation that only gentlemen need apply.

Some of the most prominent members of the Hambledon Club were members of that group which played in the White Conduit Fields in London. In 1787 two members of the White Conduit club, the ninth earl of Winchilsea and the fourth duke of Richmond, arranged that an ambitious employee, Thomas Lord, should open a private ground for their play and guaranteed his expenses. The spot, north of the Marylebone Road, was called Lord's, and it became the home of the old White Conduit group, now called the Marylebone Cricket Club.[57] In 1788 the group revised the Laws of Cricket, whereupon the M.C.C. became the recognized authority on all matters pertaining to the game, including the adjudication of gambling disputes. By 1800 mere "gentlemen" were permitted to join; and the ranks swelled to over 150.[58] Cricket clubs popped up about the country, and Lord's became the site of such major matches as the Gentlemen versus Players series (begun in 1806) and the Eton-Harrow matches (begun in 1805).

While the gentlemen maintained their control of cricket as a mass spectator sport by their positions as organizers and rule makers, the game itself was coming to be dominated by professional players. In 1807, when Surrey met and beat a team of hand-picked players from throughout England, there was not a gentleman-amateur on that county's eleven and only four on England's.[59] Likewise, in the initial matches of the Gentlemen (amateurs) versus Players (professionals) series, the amateurs succeeded in winning twice. However, the series was not resumed until 1819, and by then the Players had become too strong. During the next twenty years the Gentlemen had little success, even when using extra players or, in one instance, defending a smaller wicket. It must be emphasized that a continuing athletic series based on class distinctions is very rare in sporting history. What it suggests is not only the assurance of the ruling class within the sporting realm, but also the use of sport as a vehicle for a more democratic mythology about English society. Such matters will be examined more fully later.

SWORDPLAY AND DUELING

As in Tudor and Stuart times, swordplay was still grounded in necessity. Police protection was limited, and personal defense might be required. Of particular distress to the citizens of London were gangs, some of them composed of young gentlemen. These groups of young rakes, who assumed such names as the Hectors, Scourers, Mohocks, Hawkubites, Bold Bucks, and Hell Fires, were notorious for their practice of provoking and otherwise assaulting passersby at night. One club, composed only of young duelists, is described by Steinmetz:

> None were admitted to this club that had not fought his man. The president was said to have killed half a dozen in single combat, and the other members took their seats according to the number of their slain. There was likewise a side-table for such as had only drawn blood and shown a laudable ambition of taking the first table.[60]

As in earlier times, the gentleman learned his fencing from the masters of the Continent or from cultivated visitors who set up *salles d'armes* in English cities. The best known of these schools was established in 1759 by Dominico Angelo Malevolti Traemondo, an Italian who had learned small-sword fencing and manege riding in Paris.[61] Angelo's School of Arms became famous throughout England. People of rank would deposit their sons with him as boarders sometime before entering college. Here the young man would acquire not only skill in horse and swordplay, but also familiarity with the various political and literary luminaries who gathered at these rooms to practice. The school was continued by Angelo's descendants until 1866.

Continuing to enjoy a certain popularity was the duel of honor. Ben Truman has collected references to 196 duels during the reign of Charles II (1660–1685).[62] In these, 75 persons were killed and another 108 wounded, a toll that was increased by the fact that seconds were expected to fight as well. During the long reign of George III (1760–1820), 172 duels and 69 fatalities are recorded. While such numbers are perhaps not trustworthy indicators of an activity that was often concealed from authorities, they do provide some sort of rough comparison of the deaths by duel in the two periods. Beyond this, it is noteworthy that despite the 172 duels in George III's reign, only eighteen trials were held.[63] Of these, only three convictions for murder were rendered. This laxity of enforcement reflects the laissez-faire attitude of government toward upper-class preoccupations.

In fact, the duel was an occupational hazard for the politician, whose life abounded in opportunities for public insult. An informal stamp of approval was given the activity by a prime minister himself. As Knyveton describes in his diary:

> May 27th 1798 Whitsunday . . . Mr. Pitt has had to drive down to Putney Common to exchange shots with Mr. Tierney. High words arose between them at a recent debate in the House, Mr. Pitt accusing Mr. Tierney of raising objections to his proposals of manning the fleet in order to wreck the government, and refusing to retract his words—'tis said he was drunk at the time—this silly duel was arranged. But in the heat of their emotions, both fortunately missed and their seconds hastily separated them, declaring honour satisfied.[64]

Those who found themselves suddenly confronting a duel and were unsure of proper etiquette in the matter might consult a number of works presenting dueling codes. Such books typically informed the reader of the proper way to challenge, choose weapons, select a second, and generally conduct himself. The choice of a second was particularly important for it was the second who was charged with the responsibility of negotiating a settlement at various points in the dispute. As Robert Baldick recounts, two authorities specifically barred non-Christians and Irishmen from consideration in this capacity. The former was excluded because "it is not proper that an unbeliever should witness the shedding of Christian blood, which would delight him"; the latter because "9 out of 10 Irishmen have such an innate love of fighting that they cannot bring an affair to an amicable adjustment."[65] On the Continent, he who had been insulted (and, therefore, responded with the challenge) could dictate weapons. However, in England, the choice lay with the offender. The choice of weapons, of course, constituted a considerable advantage, as one could select a device with which he had some familiarity. After the 1760s the pistol replaced the sword as the favorite weapon in these encounters. However, the pistol was also dangerous to the user, for accidents caused by hair-triggers, overloading, and a general unfamiliarity with firearms were commonplace.

Apologists for the duel argued that the practice was an important measure of social control that ensured civility by keeping high-born bullies in check. As for the deaths resulting from the activity, an analogy was made between dueling and riding in a coach. Like the person who was killed by the upsetting of the coach, the man who died in the duel was the unfortunate victim of a socially useful practice. As Bernard Mandeville asks: "Is it not somewhat strange that a nation should grudge to see perhaps a dozen sacrificed in a twelve-month to obtain and ensure such invaluable blessings as the politeness of manners, the pleasures of conversation, and the happiness of company in general?"[66]

There was, however, little factual support for the claim that dueling promoted civility. Indeed, the English custom of allowing the bully to choose weapons seems contradictory to that ambition. By 1844 an article of war increased the penalties for dueling by its worst offenders, officers in the army and navy. This act, plus the rising attacks by the press, a new harshness of judges, and the revitalized Puritanism that was sweeping England in the 1840s, ended dueling.

FIST FIGHTS: PUBLIC AND PRIVATE

All foreign commentators seem to have agreed on at least one point: The English adored fighting.[67] A street brawl quickly produced a crowd that would begin wagering on the outcome. One contemporary describes a quarrel between two boys in the street:

> First each pulls off his neckcloth and waistcoat while a ring of spectators forms. They begin to brandish their fists in the Air; the Blows are aimed all at the Face, they kick one another's Shins, they tug one another by the Hair, etc. . . . He that has got the other down may give him one Blow or two before he rises, but no more. . . . The Father and Mother of the boys let them fight on, and hearten him that gives Ground or has the worst.[68]

Such enthusiasm for fighting is, of course, not distinctive of the English. However, in England, regulated fist fighting emerged as a public spectacle; for that reason the country is often termed the "cradle of pugilism."[69]

Like the sports discussed previously, boxing owes its development to the influence of wealthy patrons. It flourished as a spectator sport when it had the support of this group and waned when their enthusiasms turned elsewhere. Again, gambling was at the heart of the enterprise, and this led to the formation of rules and rule-making bodies. Furthermore, like cricket, boxing showcased the new, more democratic ethos that emerged at the end of the eighteenth century.

Historians of English boxing generally begin their accounts with the early 1700s when boxing was beginning to be differentiated from other forms of fighting, such as cudgel and backsword play and wrestling.[70] The activity was clearly within the tradition of those stage fights, as this advertisement from 1722 makes clear. In this case, the boxers were women:

> I Elizabeth Wilkinson, of Clerkenwell, having had some words with Hannah Hyfield, and requiring satisfaction, do invite her to meet me on the Stage, and

I Elizabeth Wilkinson, of Clerkenwell, having had some words with Hannah
Hyfield, and requiring satisfaction, do invite her to meet me on the Stage, and
box with me for three guineas, each woman holding half a crown in her hand,
and the first woman that drops her money to lose the battle.

I Hannah Hyfield, of Newgate-Market, hearing of the resoluteness of Elizabeth Wilkinson, will not fail, — willing, to give her more blows than words,
desiring home blows, and from her, no favour.[71]

The earliest of the boxing champions was James Figg, who was credited
with establishing the first English academy for boxing in 1719. Later known as
Figg's Amphitheatre, this building provided space for the exhibitions of
professional fighters and for instruction in the arts of punching and wrestling.
By 1729 a dozen such academies had been opened by Figg's pupils.[72] Furthermore, boxing booths were now common at all the larger fairs.

The next champion of note, John Broughton, came to prominence during the
1740s. Broughton had attracted the patronage of the duke of Cumberland,
brother of the prince of Wales. These early patrons, who included the Duke of
Clarence and the Prince of Wales himself, supported their fighters in training
and sometimes employed them as servants or bodyguards. Furthermore, they
wagered huge sums on their performance. With the increased betting came a
need for rules, and in 1743 these were brought out under Broughton's name.
While boxing in Figg's day had been a slugging and wrestling match that
continued without pause until one of the contestants could no longer participate,
the new rules established rounds, determined the division of prize money and the
selection of umpires, and proscribed the behavior of seconds.

Under the legitimacy offered by his patron, Broughton also opened a new
boxing school at the Haymarket in 1747. This he announced to the public in the
following terms:

Mr. Broughton proposes with proper assistance to open an academy at his
House in the Haymarket for the instruction of those who are willing to be initiated in the mystery of boxing, where the whole theory and practice of that
truly British art, with all the various blows, stops, cross buttocks, etc. in-
cidental to combatants will be fully taught and explained: and that person of
quality and distinction may not be debarred from entering into a course of
these lectures, they will be given with the utmost tenderness and regard to the
delicacy of the frame and constitution of the pupil, for which will be provided mufflers that effectually secure them from the inconveniency of black
eyes, broken jaws, and bloody noses.[73]

The "mufflers" are usually thought to be the first boxing gloves, an accommoda-
tion of the practice to the safety of noble youth.

In 1750 the duke of Cumberland lost a large sum (popularly recorded as
10,000 pounds) in backing his champion against Jack Slack.[74] Broughton then

champions re-established its creditability. Gentlemen once again learned the *ars pugnandi*. While the patronage of George III was not forthcoming, his sons were enthusiastic supporters of the ring, and this brought a crowd of other wealthy patrons to the sport. As William Boulton explains:

> As the century drew to a close, it became the fashion to take an interest in the ring and its doings amongst men who had hitherto looked upon its vulgarities with contempt. White's and Brooks' clubs did not disdain to put on the mufflers at Harry Angelo's in St. James Street. The palmy days of the ring indeed were approaching when it became the fashion for a man of fashion to keep a tame fighter of his own, the Duke of Hamilton and Lord Barrymore being two well-known patrons who enjoyed that luxury. It was the custom of the latter noblemen to introduce his gladiator to his guests after dinner at Wargrave, where they were allowed to judge the strength of his arm by the whizz of his fist an inch off their noses. By the time the 'nineties came in too, if you got caught into a street row or were hustled at Vauxhall, it was thought just as well to be able to take part with your fists, swords by that time being rarely worn.[75]

Fighters such as Humphreys and Jackson (that "corporeal pastor" of the poet Byron) styled themselves "gentlemen," though the Jewish champion Mendoza seems to have done more to advance the art of boxing itself. One contemporary writer trumpeted that to list Jackson's clients at No. 13 Bond Street "would be to write down one-third of the peerage."[76] While this claim seems excessive, another indication of boxing's popularity was the formation of a royal bodyguard of well-known boxers, decked out in scarlet and gold livery and headed by Jackson, which marched at the coronation of George IV in 1820. With such illustrious support it is not surprising that the communities around London could do little to prevent prize fights, which were attended by disorderliness and gambling.

It was in Jackson's rooms that a Pugilistic Society was formed in 1814.[77] For this purpose 120 gentlemen subscribers were accumulated with the intent of regulating fights and guaranteeing purses. Among other changes sponsored by the club was the establishment of regular venues for the fights. As we have seen, such an organization could not be without its uniform—in this instance, blue coat and buff trousers with a yellow waistcoat and "P. C." engraved on the buttons.

As Brailsford has explained, the professional boxers themselves were, as today, drawn from the poorer and more oppressed segments of society.[78] Irishmen, Jews, and American blacks were prominent during the Regency heyday of the sport, and the crafty promoter made much out of regional and even international differences. When reality could not produce the desired divisions, invention intervened. While other areas of the country, most notably Bristol, might produce the champions; the center of the sport was always London. Here was the Pugilistic Society and related conglomerations of wealth, the organs of publicity, and the possibilities for the greatest crowds.

While the preceding has focused on boxing as a spectator sport, it is worthwhile inquiring into the practical significance of boxing lessons for the upper class. It is notable that sharp disagreements between gentlemen during the eighteenth century could be settled by swords or pistols. However, if a gentleman got into a skirmish with a member of the lower classes, it was deemed most proper if he resorted to those weapons available to both—their fists. In other words, the medium of dueling was reserved for privileged equals; as the commoner could not be elevated to this level, the gentleman might venture lower. Few sights made a stronger impression on the Frenchman Henri Misson than his observation of a nobleman teaching his coachman manners by fighting in the street:

> I once saw the Duke of Grafton at fisticuffs, in the open street, with such a fellow, whom he lamb'd horribly. In France, we punish such rascals with our cane, and sometimes with the flat of the sword; but in England this is never practise'ed; they use neither sword nor stick against a man that is unarm'd: and if an unfortunate stranger (for an Englishman would never take it into his head) should draw his sword upon one that had none, he'd have a hundred people upon him in a moment that would perhaps lay him so flat he would hardly ever get up again till the Resurrection.[79]

While this image of gentlemanly fair play may have been a cherished myth that often departed from reality, it is, at any rate, clear that such academies as Broughton's and Jackson's gave the young gentleman the tools to enforce his "natural" superiority.

This attitude toward fair play became more pronounced toward the end of the eighteenth century when the glittering artifice and polish of the beau was giving way to a broader cult of "manliness." In this context the exaggerated and colorful costumes of the Enlightenment were being replaced by more sombre attire: wigs and swords, for the most part, were gone. As proof of this manliness, gentlemen would offer accounts of their own battles with the lower classes. Even the prince of Wales had a favorite story about such a combat while fox hunting:

> The scent was catching and uncertain, so that we could go no continuous pace at all. There was a butcher out, God damn me, ma'am, a great big fellow, fifteen stone, six feet two inches without his shoes and the bully of all Brighton. He over-rode my hounds several times, and I had spoken to him to hold hard in vain. At last, God damn me, ma'am, he rode slap over my favorite bitch, Ruby. I could stand it no longer but jumping off my horse, said, "Get down, you damned rascal, pull off your coat, none shall interfere with us, but you or I shall go back to Brighton more dead than alive." God damn me, ma'am, I threw off my coat, and the big ruffian, nothing loth, did the same by his. By God, ma'am, we fought for an hour and twenty minutes, my hunting field forming a ring around us, no one interfering; and at the end of

it the big bully of Brighton was carried away senseless, while I had hardly a scratch.[80]

Doubtless, this account owes more to imagination than it ought to; however, it is quite significant for its emphasis on the general ethic of manliness that frames the relationship between prince and commoner. When the German visitor Count Puckler-Muskau mounted the pavement on his horse in 1825, he collided with English custom. "This the people regard as an invasion of their rights—a huge gigantic carter held up his fist and challenged me to box with him."[81]

Thus, the readiness to fight became (at least in the eyes of boxing proponents) an indicator of true valor and the means by which Englishmen distinguished themselves from their prissier or more underhanded neighbors on the Continent. By far the most colorful and vociferous of these proponents, the journalist Pierce Egan, frames the issue in 1812:

> Let Hyper-critics "grin a horrid ghastly smile": — let the fastidious sneer and shrug up their shoulders with contempt — but never yet let Britons be ashamed of a science; yes, a SCIENCE that not only adds generosity to their disposition — humanity to their conduct — but courage to their character. A country where the stiletto is not known — where trifling quarrels do not produce assassinations — and where revenge is not finished by murder. Boxing removes these dreadful calamities; a contest is soon decided, and scarcely ever the frame sustains any material injury.[82]

As one can gather, boxing was an expression (and, indeed, a showcase) for nationalistic feelings during and after the war years with France. By this emphasis (and by its exploitation of ethnic and regional divisions) it shifted loyalties away from the class divisions that were fundamental to Georgian England.

HORSE RACING AND ITS CLUB

If cricket and boxing were becoming great spectator events, horse racing was already there. As we have seen, the more regular races of the seventeenth century were competitions for cups or plates put up by wealthy patrons or town corporations. More common were match races between wagering owners. Normally, the horses who raced were older (five years and up), and several heats might be required to settle the score.

By the end of the eighteenth century great changes had occurred—most of them spurred by gambling. As Richard Mandell has argued, English betting was, for the most part, quite different from systems in which the wagerer relied on blind luck or the intercession of the gods.[83] Rather, the gambler prized, above all else, his or her ability to calculate more or less rationally the probability of events. All the curious wagers of the age (from bets about the pregnancy of a dean's wife to estimates of rain drops hitting a pane of glass to guesses at the lifeless state of someone lying on the sidewalk) were fundamentally exercises in human judgment. The sporting wagers—about the distance a woman could ride in 1,000 hours or the time it would take a toddler to traverse the Mall—fall within this tradition. In this sense gambling paralleled the new capitalist speculation of the seventeenth and eighteenth centuries. When legitimate calculation no longer seemed adequate, "inside" information might be gathered to tip the odds in one's favor.

From a gambling viewpoint, a chief problem in horse racing was (and remains) the creation of an equitable match. Some horses are clearly superior to others; once this information is circulated, only a fool will bet against them. Hence, new, artificial difficulties had to be introduced to even the odds and thereby increase the number of horses that could run against each other. Early in the eighteenth century, then, a system of handicapping was introduced.[84] This included an adjustment of the weight carried by each sex (fillies and mares carrying slightly less) and the system known as "give and take," where weight adjustments were made according to the height of the horse. Another was the "weight for age" adjustment. Horses were required to carry increasing weight as they matured, so that a six- or seven-year-old might carry forty pounds more than his young rivals. If this seems incredible, it should be remembered that long races (four to six miles) and multiple heats tended to value stamina perhaps more than sheer speed.

Another invention of the eighteenth century was the sweepstakes. The earlier pattern was for a group of horses to run for a gold or silver object put up by some individual or corporate sponsor. Monetary rewards were usually limited to side bets or to victory in match races (where each owner usually put up half of his own winnings). The sweepstakes—to this degree like the joint-stock company—restricted individual risk, while at the same time creating the smaller prospect of great return.

Still another change was the racing of younger horses over shorter distances. During the 1720s races restricted to four-year-olds were established. By the 1730s three- year-olds were featured, then two-year-olds in the 1760s, and ultimately yearlings in the 1780s.[85] The shorter races were crowd pleasers; furthermore, they provided a quicker return on the owner's investment (the purchase, care, and training of the animal). Three-year-old sweepstakes seem to have become a favorite format, and by the close of this period the five "classic" races of this type had been established: the St. Leger at Doncaster (1778), the Oaks (1779) and the Derby (1780) at Epsom, and the One Thousand Guineas (1809) and the Two Thousand Guineas (1814) at Newmarket. Each was the result of noble or royal sponsorship.

A more complicated system of racing introduces new possibilities for cheating. Owners and jockeys might bet against themselves or even "enter into a partnership" with a prominent opponent. Furthermore, horses might be misidentified. A horse might run under different names at different tracks, two horses might share the same name, and so on. The ages of horses might be fudged to beat the handicapping system, and horses could be taught to stand with their feet apart or to shrink down slightly when being measured. Then, of course, there were the various corruptions of horses, jockeys, and judges. Men could be bribed, and horses mistreated, doped, or, in several infamous cases, poisoned. Additional weight could be hidden on a horse to make him run slower in trial races or cosmetics applied to make him appear ill. There were also rampant tactical infractions—claiming a false start if one was slow off the mark, bumping one's opponent out on the course, and the like. Such practices were more prominent at the small local meetings; however, they were common enough at the major venues as well. A whole range of imponderables and intentional misinformation was now to be added to the supposedly rational calculations of the betting public.

Two particular responses to this confusion will be noted. The first was an act of 1740, intended to slow the growth of small, local races. Henceforth, races were to have stakes of at least fifty pounds, the only exceptions being two favored aristocratic settings, Newmarket and Hambleton. The ambition here was not only to limit the gambling of poorer groups, but also to encourage the breeding of stronger horses (a portion of the act being devoted to that end).

More significant was the evolution of the Jockey Club as an organizing body for the sport.[86] The club seems to have begun around 1750 as a loose assembly of noble patrons who habituated Newmarket. They shortly built a coffeehouse there and began to assume the status of a regulatory force for its races. Through their auspices local officials were established, and the club itself became the final authority for gambling disputes. Gradually (though by a process that is not totally clear), the club became the arbiter for racing questions and controversies across the country.

Among the contributions of the club were the registering of colors in 1762, the sponsoring of a stud book (listing the lineage of true thoroughbreds), and the promoting of a series of racing calendars (announcing and reporting on races, sales, and so on). In all of these the attempt was to identify and make explicit the history of a restricted circle of competitors. Furthermore, they connected themselves to entrepreneur Richard Tattersall, who conducted open and honest sales of horses. His establishment in London included rooms for their meetings there.

One might argue that the rise of the Jockey Club corresponds to the relatively modest interest in racing shown by the first three Georges. Royal leadership (so evident in the case of Charles II and continued to a lesser degree by William and then Anne) was replaced by aristocratic association. Indeed, the Jockey Club (with membership now over 100) became strong enough that it could in effect "warn off" the future George IV from racing at Newmarket in 1791. The prince's jockey (and, thus, the prince) was accused of holding back his horse during an early race to enhance his odds in the final (which he won easily). During the investigation that followed, the prince sided with his jockey and, thus, withdrew. Not until 1805 did he resume friendly relations with the club, finally accepting a position as royal patron in the following year.

As a self-appointed body, the Jockey Club proved to be a model for the other dominant sporting associations (i.e., the Marylebone Cricket Club the Pugilistic Society) that followed. Each was quite literally a "club," with all the exclusivity, the mixing of sport and social interests, the comfortable quarters, the sponsoring of supporting institutions, and the uniforms (in the case of the Jockey Club, this was a cutaway brown coat, doeskin breeches, boots, and spurs) that we have seen in other settings. Each took its position not by any formal process, but by the collective prominence and distribution of its membership. In each case this was extensive enough to prevent the formation of rival groups of gentlemen. In a world accustomed to aristocratic leadership, the existence of such coordinating and controlling bodies, to whom disenchanted bettors might appeal, was, for the most part, welcomed. Furthermore, such organizations meant that spectator sports (at least at this "highest" and most public of levels) would remain under the control of gentlemen, rather than middle-class entrepreneurs, players, or bookmakers.

THE SUPPRESSION OF MASS SPORTS

The mass ball games of the period show rather little change from those of earlier periods. Still popularized by the lower classes and the young, they retained their connection with the holiday context, especially Shrove Tuesday. For the most part, they remained loosely organized brawls centered about a ball. What rules they followed were fundamentally local inventions, and the games never reached the level of intercity or cross-regional play. As in previous times, the property owners of the towns continued their efforts to end such activities outright or to replace them with milder diversions. However, during this period certain factors combined to make their efforts more successful.

Most descriptions of football, hurling, and camp ball during the eighteenth century attest to their continued roughness. Of such accounts, Stephen Glover's description of the Derby game, written at the end of our period, is characteristic:

> The game commences in the marketplace, where the partisans of each parish are drawn upon each side, and about noon a large ball is tossed up among them. This is seized by some of the strongest and most active men of each party. The rest of the players immediately close in upon them and a solid mass is formed. It then becomes the object of each party to impel the course of the crowd toward their particular goal. The struggle to obtain the ball, which is carried in the arms of those who have possessed themselves of it, is then violent, and the motion of the human tide heaving to and fro without the least regard to consequences is tremendous. Broken shins, broken heads, torn coats, and lost hats are among the minor accidents of this fearful contest, and it frequently happens that persons fall in consequence of the intensity of the pressure, fainting and bleeding beneath the feet of the surrounding mob. But it would be difficult to give an adequate idea of this ruthless sport: a Frenchman passing through Derby remarked that if Englishmen call this

lookers-on. The shops are closed and the town presents the aspect of a place suddenly taken by storm.[87]

As Francis P. Magoun demonstrates, the selection of sides for the Shrove Tuesday affairs was based on traditional divisions.[88] At Devonshire and Derby one parish was pitted against another. At Kingston, Ashbourne, Chester-le-Street, Dorking, and Melrose the contest featured different town wards. At Sedgefield it was the people of the town versus those of the surrounding countryside. However, other principles were used as well. At St. Ives all the Toms, Wills, and Johns played against those with other first names. At Scone, Alnwich, Wooler, Melrose, and Duns the contests featured the rivalry of married and single men.

In general, basing the teams on established social criteria heightens the dramatic possibilities of the game. In other words, such games can be flooded with meanings extending beyond the event. Not only do such activities offer uncommon opportunities to act collectively, but also they can create a sense of collective consciousness where little existed before. In short, in mass sports, people had an opportunity to act as one against some real or imagined outsider. Likewise, the games forced individuals to enact their public identities and gave them new opportunities for recognition. Indeed, Joseph Addison describes how one unmarried player comported himself so well "it was impossible that he should remain a bachelor until the next wake."[89]

It has been suggested in previous chapters that the relative license of these events sometimes had antistructural (that is, political) implications. Indeed, James Walvin has recorded several instances during the eighteenth century when football games were organized precisely for the purpose of expressing social grievances.[90] For example, in 1740 at Kettering a crowd of 1,000 was assembled on the pretext of football, but actually for the purpose of destroying some local mills. At West Haddon, Northhamptonshire, in 1764 and 1765 football matches were convened for the tearing up and burning of enclosure fences. In Lincolnshire (where we have seen the precedent for such behavior) there were three such "matches" in one month in 1768. As Walvin explains, "Such actions merely compounded authority's view of football as anti-social, dangerous, and violent: a flash point for social ills which could scarcely be imagined."[91]

During the eighteenth century, then, various town councils intensified their efforts to eradicate football. This process has perhaps been discussed best by Robert W. Malcolmson:

It was cried down at Louth in 1745 and 1754 and at Worcester in 1743, 2 s. 6 d. was paid to the bellman crying down football kicking. At Derby there were several unsuccessful attempts to suppress the Shrovetide match in the eighteenth century; a prohibition of 1747 made particular reference to "Tumults and Disorders" and "breaking windows and doing other Mischief to the Persons and Properties of the Inhabitants of this Borough." A football

"Tumults and Disorders" and "breaking windows and doing other Mischief to
the Persons and Properties of the Inhabitants of this Borough." A football
game in the market place and through the streets of Bolton on 5 January 1790
was taken into consideration by the Lancashire Quartet Sessions as a
distrubance of the peace. At Kingston-upon-Thames the several efforts during
the 1790s to put down the sport were successfully resisted.[92]

By the nineteenth century, however, these efforts were becoming more successful. The Highways Acts of 1835 provided for a fine up to 40 shillings for
playing "at Football or any other Game on any part of the said Highways, to the
annoyance of any Passenger." On this basis street football was forcibly ended
at Richmond (1840), East Molesey and Hampton Wick (1857), Hampton (1864),
and Kingston-upon-Thames (1867).[93]

In Derby the mass games were finally curtailed in 1845. As a Derby
newspaper of 1846 argued:

> . . . in a town consisting of 40,000 inhabitants, one-third of whom were
> labouring population, persons must not assemble for such low and improper
> amusements at the present day in the public streets, whatever they might have
> done when football was originally practiced—Derby at that time being a very
> small place; but at the present time the town had become very large. Persons
> from a distance occasionally residing in it, whose characters were unknown,
> availed themselves of this opportunity of injuring persons by destroying
> property, alarming the timid and well-disposed inhabitants, and putting a stop
> to all business for the greater part of two days.[94]

This seems to have been the story throughout England. In essence, growing
towns could no longer tolerate the disorderliness of village amusements. Because
the city granted too much anonymity to its residents, mass sports could too easily
devolve into riots or assaults on property. The agents of the change were the
town councils and middle-class citizens who now had somewhat more effective
laws and police to enforce them. Furthermore, they had new moral weapons in
the Evangelical and Methodist movements to pacify the poor. Still another factor
was the general decline in public play space, as land was taken over for private
housing and commercial ventures.[95] In a movement that still continues, the poor
were forced out of the fields and streets into the interiors of the city.

CONCLUSIONS

This chapter's treatment of sport was initiated with a paradox. The
Georgian period is remembered for its sanctification of private property. Private
spaces expanded as public ones shrank. Property holders could terrorize the
poor with new extensions of the death penalty. The rich tended to withdraw
into their private estates, specialized pastimes, and exclusive circles. Yet the age
is also remembered for its spectacle of class mingling. Rich and poor could be

found gambling and sporting together, elbowing their way through common crowds. Was the age more or less democratic (or at least familiar) than those that preceded it?

Let us examine first the theme of class isolation. The most spectacular instance of class protectionism is the extension of the hunting laws by the landed interests that controlled Parliament. Much of this can be traced to the growth of an ideology of private property. With the movements toward enclosure and preservation, game was seen increasingly as private property. However, even wild fowl were redefined as gentlemen's game. In so doing, a restricted set of property owners was merely following the acquisitive instincts of the age.

The privatization of the upper class was both expressed and enabled by customized sporting grounds attached to manor houses—not only deer parks, but also bowling greens, archery grounds, and, rarely, tennis courts. Another accoutrement of the period was the billiard table, the lower classes being restricted from billiards by law. Within the confines of this sporting establishment (which included facilities for horses and dogs as well), the gentlemen could entertain his friends without venturing into public.

A related issue is the development of the sporting club. The rise of the special-interest association and its shift from inns and coffeehouses to private rooms and even clubhouses is a broader theme of the eighteenth century. In archery, fox hunting, coursing, cricket, and horse racing, gentlemen-participants banded together. While sheer sociability may have been the instigation behind some of these clubs, it is significant that the members came together in the name of sport. Sport was the focus of the club, the publicly stated rationale for its existence and the substance that united a personally diverse group and greased their interaction. With the growth of private club facilities, the upper class could now hide itself away in groups as well as individually.

Plebian culture went forward, albeit on a somewhat different footing. Town fairs continued; however, some of the traditional festivities sponsored by parish churches and wealthy landlords fell away.[96] Likewise, Sabbatarianism, under the auspices of the new religious movements, was reasserting itself. Ball games, such as bowling, cricket, and their lesser-known variants remained popular; but mass games (like football and bull running) were coming under fire from the middle classes in the towns. In general, the reduction of public space and the stricter supervision of major streets meant that poorer people were forced into the alleys and interiors. The most distinctive of these settings (rivaling, in a more democratic way, the gentlemen's club) was the alehouse. Here one could find ready companions to gossip and trade poaching stories and to play such relatively sedentary games as ninepins, bowls, quoits, cards, and dice. As Hugh Cunningham has explained, the implication of this shift (from the parish church) was an increased role of drink—and gambling—in public entertainment.[97]

In summary, both patrician and plebian cultures were clearly defined and supported by distinctive institutions. However, there were important crossovers between the two traditions. First, several of the aristocratic sports (bowling, archery, cricket, and even fox hunting) had fairly humble beginnings. The upper-class contribution was then to take over and refine the activity in a way that satisfied its sense of privilege. Uniforms, special playing grounds, refinements in equipment and rules, and so on are part of this process.

A second type of crossover was the meeting of the classes in the commercial establishments devoted to entertainment (the circuses, theatres, cockpits, bear rings, bowling alleys, and gaming houses). Such pleasure domes, the creation of showmen and entrepreneurs, had a character all their own. "Public culture" under such circumstances tended to be raffish and sensational, the crowds boorish and sometimes drunk. Here the disreputable of all classes (and those seeking disreputability) found common ground. Gambling, as I have stressed, was often a part of it. The German visitor Von Uffenbach was amazed that at the cockpit "an ostler in an apron wins several guineas from a lord." In this context, he notes the presence of a large cage or basket. "If a man has made a bet and cannot pay, he is drawn up in it amidst peals of laughter."[98]

A third type of crossover occurred at the outdoor sporting events. Boxing, cricket, and horse racing were spectacles sponsored in the main by gentlemen-gamesters and their agents. For the most part, the grounds were not enclosed so that the local populace could attend. As in the description of the cricket crowd supplied above, the manners of a group of disappointed bettors could be rough. George Morland, writing in 1758 about his early experiences as a jockey, adds these comments about the racing crowd: After losing the first heat of a race, "a mob of horsemen gathered round, telling me I could not ride, which is always the way if you lose the heat, they began at last to use their whips."[99] The jockey was served no better if he won too easily. As Morland continues:

> At Margate races, I was very nearly being killed. I won the heat so completely that the other horses were half a mile behind, upon which near 400 sailors, smugglers, and fisherman, etc. set upon me with sticks, stones, wagoners' whips, fists, etc. and one man took me by the thigh and pulled me off the horse.[100]

All sports attended by betting were occasionally tarnished by fixed matches. The disorderliness of the eighteenth-century crowd merely prevented the whole production from becoming too obvious.

A fourth, and final, type of crossover occurred through shared participation. Indeed, a sport such as cricket gave contemporaries glimpses of equality that astonished them, for they were treated to scenes of gentlemen exposing themselves to the risk of failure and embarrassment at the hands of their social inferiors. Fox hunting, with its ethic of community awareness, provided another example of mingling—and an antidote to the exclusiveness of shooting. For the first time commoners were not serving simply as beaters or dogkeepers, but sometimes riding alongside (if only for a little way) their social superiors. Another example of mixed participation is racing, where gentlemen found themselves competing against and advising their own professionals. Indeed,

Daniel Defoe complained about this even at Newmarket, where "persons of quality sank to the level of grooms and riding boys."[101]

However, it is important to note that this last type of mixing was motivated by strategic interests, rather than simple good feeling. Horse racing and cricket were betting sports: gentlemen-sponsors had to field the strongest combinations possible, even if that meant playing themselves. Mixing in fox hunting, on the other hand, was motivated more by social concerns. The nature of fox hunting required the cooperation of others (even small holders) in the locality. Occasional hunts where these elements could be involved were simply good public relations.

Much was made of this class integration by upper-class sportsmen. However, true equality was never approached. Instead, the eighteenth century features what I might term "stratifed" mixing.

At the pleasure domes of the entrepreneurial class (where admission fees could be charged), seating—and standing—seems to have been segregated by social criteria. At the theater, for example, the pit was commonly reserved for gentlemen, the first stage of boxes for ladies of quality, the second for citizens' wives and daughters, and the third for common people and servants.[102] According to Cheney's Rules and Orders for Cocking in 1743, a similar stratification might be imposed at the cockpit:

> It is ordered, that Persons of the Better Rank and Quality of the Cockers, Cockmasters, and Gamesters, such as are appointed to set to Cocks, and put them fair in, and no others (without Permission of the Master of the Pit) shall set in the lower Ring; and that the said Master of the Pit shall have the authority at all times to remove such as he thinks not meet to set in the lower or second Ring, and also to make room for those of that are of the better sort and to place there at his Pleasure, according to his own Discretion.[103]

On the other hand, at prize fights and backsword fights, this order seems to have been reversed—the commoner occupied the pit or area nearest the stage. However, this arrangement may have been to prevent the gentlemen the inconvenience of having a performer fall off the stage into his lap. In this regard Boulton records the 1800 advertisement of London's Hockley-in-the-Hole where "there is lately built a pleasant cool gallery for gentlemen.[104] Concerning this, Von Uffenbach describes a sword fight where the commoners on the ground floor tried to climb up into the gallery. When they were prevented, "They cast up such monstrous showers of stones, sticks, and filth and this with no respect of persons."[105]

At horse races, too, there were ultimately grandstands to which admission fees were charged. Otherwise, the upper-class viewers were elevated by their horses and carriages. Indeed, at certain courses the principal gentlemen were allowed to ride in the last quarter mile or so alongside the contestants. It must have been quite a spectacle.

If separate viewing areas were one mechanism for keeping wealthier people apart, a second indicator of rank was costume. The cut and quality of dress, of course, marked the audience, but it was also relevant to participants. The best example of this is fox hunting, where the gentlemen-members broadcast their central role in the production. In general, uniforms for club members were a significant feature of the age. In cases where servants wore attire similar to the members, other devices (such as soft caps for the hunt servants and silk stockings for the gentlemen-cricketeers) made matters plain.

A third difference was the typical position of the gentleman as organizer or controller of the event. Gentlemen typically arranged the contests, procured the playing areas, guaranteed any expenses, provided the necessary equipment, established the rules, and so on. Furthermore, it was very often the gambling interests of gentlemen-gamesters that initiated the play. Thus, sporting organization depended on the support of wealthy patrons. Such patronage had more than economic significance. Particularly when support came from the royal family, patronage conferred a kind of legitimacy on the proceedings, which meant that they were less likely to be disputed by local constables. This support was particularly important to the development of boxing.

Increasingly, the support of the wealthy was consolidated into clubs. Not only did such clubs guarantee that gentlemen, rather than others, would control the sports at issue, but also they were a way to segregate the activities of the members. By virtue of club membership, off-the-field activities could be clearly delineated from the limited fraternization that was permitted on the field. Even after gentlemen were no longer the principal athletes in these sports (such as boxing, cricket, and racing), the major societies standardized rules, established venues, adjudicated disputes, and in general coordinated major events.

The level of class mixing in sport then was controlled, for the most part, by the upper classes. Gentlemen could go slumming at the alehouses and entertainment centers catering to the working classes, but poorer people could not return the favor. When the lower classes were allowed into the sporting events of the wealthy, it was usually on limited terms and at the discretion of the host.

Even if one concludes that sporting events of the eighteenth century featured only limited *social* integration, a quite different judgment must be reached about their role as vehicles of *cultural* integration. In other words, such public occasions as boxing and cricket matches, cockfights, and horse races were powerful ceremonies on which rich and poor alike gazed in admiration. At one level this is a fairly sobering contention, for many of the events, especially the animal sports, seem marked by their exoticism and cruelty. However, deeper reflection reveals a more fundamental set of concerns.

Most applauded by the crowd was the evidence of "bottom," meaning personal courage in the face of adversity. The baited animal was celebrated for its pluck, as was the champion cock or prize fighter. Likewise, it was the fox hunter rather than the shooter who was praised by hunting songs and poems.[106] The latter might possess great skill, but the reckless rider willingly risked his own life and that of his horse for the sake of the chase. Not surprisingly, this jaunty confidence was also applauded at the public execution.[107] Such courage could be exhibited by either king or commoner. To that extent, sport featured the celebration of *individual* traits and abilities, rather than *social* ones.

As Stephen Deuchar has shown, this view of life was celebrated in eighteenth-century sporting art.[108] In addition to the representations of social harmony, such paintings also exhibited a new attitude toward nature. In contrast to earlier visions, people were seen less as objective admirers of nature and more as participants in it. The out-of-doors was pictured as the setting where urban and courtly artifice could be set aside, where virtue (symbolized by early rising and hard riding) had a chance to find expression. Of course, the paintings were overly idealized representations of the nobility of sport; however, they fed the belief that sportsmen (especially those who had forsaken a life of idleness for sport) were somehow leading lives that were healthy, contemplative, and beneficial to the communities in which they remained.

If sportsmen applauded a more broadly human ethic, they also made much of the equality of opportunity—what came to be known as "fair play." This was thought to be, for most of the century, a peculiarly English trait. In contrast to the purportedly underhanded ways of foreigners (the world of stilettos and assassinations), the English fought each other with equal weapons in public. Furthermore, England provided opportunities for social advancement not found on the Continent. Here boxers could style themselves "gentlemen," attain some measure of economic success (under the shelter of their patrons), and even march at the coronation of a king. In keeping with this ethic of equality were the flirtations with disrespect, the suspension of deference. Gentlemen, so the mythology went, asked for no quarter from their less well placed opponents. A gentlemen could be bowled by someone else's gardener or knocked down by his boxing master. He could have his hounds ridden over by a "butcher from Brighton" or be "distanced" by a local riding boy. In short, sport was thought to be an "agreeable coffee house," uniting diverse elements of society in equal and open conversation.

It has been argued by Hay and his colleagues that eighteenth-century law was less a vehicle of personal punishment than a public spectacle that intimidated and controlled the populace.[109] The new extensions of the law gave the prosecuting upper classes unprecedented powers; yet the system allowed them to be publicly beneficent—to soften or suspend the punishments of those who had offended them. In other words, the legal system had an ideological significance greater than its regulation of daily behavior. This same set of ideas can be applied to sport, albeit on somewhat different terms. During the eighteenth century the upper classes extended their authority over certain sports, either reserving them to themselves (as in shooting) or controlling their highest levels of development (as in racing, cricket, fox hunting, archery, and boxing). Yet, despite this extension of authority, there were prominent examples of personal generosity and local familiarity. These examples were held forth to the public as symbols of English (rather than foreign) class relations.

However, just as the principles of the legal system ultimately trapped even the upper classes in its web, so the principles of sport contained an ideology all their own. Sport does, indeed, proclaim the equal opportunity of participants and the celebration of individual achievement. It does eventually embarrass those who claim that natural ability derives from high birth. Thus, even though sport may have functioned as a safety valve for class antagonisms during the eighteenth century, it also provided a new model of human relationships that could infuse the middle-class and humanitarian movements of the century that followed.

NOTES

1. See, for example, R. J. White, *The Horizon Concise History of England* (New York: American Heritage, 1971), chapter 7, "The Age of Revolutions."

2. K. B. Smellie, *Great Britain Since 1688* (Ann Arbor: University of Michigan Press, 1962), 8.

3. See E. Wingfield-Stratford, *History of British Civilization* (New York: Harcourt Brace, 1928), 652.

4. J. H. Plumb, *England in the Eighteenth Century* (Baltimore: Penguin, 1966), 11.

5. E. N. Williams, *Life in Georgian England* (New York: G. P. Putnam's Sons, 1962), 15.

6. J. M. Golby and A. W. Purdue, *The Civilisation of the Crowd: Popular Culture in England: 1750-1900* (New York: Schocken, 1984), chapter 1, "The Old Popular Culture."

7. Lawrence Stone and Jeanne Stone, *An Open Elite: 1540-1880* (Oxford: Clarendon, 1984), 408.

8. See Douglas Hay, "Property, Authority, and the Criminal Law," in *Albion's Fatal Tree: Crime and Society in Eighteenth Century England,* ed. Douglas Hay et al.(New York: Pantheon, 1975), 17-64.

9. J. H. Plumb, *The First Four Georges* (New York: Hamlyn, 1974), 8.

10. Stone and Stone, *An Open Elite,* 417.

11. Edward P. Thompson, "Patrician Society, Plebian Culture," *Journal of Social History* 7 (1974): 382-405.

12. Paul B. Munsche, *Gentlemen and Poachers: The English Game Laws, 1671-1831* (Cambridge: Cambridge University Press, 1981), 18-19.

13. For a listing of game laws, see Munsche, *Gentlemen and Poachers,* appendix. For a somewhat different accounting making the same point, see Charles C. Trench, *The Poacher and the Squire: A History of Game Preservation in England* (London: Longmans, Green, 1967), 124.

14. 3 William and Mary, ch. 10. See Chester Kirby, "The English Game Law System," *American Historical Review* 38 (January 1933): 242.

15. See Edward P. Thompson, *Whigs and Hunters: The Origins of the Black Act* (New York: Pantheon, 1976).

16. Ibid., 190-91. For a somewhat different interpretation, see John Broad, "Whigs and Deer-Stealers in Other Guises: A Return to the Origins of the Black Act," *Past and Present* 119 (May 1988): 56-72.

17. Kirby, "The English Game Law System," 254.

18. Ibid., 256.

19. Roger Longrigg, *The English Squire and His Sport* (New York: St. Martin's, 1977), 150.

20. Munsche, *Gentlemen and Poachers,* 38.

21. "The Game Laws," *Edinburgh Review* 31 (March 1819): 302.

22. Ibid., 303.

23. Hay, "Property, Authority, and the Criminal Law."

24. This obligation was given some legal footing in 1808 when the earl of Essex sued the Old Berkeley Hunt for trespassing. See Trench, *The Poacher and the Squire,* 132.

25. Stone and Stone, *An Open Elite,* 311–14.

26. Michael Brander, *The Hunting Instinct* (London: Oliver & Boyd, 1964), 114.

27. Raymond Carr, *English Fox Hunting: A History* (London: Weidenfeld & Nicolson, 1976), 35.

28. For a contemporary account of fox hunting expenses, see "English Fox Hunting," *Quarterly Review* 47 (March 1832): 216–43.

29. Guy Paget, *History of the Althrop and Pytchley Hunt* (London: Collins, 1937), 77–93.

30. See "The Early History of Fox Hunting," *Edinburgh Review* 193 (January 1901): 94.

31. See E. Hargrove, *Anecdotes of Archery from Earliest Ages to the Year 1791,* rev. Alfred Hargrove (New York: Hargrove's Library, 1845), 64.

32. See Carr, *English Fox Hunting,* 1–2.

33. John Hawkes, *The Meynellian Science.* This is the title quote and point of departure for the study of David Itzkowitz, *Peculiar Privilege: A Social History of Fox Hunting 1753–1885* (Hassocks, England: Harvester, 1977), 24.

34. "The History of Sport in Chesire," *Walford's Antiquarian* 12 (October 1887): 193.

35. Carr, *English Fox Hunting,* 8.

36. "English Fox Hunting," 227.

37. "Fox Chase of Old England," *The Knickerbocker* 12 (August 1838): 134.

38. Itzkowitz, *Peculiar Privilege,* 24–27.

39. E. Hargrove, *Anecdotes of Archery,* 269.

40. Robert P. Elmer, *Archery* (Philadelphia: Penn, 1926), 104.

41. Ibid., 88.

42. George Hansard, *The Book of Archery* (London: Henry G. Bohn, 1841), 269.

43. Hargrove, *Anecdotes of Archery,* 87.

44. Elmer, *Archery,* 87.

45. See C. J. Longman and H. Walrond, *Archery* (New York: Frederick Ungar, 1894), 183.

46. See William Bedford, "Society of the Woodmen of the Ancient Forest of Arden," *Archer's Register* (1879): 24–39.

47. Quoted in Longman and Walrond, *Archery,* 210.

48. Bedford, "Society of the Woodmen," 220–32.

49. Many of the early references are collected in G. B. Buckley, *Fresh Light on Eighteenth Century Cricket: A Collection of 1000 New Cricket Notices from 1697 to 1800 A. D.* (Birmingham, England: Cotterel, 1935). See also G. B. Buckley, *Fresh Light on Pre-Victorian Cricket: A Collection of New Cricket Notices from 1709–1837* (Birmingham, England: Cotterel, 1937).

50. H. S. Altham, *A History of Cricket,* 2 vols. (London: George Allen & Unwin, 1962), 1:31.

51. R. MacGregor, "Cricketana," *Belgravia* 42 (March 1880): 84–93.

52. See Altham, *A History of Cricket,* 1:51.

53. "Of Public Cricket Matches," *The Gentleman's Magazine* 13 (September 1743): 485–86

54. Altham, *A History of Cricket,* 1:36.

55. See Buckley, *Fresh Light on Pre-Victorian Cricket,* 208–16.

56. Neville Cardus, *English Cricket* (London: Collins, 1947), 10.

57. See John Ford, *Cricket: A Social History: 1700–1835* (Newton Abbot, England: David & Charles, 1972), chapter 3, "Patrons," and chapter 4, "Gentlemen."

58. Ibid., 76.

59. Ibid.

60. Andrew Steinmetz, *The Romance of Duelling,* 2 vols. (London: Chapman & Hall, 1868), 1:37.

61. George Paston, *Sidelights on the Georgian Period* (London: Methuen, 1902), 132.

62. Ben Truman, *The Field of Honor* (New York: Fords, Howard, & Hulbert, 1884), 35.

63. Steinmetz, *The Romance of Duelling,* 1:38.

64. Quoted in Michael Brander, *The Georgian Gentleman* (Westmead, England: Saxon House, 1973), 186–87.

65. Robert Baldick, *The Duel: A History of Duelling* (London: Chapman and Hall, 1965), 38.

66. Quoted Ibid., 5.

67. Elizabeth Burton, *The Georgians at Home* (London: Longmans, 1967), 10.

68. Duncan Taylor, *Fielding's England* (New York: Roy, 1966), 189.

69. Frank Menke, *The Encyclopedia of Sports,* 4th ed. (South Brunswick, N. Y.: A. S. Barnes, 1969), 234.

70. See Henry Miles, *Pugilistica: The History of British Boxing,* 2 vols. (Edinburgh: John Grant, 1906).

71. Quoted in J. Peller Malcolm, *Anecdotes of the Manners and Customs of London During the Eighteenth Century,* 2d ed., 2 vols. (London: Longman, Hurst, Rees & Orme, 1810), 2:155.

72. Menke, *The Encyclopedia of Sports,* 235.

73. Quoted in William Boulton, *The Amusements of Old London,* 2 vols. (London: John C. Nimmo, 1900), 2:89.

74. Miles, *Pugilistica,* 1:28.

75. Boulton, *The Amusements of Old London,* 2:97–98.

76. Ibid., 2:100.

77. See John Ford, *Prize Fighting in the Age of Regency Boximania* (Newton Abbot, England: David & Charles, 1971), chapter 5, "Development and Promotion."

78. Dennis Brailsford, "Nationality, Race, and Prejudice in Early Pugilism," in *Proceedings of the HISPA International Congress,* ed. J. A. Mangan (n. p.:1985), 17–23.

79. Henri Misson, *Memoirs and Observations of M. Misson in His Travels over England,* quoted in Christina Hole, *English Sports and Pastimes* (Freeport, N. Y.: Books for Libraries, 1949), 33.

80. Quoted in Trench, *The Poacher and the Squire,* 132–33.

81. Quoted in Ford, *Prize Fighting,* 31.

82. Pierce Egan, *Boximania: Or Sketches of Ancient and Modern Pugilism* (London: G. Smeeton, 1812), 2–3.

83. Richard Mandell, *Sport: A Cultural History* (New York: Columbia University Press, 1984), 143–45.

84. Roger Longrigg, *The History of Horse Racing* (London: Macmillan, 1972), chapter 8, "Georgian Britain: Horses and Races."

85. Ibid., 85.

86. For a brief description, see Norman Wymer, *Sport in England* (London: George Harrap, 1949), chapter 6, "Racing becomes the Sport of Kings." See also Richard Onslow, *Headquarters: A History of Newmarket and Its Racing* (Cambridge, England: Great Ouse, 1983), chapter 3, "Georgian Newmarket."

87. Stephen Glover, *The History, Gazetteer, and Directory of the County of Derby* (Derby, England: n.p., 1829), 310–11.

88. Francis P. Magoun, "Shrove Tuesday Football," *Harvard Studies in Philology and Literature* 12 (1931): 44.

89. Quoted in Montague Shearman, *Football* (London: Longmans, Green, 1899), 20.

90. James Walvin, *The People's Game: A Social History of British Football* (Bristol, England: Allen Lane, 1975), 24–25.

91. Ibid., 26.

92. Robert W. Malcolmson, *Popular Recreations in English Society 1700–1850* (Cambridge: Cambridge University Press, 1973), 139.

93. Ibid., 141.

94. Ibid., 141.

95. Quoted ibid., 144.

96. Hugh Cunningham, *Leisure in the Industrial Revolution 1780–1880* (New York: St. Martin's Press, 1980), chapter 3, "Public Leisure and Private Leisure."

97. See Dennis Brailsford, "Religion and Sport in 18th Century England: 'For the Encouragement of Piety and Virtue, and for the Preventing and Punishing of Vice, Profaneness and Immorality,'" *British Journal of the History of Sport* 1, no. 2, September 1984): 166–83.

98. Cunningham, *Leisure in the Industrial Revolution,* 86.

99. Quoted in Rosamond Bayne-Powell, *Travellers in Eighteenth Century England* (London: John Murray, 1951), 86.

100. Walter Gilbey and E. D. Cuming, *George Morland: His Life and Works* (n.p., 1907), 46.

101. Daniel Defoe, *Tour Through the Whole Island of Great Britian,* 4 vols. (n.p., 1762), 1:84.

102. Bayne-Powell, *Travellers in Eighteenth Century England,* 75.

103. Quoted in Longrigg, *The English Squire and His Sport,* 174.

104. Boulton, *The Amusements of Old London,* 1:19.

105. Bayne-Powell, *Travellers in Eighteenth Century England,* 87.

106. See Patrick Chalmers, *The History of Hunting,* 18–22.

107. See Michael Brander, *The Georgian Gentleman* (Westmead, England: Saxon House, 1973), 142.

108. Stephen Deucher, *Sporting Art in Eighteenth Century England: A Social and Political History* (New Haven, Conn.: Yale University Press, 1988).

109. Douglas Hay et. al., *Albion's Fatal Tree: Crime and Society in Eighteenth Century* England (New York: Pantheon, 1975).

7

SOCIOLOGICAL REFLECTIONS

In the social sciences, few ideas are as appealing as the concept of evolution.[1] To scan the centuries and find in them some abiding direction, even some "path of progress," is perhaps the ultimate conceit. The writer of the current work has wanted to see the preindustrial period in this way—as a prelude to the world we know. Each time I have willfully pushed forward a simple evolutionary thesis, the complexity of events and the sophistication of early people have beaten it back. The preindustrial world was clearly something other than the product of unenlightened passions or the collaboration of innocents. Correspondingly, I have found it difficult to sketch some simple linear pattern (such as rationalization or bureaucratization) across the centuries.[2] If modern people often seem egotistical and coldly calculating in their outlook, the people of earlier times could be the same way.

Nevertheless, history is not synonymous with disarray. There are patterns that characterize the ages, and these the book has tried to show. Such developments are only partly the working out of tradition in new ways. They are also the manifestation of new social and cultural inventions, demographic changes, political upheavals, environmental calamities, and so on. Like fissures opening in the earth, these forces act to centralize and decentralize social environments, to unify and divide their members along new dimensions.

The history of sport, then, is largely a history of the settings in which people have played. These settings have included the ideas that have justified or otherwise framed physical activity as well as the social structures that have encouraged and discouraged play. Most profoundly, to inquire about settings is to ask what sport has meant to the inhabitants of that realm.

As a sort of conclusion, then, I wish to consider three sociological "lessons" from preindustrial sport. Specifically, these issues are the relationship of sport to social status, the nature of normative order in sport, and the significance of sport to "society." Few sociological topics are so ordinary—or so fundamental.

SPORT AND SOCIAL DISTANCE

If there is a guiding spirit behind this work, it is the German sociologist
Georg Simmel. Among his many contributions to sociological thinking is the
concept of *social distance*.[3] The term refers to the sense of separation or
isolation between social units (between individuals, roles, groups, organizations,
and societies). Put differently, social distance denotes the extent to which social
identities are kept clear and distinct. Among the better-known uses of the idea
are Emory Bogardus's social distance scale (which measures the antipathy
between social groups in a community) and Erving Goffman's role distance (the
psychological separation individuals retain from particular roles they play).[4]

The preceding treatment of sport as an identity ceremony is indebted to
Simmel's concept as well. Throughout, my contention has been that sporting
events provide occasions for individuals (and groups) to display selected
traits—social, psychological, cultural, and physical—before others. This
opportunity for self-expression or self-definition has a dual reference. On the
one hand, each side seeks to distinguish itself against the opponent. On the
other, the partisans jointly are distinguished from the wider category of
nonplayers. Among this latter group are those who will never play the game in
question because they have been prevented (in structural terms) from doing so.
It is this latter division—between players and non-players—that has been a focus
of the study.

To take Simmel's concept seriously is to inquire into the procedures by
which social distance is maintained. This means not only the kinds or *levels* of
discrimination that exist, but also the *mechanisms* by which these are enforced.
As we have seen, the preindustrial era was an age that accepted, for the most
part, the fact of social hierarchy and the separation of ranks. Sport was one
way of expressing this sense of distinction. What the materials of the preceding
chapters indicate, then, are three fundamental levels of discrimination.

The first (and farthest-reaching) level I will call *cultural discrimination*. In
this pattern, access to an entire category of activity (for example, leisure, sport,
hunting, or shooting) is restricted. Despite a fairly basic division between
working people and a group having abundant leisure, neither leisure nor sport
was entirely fenced off during the preindustrial period. However, wealthier
groups were often suspicious of malingering by poorer people. For that reason
the larger and more public sporting events of the poor tend to appear within the
boundaries of established festivals, protected by the church or some magnanimous individual. It is this tradition that James I perpetuated with *The King's
Book of Sports*.

To understand cultural discrimination during this period, then, one must
seek a narrower focus. Even though nonaristocratic elements could participate
in the three broad categories of military sports, hunting sports, and ball play,
they were restricted as to their choices within each area. As we have seen, the
tournament was always quite exclusive, as was dueling with certain weapons.
Instead, ordinary people were constrained to practice archery and to fight with

swords and bucklers, staffs, and fists. Hunting presents a much more complicated pattern; however, in general, the wealthier groups had access to wider
territories and different species of prey. In hawking, too, they possessed the
more powerful and exotic (and, therefore, more prestigious) kinds of birds. Ball
play was not an enthusiasm of the military estate; still, kinds of activity became
differentiated here as well. Tennis and bowls were periodically protected as pursuits of wealthier groups; various street games and mass sports were left to
others.

Despite the fact that upper-class people were freer to choose their pursuits,
this freedom was not complete. Contemporary commentators from William
Fitzstephen to Joseph Strutt listed the sports that seemed appropriate to high and
low. Poor people were prevented (by law and other devices) from exceeding
their licit pastimes; richer people were fettered by their own schemes about propriety.

As the book has indicated, there were some changes in the listings of
permissible sports. Certainly, the preindustrial era was a bumptious one, and the
under classes fought to keep (and, less commonly, expand) the range of things
they were permitted to do. The tension between archery practice and ball play
or the more political connotations of mass sports are evidence of that. However,
the biggest changes seem to be associated with the drying up of traditional elite
pastimes (the tournament, hawking, and the hunting of the stag and boar) and
with the failure to maintain other, newer recreations (such as tennis and pall
mall). What this meant was that the upper class had to turn elsewhere to find
distinctive amusements. One particular source was the (sometimes neglected)
activities of commoners, such as archery, cricket, and fox hunting. These they
developed in distinctive ways. In the same sense, they brought other sports such
as horse racing and coursing to new levels of refinement. Fencing provides
another example. Upper-class fencing had its own distinctive weapon (the rapier
and then the small sword), rules of conduct, and even fencing masters (Italian
gentlemen). Finally, in the case of hunting, the upper class extended its
dominion over a diminishing population of wild animals by including some
heretofore unprestigious kinds of game birds. With the advent of "shooting
flying" and the battue, the method of killing was made class distinctive as well.

In each of these sports, the changes occurred at a different pace and for different reasons. Hunting sports were connected to the development of private
property rights and to the availability of meat within the wider population.
Military sports were a legacy of the feudal tradition; and ball play was wrapped
up in the parish holiday setting on one hand and gambling interests on the other.

As I noted above, these changes cannot be painted in evolutionary
terms—that is, as a fairly simple and steady decline in cultural discrimination.
The desire for social distinction remained strong among the ruling groups and,
to a lesser degree, among working people as well. Instead, the decline of traditional aristocratic pastimes forced that group into more precise forms of
discrimination.

A second level of restriction, then, is *social discrimination.* This means an exclusion from the social circle, the group of participants. To take a familiar example, blacks and whites in the United States have played baseball separately for many years; only in the last forty or so have they participated together widely as teammates and opponents.[5]

Two vehicles for perpetuating social discrimination among a wider class of players were the "public" sporting establishment and the sporting club. The former seems to have originated during Tudor times and was exemplified by tennis courts, bowling alleys, fencing schools, and baiting rings. Because these were managed by entrepreneurs for profit, admission fees were one way of weeding out patrons. Other social criteria might be used as well to sanitize the proceedings.

The sporting club also had dim antecedents within Tudor-Stuart times; however, its key period is the eighteenth century. In sports such as cricket, archery, fox hunting, and coursing, gentlemen gathered around a shared interest. Subscriptions were collected, clubhouses raised, and costumes and rules standardized. In addition to perpetuating cross-class distinctions, such activities articulated differences within classes. "Hunting men" were distinguished from "shooting men," coursing enthusiasts from fox hunters; Meltonians from their more provincial imitators. The preindustrial period was witness to several trends that confused status relations. The number of people with hereditary claims to gentility expanded, and there was a corresponding growth in the numbers, wealth, and power of the commercial and professional groups. Finally, London society and then the resort areas brought together this confusing mix of status aspirants. The eighteenth-century club (with its policies of invitation and exclusion) was a way to funnel interaction within this dispersed and complicated group.

The third level of restriction, *organizational discrimination,* occurs within the sporting circle itself. As has been emphasized, the seventeenth and eighteenth centuries brought the classes together on and around the field of play. Horse races, cockfights, bear baits, boxing, and cricket matches produced a hurly-burly of enthusiastic (and often wagering) observers. In addition, some of these sports matched gentlemen—or their animals—against less exalted people and theirs.

To repeat the argument of earlier chapters, such apparently democratic scenes still evidenced stratification. Even in settings controlled by middle-class entrepreneurs, special seating or standing areas, costuming, manners, and material facilities (such as horses and carriages) guaranteed that social mixing, while more prevalent than in other settings, would not be unbounded. Furthermore, it is essential to note the prominence of gentlemen (especially when gathered in clubs) as organizers and controllers of public events. Quite commonly, they arranged the meeting, established the rules, guaranteed the purse, and the like. Others who played appeared more or less at the invitation of their social superiors.

In general, then, this gradual narrowing of restrictions must not be seen as a melding of the sporting appetites of rich and poor. For the most part, wealthier people kept their own diversions private, and poorer people—in the streets and alehouses—had their settings as well. However, gentlemen also redis- covered some of the traditional pastimes of ordinary people. On certain public occasions, and especially when money was at stake, they invited the common man as participant or observer back in on their terms. By virtue of this historic patronage, gentlemen assured their position as leaders of the sporting movements of the nineteenth century.

How were these patterns of discrimination maintained? As today, stratifica- tion was based on the control of four central resources—knowledge, prestige, power, and wealth.[6] To take a contemporary example, a potential applicant to a club may be kept out because he or she lacks knowledge of the club's exis- tence, its rules, its manners, or even the game that is its centerpiece. Likewise, a person may be excluded for social or prestige reasons; membership is deemed inappropriate for a person of that "type." Power refers to the coercive abilities of individuals (the ability to force their will upon reluctant others), and wealth, of course, represents a more positive set of inducements that can be offered. In short, one can be excluded because he or she is too ignorant, too disreputable, too weak, or too poor.

The modern industrial West, with its class system, tends to emphasize economic distinctions. Money and property open doors to the other kinds of resources—if not for oneself at least for one's children. However, in less fluid and less complicated systems, the other elements rise in prominence. When all four resources are controlled by a hereditary elite, the result can be a terrific set of barriers to social interaction and mobility.

In the preindustrial world, with its more sharply defined and restricted stations of life, differences in knowledge were a significant block to communica- tion. Indeed, special knowledge in religion, economics, and statecraft might be jealously guarded. For those not situated in the households of the eminent, the processions of the Anglo-Norman rulers—with their strange gibberish and cos- tumes and customs—must have been an awesome sight. In this context, sports were badges of station. The special traditions of noble hunting and hawking were not accessible to all. The military tournament was generally blocked to the nonfeudal classes. These matters changed somewhat with the revolutions in printing and mass literacy. Now the secrets of aristocratic behavior could be spread.

The second criterion is prestige, the social estimate of personal quality. During the preindustrial era societywide prestige derived less from individual accomplishment than from group affiliation. People partook of the prestige of the family, guild, order, town, village, or other entity to which they belonged. To the extent that some of these memberships were determined by hereditary criteria, a fairly stable system of social ranking, perpetuating conceptions of in- alienable qualitative differences between human categories, was established. Sports were, thus, the hallmarks of groups. A collection of tradesmen aping the tourney or a bishop chasing a football was a pretender to a status he did not possess.

In societies that respect tradition, the force of custom is sufficient to restrict access to social activities. During times of change and dissension, other measures are required. A key (and, to the modern eye, most curious) mechanism was the use of power—especially governmental authority—to enforce sporting habits. Sporting legislation appeared throughout the period; however, such laws typically were not expressions of some coordinated governmental program regarding sports, but rather reactions of those in power to the failure of custom or earlier laws. Poaching laws were justified by accounts of new incursions against the time-honored hunting privileges of property owners; property qualifications in general were attempts to stifle the aspirations of working groups with money in their pockets. As we have seen, power (or the threat of it) could also be used to defend the customs of these working people. The spirited defense of mass games or holiday revels was usually a reaction to threats (by the property-owning classes) against longstanding traditions.

Money and property were used as well. Wealth (both source and amount) in the form of membership dues, admission fees, and property qualifications was a way of restricting access to social activities. In another way the ownership of buildings and enclosures (such as clubhouses, deer parks, and tennis courts) was a way of guaranteeing privacy. Furthermore, the connection of sports with elaborate material requirements—horses, dogs, costumes, equipment, and so on—was a way of safeguarding upper-class sports from meaningful imitation. Finally, the centrality of the upper groups in public sporting events was assured by their economic patronage. In modern capitalist countries, considerations of expense become the key (though certainly not the only) constraints on sporting participation and spectatorship.

Even though this listing of the levels and mechanisms of discrimination derives from a study of the past, it is more valuable as a tool for interpreting the present. In particular, it provides a way of registering the depth of assimilation of different categories of people in sport and the devices that are used against them. For example, women in the United States still have relatively little access to a variety of sports that men play (that is, cultural discrimination exists). When they do participate in sports men play, each sex commonly plays alone and before separate audiences. Ideas about social propriety, access to material facilities, availability of players and sponsoring organizations, sheer knowledge about the game itself, and even laws about the allocation of funds in schools become issues.[7]

American black men likewise experience some cultural discrimination (for example, they are concentrated in only a handful of sports at the professional level), and social discrimination is maintained largely by segregated residential patterns and by the policies of clubs and other organizations sponsoring play.[8] However, much more is now being written about their experience of organizational discrimination (historic "stacking" at certain positions or failure to obtain leadership positions on and off the field).[9] Clearly, the preceding materials are intended to invite a more detailed history of the minority experience in sport.

RITUAL AND PLAY: COMMENTS ON NORMATIVE ORDER IN SPORT

If the people find distinction in the sports they play, they are also marked by the way they play them. Indeed, sporting events (and sportsmen) seem to be pulled by two contradictory tendencies. On the one hand, sports are commonly considered to be a species of play, an opportunity for creative and indulgent personal expression. Indeed, games are characterized by a contentious, spontaneous quality. On the other hand, games have as their defining characteristic a set of (quite artificial) rules that restricts free expression. Operating within this structure requires deference and discipline and a certain fairness to others. In short, behavior in games can drift between an almost unbridled partisanship and a ritualistic obedience to the formalities surrounding the game.

Although we must be a bit suspicious of the accounts provided by preindustrial reporters, it is generally conceded that the mass sports of village folk tended toward the former extreme. There were, it seems, few rules or officials, and because of the size of the sides and the expanse of the playing area, regulation would have been nearly impossible anyway.

However, two points should be made. First, as Richard Carew's comments in Chapter 5 indicate, there were also some more regulated forms of these games played by villagers. Second, partisan excesses were not confined to working people. The mass games of the early military class—the melees—were also fairly unregulated. Fighting stretched over miles and much of the behavior (for example, ganging up on one competitor and entering the fray after others had tired) seems by later standards unsportsmanlike. With this background, then, it is worth inquiring into the sources of normative regulation in sport and (somewhat differently) the willing acceptance of these rules by the players themselves.

In a recent book Norbert Elias and Eric Dunning have commented on these issues.[10] In their view, self-control (and violence regulation) in sport was part of a broader "civilizing process" affecting manners in general. A key source of the new ethic was the development of court life during the Renaissance.[11] In England, as on the Continent, diverse and rivalrous aristocrats were brought into a circle that not only set standards for, but also made a contest of, "decorum." Likewise, sports—as sublimated forms of rivalry—were given a center for their evolution and dissemination.

This pattern accelerated during the seventeenth century with the development of a London "society" season. Again, a dispersed governing class was brought together and exposed to such models of regulated competition as gambling, debates, gossip, and sport. By the end of the century a parliamentary regime provided yet another model of how antagonisms could be worked out in peaceful ways. An associational concept of social life was applied to clubs of many kinds, including sports clubs. In their resounding terms, the "parliamentarization of the landed classes" led to "the sportization of their pastimes."[12]

By their own account this portrait is offered less as a "causal analysis" of the changes in sport and more as a depiction of broad societal transformations that accompanied these changes. Nevertheless, the preceding chapters make some minor modifications in their position plausible. First, qualities of violence regulation and self-control seem apparent from earlier centuries as well. Marcelle Thiebaux's descriptions of aristocratic hunting during the thirteenth and fourteenth centuries (see Chapter 3) and Juliet Barker's comments about the evolution of the tournament (Chapters 2 and 3) make it clear that behavior in certain circles was becoming fairly ritualized. Wholesale violence (as in the melee) was being narrowed into socially permissible channels. Furthermore, the emphasis was shifting from the moment of physical confrontation itself to the activities surrounding it—feasts, parades, courtly gestures, dances, songs and stories of the event, ritualistic division of the spoils, and so forth. In the *à plaisance* tourneys, even the moment of truth itself was softened.

To continue in a somewhat different direction, the "demilitarization" of the landed classes was probably as important to sporting life as "courtization" or "parliamentarization." When elite sports (again, primarily hunting and the tournament) lost their rationale as military exercises, they shed some of their connection to ferocity and endurance as well. Success in the more pacified world of the Tudors required other, largely nonmilitary skills. Recalling Dennis Brailsford's remarks from Chapter 4, it was more prudent for the gentleman to be a spectator to acts of violence by others (such as professional swordsmen or animals) than to perpetuate them himself. Correspondingly, softer pastimes such as bowls or tennis now suited the aristocratic ideal.

To return to the development of rules (and rule adherence) in sport, it seems to me that this process accompanies the growth of recognized communities or groups transcending the partisans themselves. To cite an example, interparish or interward football games remained fairly unregulated because there was no substantial affiliation beyond the locality.

To put the matter more strongly, regulations in sport arise when a wider group (or its leader) has a vested interest in the corporate cooperation or efficiency of the partisans. Some of the earliest regulations are, thus, attributable to the political aspirations of kings or nobles. The initial efforts of the kings to prevent—and then to pacify or otherwise regulate—the tourney were reflections of their anxiety about the event spilling over its boundaries and causing mayhem. However, military training was needed. As the event developed during the later Middle Ages, it became largely a parade ground for invited notables who were enveloped within a broader mythology sponsored by the host. The actual fighting itself (often with dulled weapons) became overrun by days of feasting, pageants, and fellowship. The royal commitment to military efficiency and public duty was also expressed in the regulations about archery practice.

Henry VIII's requirement that archery contests include shooting at distances over 200 yards and at varying targets was related to his views of warfare.

If the political considerations of a leader represent one source of regulations, another was the development of economic interests in games. Richard I's scheme for organizing the tournament in England included some ways of making money from participants. Likewise, the ransoming system of the early tourneys made regulations regarding the capture (for example, the appropriate use of squires) and return of prisoners necessary.

In this light, perhaps the greatest source of rule making in sport has been gambling. The concern of government and religious officials about the gambling of the poor was a source of many of the legal prohibitions regarding sport and of the licensing of sporting houses. However, gambling also instigated more positive directions—"house rules" of the sporting entrepreneurs or "articles of agreement" drawn up by gamesters. With great sums riding on the outcome of cockfights, boxing matches, horse races, and cricket matches, disputes were inevitable. Prior agreements over the nature of the playing field, length and number of "rounds," eligibility of contestants, fair and foul maneuvers, selection and authority of officials, and procedures for handling bets mollified these disputes somewhat.

Predictably, then, the gambling sports of the seventeenth and eighteenth centuries produced some of the more widely recognized sets of rules. These included the duke of Norfolk's Laws of the Leash for coursing (late sixteenth century), Kiplingcote's Rules in horse racing (1619), Cheney's Rules and Orders for Cocking (1743), Broughton's Rules in boxing (1743), and the first Laws of Cricket set forth by the London Club in 1744. Notably such rules were not only the result, but also the source of wider participation; local rules were being replaced by more standardized forms. Rules also were useful in building an audience for sport. By the end of the preindustrial period a sporting crowd or "fancy" knowledgeable in the traditions of the game was replacing the earlier collections of curiosity seekers.

Gambling was, furthermore, a force for the spread of sporting organizations. Following the success of the Jockey Club in the 1750s, associations of gentlemen in cricket and boxing stepped forward to attempt regulation of their sports as well. Such clubs discouraged sharp play, in part by serving as a court of appeal of sorts for disconcerted bettors. Just as these bodies provided an aura of legitimacy to their sports, so they oiled the gambling machine. In essence, the reputation for fairness at a venue facilitated betting and furthered the popularity of a sport. The public acclamation of scandal (a factor that affected boxing several times) could deaden both. In brief, regulation was in the interest of the broader betting community.

If political and economic forces were sometimes behind rules, so was "social" capital. Sporting events within the upper class became thoroughly artificial vehicles for class solidarity and class consciousness. Standards of behavior were set forth, and people were judged by their ability to adhere to these. Uniforms and clubhouses proliferated. This pattern is pronounced in a nongambling sport, archery. Here new standards brought out by the prince of Wales facilitated contests between the various societies that had formed. In such settings sociability was the keynote. Likewise, good form was elemental to fox hunting, a sport where much of the work was carried on by the dogs and the hunt servants. Most of the riders were merely participants in collective pageantry. Again, food, stories, and general good fellowship swept around the event.

Self-regulation occurs when the interest of the participants is tied to the interest of the wider group. When prestige accrues not merely from competitive success (winning), but also from social deportment, the individual has a different stake in the contest. "How one plays the game" (meaning the ability to enact group standards), thus, became central to the amateur tradition. Not surprisingly, this emphasis on rules and rule observance became predominant in the more public sports. The private sports, such as shooting and fishing, were, for the most part, unceremonious. As indicated previously, hunting manuals were less statements of decorum than sets of techniques. When an effective method (for example, stalking prey by hiding behind one's horse or baiting the leg of a goose) is discovered, it is recommended. Group sport (including hunting) changes the ambiance. Contest is now also performance.

SPORT AND SOCIETY: THE INSTITUTIONALIZATION OF SPORT

It is surely peculiar that the two most inimical viewpoints in sociology—functionalism and conflict theory—share much in their treatment of sport.[13] On the surface, of course, the differences are real enough. Functionalism (at least in its structural or "social" variant) emphasizes processes that sustain and stabilize societies. What is marvelous about society, in the functionalist view, is its relative orderliness. Society absorbs all kinds of shocks and strains and somehow regains its footing; consent, cooperation, and continuity prevail. Conflict theory, predictably enough, emphasizes what remains—the collisions of interests, the gnawing scarcity, the endless discontent. From such a viewpoint, consent is commonly unrecognized coercion, cooperation is only uneasy alliance, continuity is merely the stranglehold of the powerful.

From the functionalist vantage point sport has been viewed as a setting in which major cultural themes are rehearsed and reaffirmed.[14] Sport facilitates interaction among people and builds solidarity at various levels. It promotes health and physical stamina. It sponsors the development of socially admired personality traits. It accustoms people to the vicissitudes of success and failure.

Conflict theorists, on the other hand, are less likely to speak of "society" as a meaningful entity. Rather, they emphasize how prominent groups in society use sport (as they use religion, politics, or education) to exploit the disadvantaged.[15] Sport promotes the survival of the dominant group; it does not benefit society as a whole. In the most evocative image, sport is pictured as an "opiate" that distracts poorer people from their true (that is, class-based) interests. More particularly, big-time sport in capitalist societies (the focus of Marxian analyses) is a fantasy world proffering crass, commercial values and narrowly personal visions of success. In this way sport constitutes a vehicle for social control. It misdirects human energy into pointless rivalries and, thus, prevents the recognition of more substantial shared interests.

How are such opposed views similar? Both agree that sport provides opportunities to rehearse major cultural themes and promotes solidarity and stability. What is debated is the question of who benefits from and promotes these events as well as the propriety of the various forms of stability and solidarity that are created. More significantly, both theories see sport as a piece of some broader puzzle—as a prop for some wider or more established aspect of social structure.

This tendency to depict sport as a characteristic or feature of wider societal patterns can be called the "mirror of society" or "microcosm" view of sport.[16] In this model, sport evinces traits (values, rewards, norms, ranking patterns, and so on) that are anchored in the structure of society. In other words, one learns about a society by attending to its sporting habits.

Certainly, much about the sporting life of the preindustrial period can be looked at in this way. Sporting activities were quite often "pastimes"—relatively unorganized and participant-motivated recreations fitted within daily routine. For the elite, sport was commonly an extension or expression of routine social identity. The early tourney or hunting and hawking was part of a broader life style, not apart from it. Conversation about and preparation for these occasions were significant parts of daily life, and sporting implements themselves (such as horses and dogs, pet falcons, and special clothing) were familiar elements of the domestic scene. Furthermore, sports could be linked to personal (and group) interests beyond the playground—that is, to the maintenance of military status or the provision of food. In short, practicality was interwoven with amusement.

With the rise of thoroughly impractical sports (ball play, gentlemanly archery, and fox hunting) social and cultural issues became central. Elite pastimes became occasions for intra-class mixing and opportunities to confirm upper-class ideals. Sports provided "models of sociability" for the more individualistic conditions of the seventeenth and eighteenth centuries.

Although the "mirror of society" approach fits elite sport fairly well, folk sports follow a somewhat different pattern. Ordinary people commonly played sports during times stolen from working life, either illegitimately (taken from daily routine) or legitimately (within the holiday context). While sport served many of the same functions for working people as it did for the elite, it also functioned as a safety valve or even "antistructure."[17] In other words, sports allowed individuals and groups chances for assertion or aggression that contrasted with or even counterpointed social routine. To rephrase the matter, sporting pastimes for the elite were quite often an idealization of existing reality—a ritualistic celebration of stability and prosperity and the generosity of the host. Sport for poorer people could follow this pattern; but it was more often a realization of ideals—an opportunity to experience personal achievement away from a hierarchical, largely ascriptive world.

The best example of such play is the mass ball games. Especially in their holiday context, such events became associated with the freedom of subordinate groups, such as peasants, apprentices, and schoolboys. Over the objections of property holders, games were played, and villages and towns taken over. Of special note is the turbulent quality of such games. Rules were not cumbersome, and regulation, once the game had begun, was often impossible. If the previous discussion emphasized the importance of cooperation and the development of a broader class ethic, the focus here is on the joy of competition.

In this light the sports of the under classes (or the dissatisfied of any rank) could have specifically political connotations. Poaching (to the extent that this can be considered sport) was not only an economic activity but also a confounding of authority. Poaching was always a stealing of food; however, heads of animals were put on poles facing the mansion house of the owner, deer park palings destroyed, haystacks and barns burned, dogs killed, and shots exchanged. In a milder sense the comic assaults on the quintain or the "jousts" performed on ice skates or in boats can be looked at in a political context. As part of the medieval tradition of foolery, such acts demean not only the participants, but also the more elaborate events of which they are an imitation.

Even when it entails specifically antisocial themes, sport is more often a safety valve than an effective agency for change. Nothing is produced. Energy is spent. The game concludes. Much of folk sport can be seen in this way. Traditional habits of deference or other obligations are suspended; order is replaced by disorder, and corporate restraint by individual excess. Again, such formlessness in sport denotes a group of players who look to leisure not as an opportunity to cement a comfortable position in society, but as an occasion to counter traditional identities.

Both the elite and the folk traditions can be fitted within the two theoretical perspectives. From a functionalist viewpoint, the use of sport to reaffirm elite values and to facilitate interaction diminished undue rivalry among society's leaders and thereby contributed to overall societal harmony. Likewise, the use of sport as a safety valve exhibits societal tension management—channeling and releasing in harmless ways the frustrations of the unsuccessful. From a conflict viewpoint the building of upper-class solidarity through sport had more malevolent implications. Furthermore, upper-class patrons were behind many of the folk festivities. Ordinary people were set against one another in pointless rivalries, all to the benefit of the ruling group.

Furthermore, many of the spectator sports of the era can be looked at in this latter way. Wealthy hosts initially sponsored events that paraded the wealth, sophistication, and martial ferocity of their class before the gawking representatives of the other estates. Much later, they sponsored spectator sports that put common people (even servants) into their midst. Indeed, these commoners (as boxers, jockeys, and cricketeers) could occupy center stage. What such sports provided was another model—of affable interclass mixing and the celebration of purely personal character and achievement. From a conflict perspective such occasions can be interpreted as a democratic smoke screen cast over a fiercely protectionist age.

In contrast to the preceding views, my own inclination is to emphasize the growing independence of sport as a realm of culture. Talcott Parsons (himself a functionalist) has called attention to a process of "differentiation," which, he feels, characterizes the evolution of modern societies.[18] For our purposes this means the growing separation and independent development of the various social institutions (the economy, education, health care, and so forth). Within each area, specialized organizations arise, and these promote values and norms that are germane to their purposes alone. People (themselves increasingly differentiated) contract with these organizations for their needs; and society itself exists primarily as a web of interdependency among specialists.

In terms of this viewpoint, how might sport (at least at some levels) have emerged as a relatively independent part of society? For most of the preindustrial period, sports were basically exercises or pastimes existing under the principles and auspices of other institutions. Peasant festivities were commonly part of the holiday context legitimized by the church. Like the church itself, these events subverted (in mild ways) the claims of secular authorities. Many other activities (such as archery and the tourney) were justified as military exercises; others (such as hunting and hawking) combined military and economic rationales.

Yet another institutional context was, for want of a better term, "sociability." Sports were reconstrued as occasions for social integration. The later tournaments and noble hunts, archery, fox hunting, and the like became dominated by the aforementioned precepts about good manners. Gentlemen were expected to retire amicably after the event was over.

A growing force, which others have commented on, was the commercialization of sport.[19] Sports were connected to drinking and gambling in alehouses. Some spectator sports were enabled by wealthy gamesters. Others were products of entrepreneurs who promised a bloody and exotic show.

The history of sport, then, is very much the history of shifting institutional contexts. During the nineteenth century, education took sport under its wing, and sport was put to further use by the government in the form of intercounty and international competitions. However, is there a sense in which the balance between sport and these other institutional contexts tipped—so that sport was no longer in service to outside organizations and institutions, but rather stood more or less on its own terms? In other words, when did "sport for sport's sake" become prevalent?

To study how any activity becomes institutionalized is to inquire into the processes by which that activity is established and accepted in society. Key elements in this development are distinctive organizations, roles, and normative elements (that is, values and rules for behavior).

As I have already indicated, I believe that two social inventions were essential to the development of sport. The first was the commercial sporting establishment (tennis courts, bear and bull rings, cockpits, fencing and boxing schools, and so on). While mixed with other pleasures, sport or sporting skill was the principal item for sale. Furthermore, these establishments provided continuous, specific settings for sport, something that had heretofore been missing. The second invention was the sporting club. Such clubs were vehicles of sociability, but they were also settings where sports could be collectively refined and exalted. As suggested before, sport was now the terms by which a dispersed group of people came together. Likewise, sport acquired new levels of permanence and standardization. Personal whim was replaced by officers, bylaws, clubhouses, and venues.

Along with recognized and continuous centers for sport came changes in social roles. There were the elected heads of the sporting clubs and the often autocratic "masters" (of fox hunting, fencing and riding schools, and the like) who supervised participants. Likewise, a host of supporting roles (such as bookmakers, animal trainers and handlers, grounds keepers, and equipment manufacturers) arose. Another role coming into view was that of the spectator or "fancy," as was its complement, the sporting hero. Perhaps most significant, the category of the "sportsman," as a gentleman who is recognized for his skill and devotion to sport, was emerging as well.[20] Such sporting squires as George Osbaldeston, Peter Beckford, John Mytton, Hugo Meynell, and Thomas Assheton Smith had wide reputations.[21]

Just as the sporting world became peopled with a cast of often colorful characters, so sport sprouted its own ideology. This myth was not simply grafted onto sport, but was largely inherent in it. Upon the development of this ethic, the sporting world could exist not only as a mirror of society, but also as a model for it. England, of course, was not alone in developing physical exercise in the form of contest—or in exploiting the specifically social possibilities of games. However, among contemporary societies England was preeminent in formally organizing sports and in sponsoring large-scale events for public consumption. These displays were basically celebrations of individual accomplishment in competitive settings. Moreover, that accomplishment was attributable to physical and psychological qualities, rather than to social ones. Unlike the rest of society, the sporting world proclaimed an equality of opportunity for competitors. Advantage of birth or social breeding was presumably set aside. When one horse or a cricket eleven was too strong, it might be handicapped to even the odds.

Sporting events, thus, played out the possibilities for an achievement ethic within what was still largely an ascriptive society.[22] Moreover, this competitive exercise pattern modeled relations in the economic and political spheres. Social order, such as it was, appeared as a fragile and ever-changing artifact resulting from the negotiation of contending individuals and groups. Players met on a common field, "articles of agreement" regulating their behavior were drawn up, and temporary hierarchies in the form of victor and loser were established. In this scheme of things partisanship was seen as somehow morally elevating, success and failure inevitable, and social harmony an agreement about the boundaries of strife. In short, sport provided a thoroughly secular ethic for a society grown suspicious of religious authority and the divine right of kings.

A work of this sort raises perhaps more questions than it answers. Indeed, the more inquisitive reader will wonder about the details behind so broad a sketch of so many centuries. What about regional, ethnic, rural-urban, age, religious, and gender variations in sports. Who were the entrepreneurs of the sporting establishments? Who were the professional athletes?[23] How were they trained?[24] How were sporting clubs organized, and how were they interrelated? To what extent did a broader sporting community transcend the organization of individual sports? To what extent were the ideological possibilities of sports recognized by contemporaries? Some of these themes have been broached by other works, both cited and uncited. However, for the most part, such matters lie in waiting for the new generation of historians and social scientists.

NOTES

1. Although evolutionism is primarily a nineteenth-century idea (evidenced by such writers as Karl Marx, Auguste Comte, Herbert Spencer, Edward Tyler, and L. H. Morgan), it has been put forth more recently as well. See, for example, Talcott Parsons, *Societies: Evolutionary and Comparative Perspectives* (Englewood Cliffs, N. J.: Prentice-Hall, 1966).

2. See the debate about the rationalization process in sport in John M. Carter and Arnd Krueger, eds., *Ritual and Record: Sports Quantification in Pre-Industrial Societies* (Westport, Conn.: Greenwood Press, 1989).

3. See Donald Levine, Introduction to *On Individuality and Social Forms* by Georg Simmel (Chicago: University of Chicago Press, 1971), xxxiv–xxxv.

4. See Emory Bogardus, "*Social Distance* and Its Origins," *Journal of Applied Sociology* 9 (1925): 216–26, 299–308; and Erving Goffman, *Behavior in Public Places* (New York: Free Press, 1963).

5. See D. Dodson, "The Integration of Negroes in Baseball," *Journal of Educational Psychology* 28 (October 1954): 73–82.

6. For a general treatment of this issue, see Richard Gruneau, "Sport, Social Differentiation, and Social Inequality," in *Sport and Social Order*, ed. Donald Ball and John Loy (Reading, Mass.: Addison-Wesley, 1975), 117–84.

7. See William Beezley and Joseph Hobbs, "Nice Girls Don't Sweat: Women in American Sport," *Journal of Popular Culture* 16 (Spring 1983): 42–53. See also M. Marie Hart, "On Being Female in Sport," in *Sport in the Socio-Cultural Process,* ed. M. Marie Hart (Dubuque, Iowa: William C. Brown, 1972), 291–320.

8. See the works of Harry Edwards, especially *The Sociology of Sport* (Homewood, Illinois: Dorsey, 1973), chapter 7.

9. See Norman Yetman and D. Stanley Eitzen, "Racial Dynamics in American Sport: Continuity and Change," in *Majority and Minority: The Dynamics of Race and Ethnicity in American Life,* ed. Norman Yetman (Boston: Allyn & Bacon, 1982).

10. Norbert Elias and Eric Dunning, *The Quest for Excitement: Sport and Leisure in the Civilizing Process* (New York: Basil Blackwell, 1986).

11. Ibid., 63–90.

12. Ibid., 34.

13. See Jay Coakley, *Sport in Society: Issues and Controversies* (St. Louis: C. V. Mosby, 1982).

14. See Gunther Luschen, "The Interdependence of Sport and Culture," in *Sport in the Socio-Cultural Process,* ed. M. Marie Hart (Dubuque, Iowa: W. C. Brown, 1972), 67–77.

15. See Paul Hoch, *Rip Off the Big Game* (New York: Doubleday, 1972). See also John Hargreaves, *Sport, Power, and Culture* (Oxford: Basil Blackwell, 1986).

16. Users of this imagery include Robert Boyle, *Sport: Mirror of American Life* (Boston: Little, Brown, 1963); Henry Morton, *Soviet Sport: Mirror of Soviet Society* (New York: Collier, 1963); and Timothy Curry and Robert Jiobu, *Sports: A Social Perspective* (Englewood Cliffs, N. J.: Prentice-Hall, 1984), 17.

17. For an example of this approach, see Clifford Geertz, "Deep Play: Notes on the Balinese Cockfight," in *The Interpretation of Cultures* (New York: Basic Books, 1973), 412–54. The idea of antistructure is usually attributed to the anthropologist Victor Turner; see *The Ritual Process* (Chicago: Aldine, 1969).

18. Parsons, Societies.

19. J. H. Plumb, *The Commercialization of Leisure in Eighteenth Century England* (Reading, England: University of Reading Press, 1973); Hugh Cunningham, *Leisure in the Industrial Revolution 1780–1880* (New York: St. Martin's, 1980).

20. See Ikuo Abe, "A Study of the Chronology of the Modern Usage of 'Sportsmanship' in English, American, and Japanese Dictionaries," *International Journal of the History of Sport* 5, no.1 (May 1988): 3–28.

21. See Roger Longrigg, *The English Squire and His Sport* (New York: St. Martin's, 1977).

22. The achievement-ascription distinction is developed in Talcott Parsons, *The Social System* (New York: Free Press, 1951), 151–200.

23. For an analysis of professional boxers, see Dennis Brailsford, "Nationality, Race, and Prejudice in Early Pugilism," in *Proceedings of the XI HISPA International Congress*, ed. J. A. Mangan (Glasgow, 1985), 17–23.

24. See Peter Radford, "The Art and Science of Training and Coaching Athletes in Late-18th and Early 19th Century Britain," in *Proceedings of the XI HISPA International Congress,* ed. J. A. Mangan (Glasgow: 1985), 80–83.

SELECTED
BIBLIOGRAPHY

Works as broad in scope as this one tend to exist along the ridges of historical understanding. Supporting the observations made here is a great mass of historical detail which, for the most part, must be found elsewhere. While hardly exhaustive, the following is a list of writings I have found especially useful. These works generally deepen the understandings of the preceding pages. However, they contain as well many alternative themes that have not been developed here.

Abe, Ikuo. "A Study of the Chronology of the Modern Usage of 'Sportsmanship' in English, American, and Japanese Dictionaries." *International Journal of the History of Sport* 5, no.1 (May 1988): 3–28.

Aberdare, Lord. *The Story of Tennis.* London: Stanley Paul, 1959.

Altham, H. S. *A History of Cricket.* 2 vols. London: George Allen & Unwin, 1962.

Anglo, Sydney. *The Great Tournament Roll of Westminster.* Oxford: Clarendon, 1968.

———. *Spectacle, Pageantry, and Early Tudor Policy.* Oxford: Clarendon, 1969.

Aylward, J. D. *The English Master of Arms: From the Twelfth to the Twentieth Century.* London: Routledge and Kegan Paul, 1956.

Bailey, Peter. *Leisure and Class in Victorian England: Rational Recreation and the Contest for Control.* London: Routledge and Kegan Paul, 1978.

Baker, William J. "The State of British Sports History." *Journal of Sport History* 10, no.1 (Spring 1983): 53–66.

Baldick, Robert. *The Duel: A History of Duelling.* London: Chapman & Hall, 1965.

Barber, Richard. *The Knight and Chivalry.* London: Butler & Tanner, 1970.

———. *The Reign of Chivalry.* New York: St. Martin's, 1980.

Barker, Juliet. *The Tournament in England: 1100–1400.* Wolfboro, New Hampshire: Boydell, 1986.

Barrington, Daines. "Some Observations on the Practice of Archery." *Archaeologia* 7 (1785): 46–68.

Boulton, William. *The Amusements of Old London.* 2 vols. London: John C. Nimmo, 1900.

Brailsford, Dennis. *Sport and Society: Elizabeth to Anne.* London: Routledge and Kegan Paul, 1969.

———. "Religion and Sport in 18th Century England: 'For the Encouragement of Piety and Virtue, and for the Preventing and Punishing of Vice, Profaneness and Immorality.'" *British Journal of the History of Sport* 1, no. 2 (September 1984): 166–183.

————. "Sport and Class Structure in Elizabethan England." *Stadion* 5, no.2: 244–52.

Brander, Michael. *The Hunting Instinct.* London: Oliver & Boyd, 1964.

————. *The Georgian Gentleman.* Westmead, England: Saxon House, 1973.

Buckley, G. B. *Fresh Light on Eighteenth Century Cricket: A Collection of 1000 New Cricket Notices from 1697 to 1800 A. D.* Birmingham, England: Cotterel, 1935.

————. *Fresh Light on Pre-Victorian Cricket: A Collection of New Cricket Notices from 1709–1837.* Birmingham, England: Cotterel, 1937.

Cardus, Neville. *English Cricket.* London: Collins, 1947.

Carew, Richard. *A Survey of Cornwall.* London: n.p., 1602.

Carr, Raymond. *English Foxhunting: A History.* London: Weidenfeld & Nicolson, 1976.

Carter, John Marshall. *Ludi Medi Aevi: Studies in the History of Medieval Sport.* Manhattan, Kan.: Military Affairs, 1981.

————. "Muscular Christianity and Its Makers: Sporting Monks and Churchmen in Anglo-Norman Society, 1000–1300." *British Journal of Sports History* 1, no.2 (September 1984): 109–24.

————. *Sports and Pastimes of the Middle Ages.* Columbus, Ga.: Brentwood University, 1984.

Castiglione, Baldassare. *The Book of the Courtier,* translated by Thomas Hoby. London: J. M. Dent, 1928.

Castle, Egerton. *Schools and Masters of Fence from the Middle Ages to the End of the Eighteenth Century.* London: Arms & Armour, 1885; reprint, 1969.

Chalmers, Patrick. *The History of Hunting.* London: Seeley, Service, 1936.

Clephan, R. Coltman. *The Tournament: Its Periods and Phases.* London: Methuen, 1919.

Coulton, G. G. *Medieval Panorama.* Cambridge: Cambridge University, 1939.

Cousins, Geoffrey. *Golf in Britain: A Social History from the Beginnings to the Present Day.* London: Routledge and Kegan Paul, 1975.

Cox, Harding, and Lascelles, Gerald. *Coursing and Falconry.* London: Longmans, Green, 1892.

Cox, R. W. "A Survey of the Literature of the History of Sport in Britain." *British Journal of Sports History* 1, no.1 (May 1984): 41–59. (periodic bibliography that continues in *International Journal of the History of Sport*).

Cripps-Day, Francis. *The History of the Tournament in England and France.* London: Bernard Quaritch, 1918.

Cuming, E. D. "Sports and Games." In *Johnson's England,* edited by A. S. Turberville. 2 vols. Oxford: Clarendon, 1933, 2:362–83.

Cunningham, Hugh. *Leisure in the Industrial Revolution 1780–1880.* New York: St. Martin's, 1980.

Daniel, William. *Rural Sport.* London: Bunny and Gold, 1801.

Denholm-Young, Noel. "The Tournament in the Thirteenth Century." In *Studies in Medieval History Presented to Frederick Maurice Powicke,* edited by R. Q. Hunt et al. Oxford: Clarendon, 1948.

Deucher, Stephen. *Sporting Art in Eighteenth Century England: A Social and Political History.* New Haven: Yale University Press, 1988.

Duby, Georges. *William Marshal: The Flower of Chivalry.* New York: Pantheon, 1985.

Dunning, Eric, and Sheard, Kenneth. *Barbarians, Gentlemen, and Players: A Sociological Study of the Development of Rugby Football.* New York: New York University Press, 1979.

Edward, Second Duke of York. *The Master of Game,* edited by W. A. Baillie Grohman and F. Grohman. London: Ballantine, Hanson, 1904.

Egan, Pierce. *Boximania: Or Sketches of Ancient and Modern Pugilism.* London: G. Smeeton, 1812.

Elias, Norbert, and Dunning, Eric. *The Quest for Excitement: Sport and Leisure in the Civilizing Process.* New York: Basil Blackwell, 1986.

Featherstone, Donald. *The Bowmen of England.* New York: Clarkson and Potter, 1967.

Ferguson, Arthur. *The Indian Summer of English Chivalry: Studies in the Decline and Transformation of English Chivalric Idealism.* Durham, N.C.: Duke University Press, 1960.

Fitzstephen, William. "Description of the City of London (1170–1183)." In *English Historical Documents: 1042–1189,* edited by David Douglas. London: Eyre & Spottiswoode, 1968.

Ford, John. *Prize Fighting in the Age of Regency Boximania.* Newton Abbot, England: David & Charles, 1971.

————. *Cricket: A Social History 1700–1835.* Newton Abbot, England: David & Charles, 1972.

Frederick II. *The Art of Falconry Being the De Arte Venandi Cum Avibus of Frederick II.* translated and edited by Casey Wood and Marjorie Fyfe. Stanford, Calif.: Stanford University Press, 1943.

Froissart, Jean. *The Chronicle of Froissart,* translated and edited by Sir John Bouchier and Lord Berniers. 6 vols. London: David Nutt, 1902.

Gautier, Leon. *Chivalry.* London: Phoenix House, 1959.

Gillmeister, Heiner. "The Flemish Ancestry of Early English Ball Games." In *Olympic Scientific Congress 1984. Official Report Sport History,* edited by Norbert Muller and Joachim Rühl. Niederhausen: Schlors-Verlag, 1985, 54–75..

————. "The Gift of a Tennis Ball in the Secunda Pastorum: A Sport Historian's View." *Arete: The Journal of Sport Literature* 4 (1986):105–19.

————. "Medieval Sport: Modern Methods of Research—Recent Results and Perspectives." *International Journal of the History of Sport* 5, no.1 (May 1988): 53–68.

Glasier, Philip. *Falconry and Hawking.* London: B. T. Batsford, 1978.

Golby, J. M., and Purdue, A. W. *The Civilisation of the Crowd: Popular Culture in England: 1750–1900.* New York: Schocken, 1984.

Hanawalt, Barbara. "Men's Games, King's Deer: Poaching in Medieval England." *Journal of Medieval and Renaissance Studies* 18, no.2 (Fall 1988): 175–94.

Hansard, George. *The Book of Archery.* London: Henry G. Bohn, 1841.

Hardy, Robert. *Longbow: A Social and Military History.* Cambridge, England: Patrick Steves, 1976.

Hargrove, E. *Anecdotes of Archery From Earliest Ages to the Year 1791,* revised by Alfred Hargrove. New York: Hargrove's Library, 1845.

Harris, H. A. *Sport in Britain: Its Origins and Development.* London: Stanley Paul, 1975.

Hay, Douglas, et al., eds. *Albion's Fatal Tree: Crime and Society in Eighteenth Century England.* New York: Pantheon, 1975.

Hoffman, Richard. "Fishing for Sport in Medieval Europe: New Evidence." *Speculum* 60, no. 4 (1985): 877–902.

Hole, Christina. *English Sports and Pastimes.* Freeport, N. Y.: Books for Libraries, 1949.

Holt, Richard. *Sport and the British: A Modern History.* Oxford: Clarendon, 1989.

Hoskins, C. H. "The Latin Literature of Sport." In *Studies in Medieval Culture,* 105–23. New York: Frederick Ungar, 1958.

Huizinga, Johan. *Homo Ludens: A Study of the Play Element in Civilization.* Boston: Beacon, 1955.

Itzkowitz, David. *Peculiar Privilege: A Social History of Fox Hunting 1753-1885.* Hassocks, England: Harvester, 1977.

James, E. O. *Seasonal Feasts and Festivities.* New York: Barnes & Noble, 1961.

Jeffreys, Stephen. *Tourney and Joust.* London: Wayland, 1973.

Keen, Maurice. *Chivalry.* New Haven, Conn.: Yale University Press, 1984.

Kirby, Chester. "The English Game Law System." *American Historical Review* 38 (January 1933): 240–62.

Lang, Andrew. "Cricket." *English Illustrated Magazine* (August 1889): 47-57.

Longman, C. J., and Walrond, H. *Archery.* New York: Frederick Ungar, 1894.

Longrigg, Roger. *The History of Horse Racing.* London: Macmillan, 1972.

———. *The History of Foxhunting.* London: Macmillan, 1975.

———. *The English Squire and His Sport.* New York: St. Martin's, 1977.

MacGregor, Robert. "The Game of Bowls." *Belgravia* 36 (September 1878): 352–59.

———. "Cricketana." *Belgravia* 42 (March 1880): 84–93.

McLean, Teresa. *The English at Play in the Middle Ages.* Windsor Forest, England: Kensal Press, 1984.

Magoun, Francis P. "Football in Medieval England and in Middle English Literature." *American Historical Review* 35 (1929–1930): 33–45.

———. "Shrove Tuesday Football." *Harvard Studies and Notes in Philology and Literature* 12 (1931): 9–46.

———. *The History of Football—From the Beginnings to 1871* (Bochum-Langendreer: Verlag Heinrich-Poppinghaus, 1938.

Malcolmson, Robert W. *Popular Recreations in English Society: 1700–1850.* Cambridge: Cambridge University Press, 1973.

———. "Sports in Society: A Historical Perspective." *British Journal of Sports History* 1, no.1 (May 1984): 60–72.

Mandell, Richard. *Sport: A Cultural History.* New York: Columbia University Press, 1984.

Mangan, J. A., ed. *Pleasure, Profit, Proselytism: British Culture and Sport at Home and Abroad: 1714–1914.* London: Frank Cass, 1988.

Manwood, John. *A Treatise and Discourse on the Laws of the Forest.* 4th ed. London: n.p., 1717.

Marshall, Julian. *The Annals of Tennis.* London: Horace Cox, 1878.

Miles, Henry. *Pugilistica: The History of British Boxing.* 2 vols. Edinburgh: John Grant, 1906.

Munsche, P. B. *Gentlemen and Poachers: The English Game Laws 1671-1831.* Cambridge: Cambridge University Press, 1981.

Noel, E. G., and Clark, J. O. M. *A History of Tennis.* 2 vols. London: Oxford University Press, 1973.

Oakeshott, R. Ewart. *A Knight and His Horse.* London: Lutterworth, 1962.

Onslow, Richard. *Headquarters: A History of Newmarket and Its Racing.* Cambridge, England: Great Ouse, 1983.

Painter, Sidney. *William Marshal: Knight-Errant, Baron, and Regent of England.* Baltimore: Johns Hopkins, 1953.

Plumb, J. H. *The Commercialization of Leisure in Eighteenth Century England.* Reading, England: University of Reading Press, 1973.

Poole. A. L., ed. *Medieval England.* 2 vols. Oxford: Clarendon, 1958.

Reay, Barry, ed. *Popular Culture in Seventeenth Century England.* New York: St. Martin's, 1985.

Rudorff, Raymond. *Knights and the Age of Chivalry.* New York: Viking, 1974.

Rühl, Joachim. "Religion and Amusements in Sixteenth and Seventeenth Century England: 'Time might be better bestowed, and besides we see sin acted.'" *British Journal of Sports History* 1, no.2 (September 1984): 125–65.

Strong, Roy. *The Cult of Elizabeth: Elizabethan Portraiture and Pageantry.* London: Thames & Hudson, 1977.

Strutt, Joseph. *The Sports and Pastimes of the People of England.* London: Metusen, 1801; reprint, edited by J. C. Cox, 1901.

Thiebaux, Marcelle. "The Medieval Chase." *Speculum: A Journal of Medieval Studies,* 42, no.1 (January 1967): 260–74.

Thiebaux, Marcelle. *The Stag of Love: The Chase in Medieval Literature.* Ithaca, N. Y.: Cornell University Press, 1969.

Thompson, Edward P. "Patrician Society, Plebian Culture." *Journal of Social History* 7 (1974): 382–405.

———. *Whigs and Hunters: The Origins of the Black Act.* New York: Pantheon, 1976.

Trench, Charles C. *The Poacher and the Squire: A History of Game Preservation in England.* London: Longmans, Green, 1967.

———. *The History of Marksmanship.* London: Longman, 1972.

Twiti, William. *The Art of Hunting,* edited by Bror Danielsson. Uppsala: Almquist & Wikell, 1977.

Vale, Juliet. *Edward III and Chivalry: Chivalric Society and Its Context: 1270–1350.* Woodbridge, England: Boydell, 1982.

Vale, Marcia. *The Gentleman's Recreations: Accomplishments and Pastimes of the English Gentleman 1580–1630.* Totowa, N. J.: Rowman & Littlefield, 1977.

Vamplew, Wray. *The Turf: A Social and Economic History of Horse Racing.* London: Allen Lane, 1976.

Walvin, James. *Leisure and Society: 1843–1950.* London: Longmans, 1978.

Whitaker, W. B. *Sunday in Tudor and Stuart Times.* London: Houghton, 1933.

Whitman, Malcolm. *Tennis: Origins and Mysteries.* New York: Derrydale, 1932.

Wymer, Norman. *Sport in England.* London: George Harrap, 1949.

Young, Charles. *The Royal Forests of Medieval England.* Philadelphia: University of Pennsylvania Press, 1979.

Zeigler, Earle, ed. *A History of Sport and Physical Education to 1900.* Champaign, Ill.: Stipes, 1973.

INDEX

About the Author

THOMAS S. HENRICKS is Professor of Sociology at Elon College in North Carolina. Specializing in the sociology of sport and popular culture, he is the author of numerous articles and reviews.